rock on wood

rock on wood
the origin of a rock & roll face
ronnie wood

Terry Rawlings

B◼XTREE

First published 1999 by Boxtree

an imprint of Macmillan Publishers Ltd
25 Eccleston Place, London SW1W 9NF
Basingstoke and Oxford

www.macmillan.co.uk.

Associated companies throughout the world

ISBN 0 7522 1164 1

Copyright © 1999 Terry Rawlings

9 8 7 6 5 4 3 2 1

A CIP catalogue record for this book is available from
the British Library.

Cover design and artwork by
Terry Rawlings, Paul McEvoy
at MC80 Grahpic Design. Original
silkscreen adaptations by Terry Rawlings

Typeset by SetSystems Ltd, Saffron Walden, Essex
Printed and bound in Great Britain by
Mackays of Chatham plc, Chatham, Kent

Contents

Acknowledgments

A cknowledgments and thanks:
firstly to Ron and Jo Wood, for finding time; Art and Angie Wood, for their encouragement; Lizzie Wood for making time to remember "well, almost everything"; Paolo Hewitt for a very much appreciated introduction to a very receptive publisher, in one Clare Hulton; Richard (Barney) Barnes, for those stories that would have been great if only he'd remembered them – cheers, Barn! Roch The Mod Vidal, France's most famous Mod, for Birds memorabilia; Richard and Sue Cunningham, for being so open and friendly; Nick Cowan for being so helpful; Reg Pippet, for some great pics. Kenney Jones was invaluable, as was Jessie Wood. Thanks to Micky Waller for the use of his diaries. A Shameless Plug for Kim Gardner and the Cat & Fiddle, 6530 Sunset Boulevard, Hollywood, Calif., USA. Thanks also to Tony Monroe and Kim Gardner for priceless photos, memories and memorabilia. To Jaap Hoetsman, Jack Jones, Bob Gardner and Eddie Philips, Mod Gods all. To Mandy and Steve Hume for tireless help in transcribing; Dougal Butler for yet more unprintable stories; Krissie Wood for being so open; and Sandy Sarjeant for her down-to-earth frankness. To John Gray, Marilyn Kenney and Gary Millard at *Smiler* magazine; Nigel Foster 'It's the military training', who wants a mention for Tara and Sacha. Shameless Plug Number 2: Mike Stax and everyone at *Ugly Things* magazine, 3707 Fifth Avenue, 145 San Diego CA 92103. Thank you, Shirley Arnold, for some great and not so great memories. Thanks to Dave Wedgbury, a great photographer who's sorely missed, and his widow, Mary, for all her encouragement. Ian McLagan was also supportive. Thanks to John Hellier, the last word in all things Small Faces; to Shel Talmy for being forgiving whenever I forgot the eight-hour time difference; Donovan, for being a gent; Steve Spears; Jim McCarty, Keith Grant, Roman Saliki, Paul Newman and Jimmy Page for all their help . . . and to Keith Badman, an old partner in printed crime. Thanks also to Andy Neil, Jerry Stone, Mandy the Mod, Steve McNerney and Paul Hallam. A relieved, we-made-it thanks

to Paul McEvoy and all at mc80: Andy, Julian, Ted, Jo, little Andy, Allan and Ben. Special thanks to Geraldine Brice. Also to Tadhg Meehan for helping save the day. And before the final dedication, a very special Thank You with love to Lesley (Benson) Rawlings and our daughters Molly and Nancy.

And the envelope please . . .

This book is dedicated to Lizzie Wood, Gawd Bless Ya!

Introduction

It's one o'clock in the afternoon on 6 July 1997, and the Wood clan has good-naturedly gathered for Art's sixtieth birthday party. Art, the eldest of the three Wood brothers, has chosen the Blues Club in West Kensington for his celebratory bash. Back in the 1950s, he was one of those musicians who helped bring R&B to an avid Britain. Ted, the next youngest brother, was and still is well known on the jazz circuit. And their baby brother, Ronnie, is now lead guitarist with the Rolling Stones. So it was either the Blues Club or Wembley Stadium.

Art has even managed to re-form the short-lived cult band Quiet Melon for the night – or rather revamp it, since Rod Stewart couldn't make it and ex-Kink Mick Avory is guesting on drums. But bass guitarist Kim Gardner, once of Ashton, Gardner and Dyke, is there, and Ronnie will arrive at any moment. This will be the first time Kim and Ronnie have played together since their days in the Creation, which should have been the first super-group until its auto-destruction back in the late sixties. And both also played with the legendary R&B band the Birds, which also died, albeit in a quiet sort of way: everyone went on holiday one day and never came back. The Creation, the Birds, the Jeff Beck Group and the Faces: Ronnie's more than a great musician; he's got great taste.

Excitement flares in the club as he enters. These are his own family and friends standing up and craning their necks for a better view. People he has known all his life cluster around, needing him to remember when and where they were last together. He is grabbed and pulled from one side of the tiny venue to another by nieces, nephews, aunts, uncles, cousins, and relatives more times removed than Pickford. Likewise musician mates – and the few obligatory hangers-on without whom no musician's party is truly complete. He works the crowd like a pro, careful to speak to each and every one of them, his laugh cracking above the excited hum and a band who have actually begun to play better. Ronnie is careful to remind everyone that this is Art's night, not his. This is not false modesty, for family is all-important, especially for the Wood brothers. If you scratch one, they all bleed – and so, ultimately, will you.

The welcome isn't just for a member of the world's greatest rock band, nor yet a multimillionaire who has partied with kings without ever losing the common touch. People would want Ronnie to like them whatever he did in life, although the other stuff probably does help, just a little. They want to feel that they're the centre of his universe for a few brief, sweet minutes. Ronnie Wood has got something indefinable, and everyone wants a piece.

Art, Ted and the other musicians roll their eyes indulgently as tempers suddenly flare. He's mine . . . No, he's mine . . . No, mine. For some, the mood has swung the other way. Krissie Wood has commanded the stage and is colourfully explaining why her ex-husband is not such a wonderful guy after all. The explanation dissolves into tears and she's led away to be comforted by Ronnie's present wife, Jo. You get the impression that Jo has done a great deal of comforting over the years. It always comes as a shock when a person discovers that they are not, as they thought, the centre of Ronnie's world

For a moment, Ronnie's composure snaps. 'Nice fucking speech, Kris!' he says, before leaping on stage and barking a request to the Quiet Melons' bemused guitar player, and then to current Krissie beau Ray Majors. A minute later Ronnie breaks into a long riff on a borrowed guitar, as a grinning Kim Gardner – always an innovative player – answers back with his bass, and drummer Mick Avory takes a minute to recognize the tune.

The mood in the club suddenly lightens. The rock scene's inimitable party man has ensured that the good times roll. Who the hell could ever refuse him?

Art orders another round of drinks, still grinning at the memory of Ronnie's almost anguished cry: 'Give me a fuckin' guitar or I'm gonna fuckin' kill someone!'

Music is the centre of Ronnie's world, and always will be.

1

'My mum can outknit anyone else's mum, so there!'

That bright Sunday, 1 June 1947, only one boy was born at West London's Hillingdon Hospital. One baby boy among seven baby girls – not exactly an omen, but still a novelty.

Boys were still the future breadwinners in those days, and besides, too many men had been killed in the world war that had finished only eighteen months earlier. So a single boy baby was an event, to be admired and clucked over by all the other mothers. All, that is, apart from the one who came back from the nursery with a worried expression on her young face and called out:

'Mrs Wood? Mrs Wood?'

Lizzie Wood put up her hand.

The young mother sat on Lizzie's bed and told her: 'I've just seen your little baby son.' There was a long, maybe even pregnant, pause. 'I must ask you, Mrs Wood: have you had something to do with a Jew?'

Lizzie Wood could laugh about it later, but at the time came close to hitting the woman with a bedpan. True, the war had relaxed traditional morality, and the father's name on a birth certificate was often a triumph of expediency over truth. But the Woods were as respectably devoted a couple as you could ever hope to find – Lizzie had even been chaperoned when they first went out together. Yet the inescapable truth was that her son did look a little exotic.

Nothing so mundane as the standard baby's squashed-button nose. Instead he had the prominent family hooter and a mass of sticking-up black hair – a miniature version of how he'd look fifty years later, give or take a wrinkle or twenty.

Ronald David Wood was born with a look that would spawn a thousand imitations.

He came as a bit of surprise, too, for as Lizzie used to explain, she'd 'shut up shop'. She and Arthur – her husband, not Jewish, but a water gypsy – had already brought up two boys during the war, with all its bombing, and were sure they didn't want to bring another child into such an inhospitable world. Besides, she was in her mid-thirties, and in those days that was considered a little old for motherhood.

Baby Wood had other ideas. And along with the family nose, he inherited the family's luck and creativity.

Lizzie was born Mercy Leah Elizabeth Dyer in 1911, on a narrow boat called the *Orient*, which was moored in Brentford Dock. Like her husband-to-be, she came from a long line of water gypsies who had worked the canals for generations. The *Orient* was a working craft, and she had family spread all along the length of the Grand Union Canal.

Arthur Wood was born in 1908, at 40 Dock Road, Paddington, the son of a tugboat skipper. He started work at fourteen, helping his father and grandfather transport timber from London to Manchester and by the mid-1920s he was skipper of a tug named the *Antelope*. As well as being an excellent waterman, Arthur – 'Arch' to his mates – was an enthusiastic and gifted amateur musician, if just a little eccentric. Who else would put together a twenty-four-piece harmonica big band? Or as he used to describe it, twenty-four musicians and a drummer. Even in those days, people found it hard to take drummers seriously.

Not that Arthur took his musical career all that seriously himself. 'Booze, racetracks and women' was the band's motto, and they could be found blowing up an inebriated storm next to the winning posts at Goodwood, Kempton Park, even Royal Ascot. 'Blaze Away' was their signature tune, and they did. But if they had a name, Lizzie Wood can't remember it. 'Really, they only did it for a bit of a lark. They'd have a big day out at the races, or play at the Bricklayer's Arms pub in Yiewsley, where they had a back room to rehearse in. Or the Crown pub, where my parents sometimes went.'

Lizzie's father, Fred, was working with Arthur's father, Sylvester, and both families would often meet at the weekend in the Crown. That was where Ronnie Wood's parents first met.

It was the Whitsun Bank Holiday of 1932, and Arthur had won a darts tournament at the pub, for a first prize of a leg of pork. Arthur was still carrying it when he was introduced to Lizzie, Fred Dyer's twenty-one-year-old daughter. You don't spend your spare time playing the mouth organ at Royal Ascot without learning a thing or two about chivalry. Arthur, instantly smitten, offered her his prize, the gesture of a man who wanted to be taken seriously. With Fred, her mother Leah and younger sister Mary looking on, Lizzie accepted the leg of pork. After the pub closed, they all went back to the Dyers', where it was cooked and eaten; the crackling tasted particularly good.

Lizzie and Arthur began walking out together at weekends. At first they were always accompanied by a chaperone – Lizzie's mother or an aunt – for the people who worked the canals were very strict. Two years later, on Christmas Day 1934, the couple were married. Arthur had his own river tugboat by then, the *Fastnet*, and they were able to move into a comfortable two-up, two-down, 8 Whitethorn Avenue, Yiewsley, on the edge of West London. The 'two-up' were bedrooms plus a small boxroom, the 'two-down' a front room and small back room plus a tiny kitchen. The lavatory was outside. A house of this kind was widely considered fairly luxurious for Britain's working class in the thirties, and some people in authority worried that such comfort might even spoil them. It was solidly built and, unlike a narrow boat, had stairs. And so Lizzie became the first Dyer for generations to decamp to dry land. She found a job as a polisher at the giant HMV plant in nearby Hayes, working Monday to Friday from 7.30 a.m. to 7 p.m. and on Saturday until 12.00 p.m. – for the princely sum of thirty shillings and seven pence, with no sickness pay or pension.

When their first child, Arthur (Art), was born, on 7 July 1935, Lizzie happily exchanged the monotony of the conveyor belt for cotton nappies and wooden teething rings. In the thirties, few women in their right mind preferred factory work to being a housewife. Four years later the family would further rejoice when Edward (Ted) was born, on 24 June 1939. But it was a short-lived celebration, for three months afterwards the Second World War began.

Canal work was a reserved occupation during wartime. Men like Arthur Wood were exempted from being called up because they were responsible for transporting supplies to and from London. The canals became one of London's lifelines – a fact quickly realized by the Luftwaffe, who tried very hard to bomb them and men like Arthur out of existence. On the one hand, Lizzie knew that she and her husband would be spending the war years together, unlike so many other thousands of couples. On the other, she realized that Arthur faced almost daily bombing until the closing stages of the war.

Nor was it that much easier at home, for Yiewsley was close to both the canal system and the RAF airstrip that would later be developed as Heathrow Airport. After the Blitz the area would become an obvious target for unmanned flying bombs: the V-1 rocket and its successor the V-2. Several doodlebugs hit Whitethorn Avenue, and one destroyed the house opposite Arthur's mother-in-law. Worse, another destroyed the

Black Bull in Falling Lane. The Englishman is a forgiving soul – but destroy his favourite pub and you make an enemy for life.

The Wood family had spent many nights huddled together in the Anderson shelter in the back garden. This was a corrugated-iron structure which was sunk into the ground and then covered with up to three feet of earth. They were damp, cold and usually effective only against small bombs and debris.

When Art and Ted came down with severe whooping cough, it was decided that long nights in an Anderson shelter were not a good idea, and the boys were too ill and too young to be evacuated from London. So one day Arthur and some of his mates from the pub dug up the shelter and moved it into the small back room next to the kitchen. The earth stayed outside.

Now, without dirt piled on top of it, an eighth of an inch of corrugated iron isn't going to stop a bad cold, let alone a bomb. But Arthur and his pals had thought of that, and built a wooden shell around the shelter, and another wooden roof on top of that. So it was a shelter-inside-a-shelter-inside-a-shelter, and to hell with the doodlebugs. But that didn't stop the Black Bull being destroyed by one – it had probably piqued the Nazis that the Woods weren't being cold and miserable along with everyone else.

Instead the family were warm and miserable, crammed together in the improvised shelter as bombs fell around them, knowing, like so many others, that the sound of the explosion that destroyed a home nearby was horribly preferable to the final split second of light and noise that would herald their own deaths.

It was all thanks to doodlebugs and the Blitz that young Art discovered he was an artist, as his younger brother also would many years later – a talent which would lead Ronnie to become one of the world's most enigmatic and copied rock musicians. Lizzie explains it best: 'During the endless hours we spent in that shelter waiting for the all-clear, Art and Ted first learned to draw, because the shortage of metal or lead meant you couldn't buy any toys like a box of soldiers or cars and trains. The only thing that you could get hold of was paper pads and crayons. So that's what they got, that was their experience. I would take them down the shelter with their drawing books and try to take their minds off the bombings, which was very difficult, as you can imagine. But it would prove to be a very big part of all their lives. A part that has remained with them all even to this day.'

With the war at an end, in 1945 England faced up to the mammoth task of rebuilding. Ration books remained in place (cream ones for parents, green for children), so that for even the most basic of household items the queues still stretched around the block. The memories are still extremely vivid to Lizzie. 'My Mother Leah would save up all her sweet rations and store them in a big yellow biscuit tin which she'd keep on top of her dresser. All the children in the street knew about it and they would ask her "Have you got any sweets for us?" and she would hand them out. Everything came in two ounces. Two ounces of tea, two ounces of butter. ONE EGG? What were you expected to do with two ounces of anything amazed me. It was a terrible struggle, especially if you had children. It was heartbreaking to see them go without. But people did make the most of it and try and help each other out as much as they could, especially at Christmas or birthdays. Someone would make toys out of wood or make soft toys from fabrics, but mainly it was the drawing materials that the boys got because of the lack of resources. Arthur, their Dad, played a big part in developing their imagination and their love of art. He was a very good critic. They used to sit and draw for ages and eventually bring their pictures up to him and say, "Look, Daddy, look what we've drawn." And he would say, "Now, son, you wouldn't see a horse with legs like that, would you?" or "You wouldn't ever see a dog with a tail like that" and so on, you see? Whereas I would say, "Draw me a nice picture" while I was getting the tea or something, and they'd bring it back to me and I'd say, "Oh yes, that's lovely, now draw me something else." I didn't pick fault with it, whereas Arthur did, in order to encourage them, but they took notice of him, and it worked.'

It certainly did for Art Wood, now a successful commercial artist and no mean musician himself. 'Dad didn't have any training in teaching,' he recalls, 'but he had a natural flair for drawing, which made us eager to please him, so we'd strive to get every picture right so that he'd say, "That's much better", but he'd never say. "That's excellent" or "That's good!", always "Much better". Whereas Mum would say, "That's lovely" whatever we did. Nothing was ever rotten with Mum, even the worst pictures were lovely. "That's nice, Artie, now draw me a swan," she would say. So when little Ron was finally born, drawing and painting were already a firmly established part of our family and our growing up.'

It was on his mother's thirty-sixth birthday that Ronnie was taken home to see his two elder brothers. Neither parents had expected any more children. 'I'd shut up shop' Lizzy claims. In those days, motherhood at thirty-six was considered a little on the old side. It isn't clear what Art and Ted expected. Ten is an awkward age for boys – and it stays that way for the next forty years or so – while seven isn't much easier. Both brothers had known the warmth of a close-knit, loving family where all the attention was focused on them. And while ten-year-olds in 1947 were less sophisticated than today's, Art was undoubtedly aware of the first stirrings of adolescence. One moment he was on the threshold of man's estate, the next he was expected to admire something that squeaked, puked and burbled.

Lizzie and her new-born son were carried indoors by two ambulance men, followed by the midwife – there was no emergency: that was just the way the National Health Service worked in those halcyon days – and were met by Art and Ted shouting, 'Happy birthday, Mum! Happy birthday!' And as the stretcher paused to negotiate a bend in the stairs, the two boys piled it high with the presents and cards they'd made for their mother. And from Auntie Alma there was a much-prized Pyrex dish – in the late forties, oven-proof glassware was a rare luxury. So it was, after this triumphal procession, that Ronnie arrived at the cot in his parents' bedroom.

Mother and son duly installed, it was time for Art and Ted to be formerly introduced. The boys' grandmother, Leah, told them to come up one at a time and meet their new brother. Lizzie remembers: 'Art came storming in first, like he always does, walked round the bed, face white like a sheet, and just stared at Ronnie. "Well," I asked him, "what do you think?" And with that he just turned round and stomped off. Stomp, stomp, stomp, down the stairs, out through the kitchen and slam! out the back door.'

Ted arrived next, his face bright red. Lizzie remembers him giving Ronnie exactly the same look as Art: embarrassment, shock and deep suspicion. But at least he spoke.

'What do you think of your new baby brother?' asked Leah.

'All right,' Ted muttered, before stomping off to join Art out in the back garden.

With the new arrival, Art's older-brother status won him promotion to the privacy of the boxroom, whereas Ted suddenly found himself lumbered with a much smaller room-mate who gurgled and smelled.

But it was a short-lived rejection, according to Art, who remembers he and Ted adopting an almost overprotective attitude towards their little brother – at least, outside the family, in the street. At home it was understandably a little different, and Art remembers asking his mother to take Ronnie back to the shop where she'd brought him. Art wasn't really that unsophisticated, but it was far kinder than suggesting, say, that the newcomer should be abandoned to the wolves. Even if he had been, Ronnie's luck would probably have ensured that the wolves brought him straight back. As it was, Art and Ted swiftly discovered the joys of babysitting – 'which you don't always want to do when you're young', Art remembers – and while Ronnie might have been a nuisance he was family. That excused everything, just as it does today.

Ronnie was cute, often unbearably so, which explains the request, when he was about two, to take him back to the shop. Art and Ted had walked all the way to Uxbridge to buy goldfish, and walked back with two innocent invertebrates swimming happily in a jamjar. Dogs and cats are fine, but there's nothing quite so pleasingly traditional as a boy and his fish. Loyalty, affection – albeit one-sided – and hours of harmless fun teaching it tricks, like 'Sink!' or 'Swim!' These and other excited plans ran through Art and Ted's minds as they sat talking to their mother. But then their little brother toddled in.

'Fish, Mummy, fish,' Ronnie said, pointing behind him. 'Gone to sea.'

And then Ted remembered with horror that he'd just heard a lavatory flush.

To this day, Ronnie remains convinced that he was only trying to liberate them.

With money for luxuries in short supply in the years after the war, toys were carefully shared out among the three boys. They played with the same tin soldiers and battered old football, and this made Ronnie identify even more with his two elder brothers, whom he already adored. But there was also a steady stream of drawing books and crayons to stimulate the youngsters' imaginations. Ronnie grew to inherit his older brothers' love of art, immersing himself in drawing and painting with results that greatly impressed the entire family. The two older boys would sit at opposite ends of the small kitchen table, happily drawing away, as Ronnie would quietly edge his chair between them. At first he would content himself with merely glancing from one to another. But inevitably he would begin jogging the table as he leaned to the left or the right for a better look. This led to complaints that he was being a fidget – a criticism that all older brothers feel safe to make about a younger sibling – and Lizzie would have to wedge Ronnie in the armchair with a tray to draw on. And there he would sit, copying perfectly the pictures he'd watched being drawn by Art and Ted – until he began to develop his own style and interests, when he was about five. 'It was always Cowboys and Indians,' Art remembers, 'because Ronnie loved to draw horses and Indians. It was the thing that impressed his art teachers later on, these amazing pictures!'

Although one of Ronnie's earliest memories was of a bridge painted in the style of Van Gogh – whether this was pure coincidence or it was taken from a book isn't known – horses were a speciality; as was an early fascination with the Wild West.

'I loved to draw American Indians, I still do,' Ronnie says. 'I think it's because I've always thought I was part Indian. I mean, I do realize I look like one. I've always wanted to trace my roots to see if I have any genuine Indian blood in me. But I'm a little scared of what I'd find if I dug too hard!'

Push him further and he changes the subject or pours you another drink. Maybe it's to do with being a water gypsy. If so, there's nothing to worry about: water gypsies were directly descended from Romanies, as distinct from travellers, and were 'horse whisperers' long before it became fashionable. Thousands of years ago they were one of the many nomadic tribes who reached Europe from Central Asia and developed a near-mystical understanding of the horse, most evident today in the Camargue in southern France.

When Britain began building canals in the eighteenth century it was natural for the Romanies to become involved in running them: they had the horses needed for towing barges, while the very life of moving from one town to another appealed to their wandering spirit. Music is one of the great Romany gifts to the world, particularly flamenco. Another of their great loves, partying, is more universal, although no one really parties like them.

'I was brought up on tinned milk and the canals,' remembers Ronnie. 'It was a happy home life. We used to have parties with fifty people crammed into our tiny little semi-detached house ... parties every weekend, with the music shrieking out.'

The guiding spirit behind these gatherings was Arthur, the boys' dad. Arthur loved to make music, with his harmonica band or anything else that came to hand, loved horses and loved people. Weekdays were for working, weekends were for playing music and for parties. And his sons grew up thinking it was all quite normal, never really wondering why many of their friends seemed to spend more time at the Wood house than their own.

By 1950, when he was fourteen, Art Wood's own artistic abilities had taken him to Ealing School of Art. In those days art schools taught both practical and purely creative subjects. They produced as many typographers and illustrators as they did sculptors or painters, and gave all children from all backgrounds the chance to succeed.

Art settled down to a regime divide equally between academic studies and art. At sixteen he would begin specializing in a specific subject – the aforesaid typography or illustration, even fine art – secure in the knowledge that Ealing's contacts would always help find him a job, if he wanted one. It was a perfect existence, although not quite in the way the educational authorities envisaged.

The art school had built up a reputation as one of the best London had to offer. This might appear strange, for even today the suburb of Ealing gives the impression that the pavement will be rolled up at 9 p.m. sharp. It didn't seem like the sort of establishment that would eventually boast alumni like Art, Ted and Ronnie Wood; David Bowie; Pete Townshend; and Freddie Mercury. But then Ealing School of Art drew on all of West London, from Shepherd's Bush out to Uxbridge and West Drayton. For fine art, it was the place you went to before perhaps going on to do postgraduate work at the Slade, Chelsea or the Royal College of Art. In terms of graphic design, Ealing graduates were assured of jobs in advertising or the media. That began to change in the early fifties.

'Ealing was very unusual,' Art explains. 'It was constantly evolving at an alarming rate. It was a straight art school when I first went there in 1950. But it soon started to get this very musical feel to it. Everyone was getting very experimental – after all it was the "beatnik" era. The sexy French look for girls, the beginnings of what would become skiffle, it was all happening, so anyone who had even the remotest artistic or musical bent was just carried away!'

In other words, people began to go to Ealing as much for the music as the art. For new ideas, too. Fifties students would discover Camus, Jack London, Sartre, Hank Janson and Mickey Spillane. Musical influences – aside from Juliette Greco – were predominantly American: skiffle, blue-grass, trad jazz and the blues. Later it was Chicago jazz, Buddy Holly and Elvis. British students were no respecters of other people's traditions and quite happily mixed and matched – although there some purists, most of whom vanished into the folk-music scene – until, perhaps adding their own particular spin, they got the result they wanted. But all that was still in the future. All that little Ronnie knew was that his big brothers – for Ted followed Art to Ealing – would bring home the most amazing, motley group of friends that any child could hope to gawp at. By the time he was eight or nine, he knew exactly what he wanted out of life: sex.

'Art and Ted would always have their schoolmates over at our house,' Ronnie remembers. 'Artists, musicians and wild bohemians with shades, drainpipe trousers, suede brothel-creepers and big overcoats. They'd have all these nice-looking "chicks" with them and they'd lock themselves in the front room with all their instruments. We had a serving hatch in the wall between there and the kitchen and they would pass drinks through it. I was like a puppy scratching at the door from outside. What went on in there is nobody's business, but I would see photographs of fifteen or sixteen people sprawled on the sofa. I knew that was the life for me. I wanted to emulate my brothers. I wanted to get into Ealing as soon as possible, mainly because I fancied their art-school girlfriends.'

Ronnie left St Stephen's Primary School at the age of seven, moving to the tiny St Matthew's Secondary, which was attached to the parish church in Yiewsley High Street. Here those early lessons around the kitchen table bore fruit and he was asked to paint a frieze along the walls of the school's entrance corridor. The painting, depicting St Francis and the animals, greeted parents and visitors on the next school open day. Lizzie remembers it as the most wonderful picture she'd ever seen: 'It was a lovely day because all the teachers were telling us how good he was and how proud they were – which was more than could be said of the other two at that time!'

This isn't to say that Art and Ted were running riot, although they did enjoy far more freedom than their friends. But, as the boys finally realized years later, their parents hadn't been weak, merely thoughtful. Arthur in particular believed in allowing his sons to think for themselves, and contented himself with throwing in a bit of sensible advice from time to time: 'That didn't make him weak, or suggest he didn't care. Because our dad did care; he cared a lot. Dad was just very loose with us.'

Not surprisingly, the Wood household became a magnet for all of Art and Ted's friends – although the endless supply of food probably had something to do with it. Sometimes their mother felt she spent her entire time in the kitchen, making sandwiches, beans on toast or boiling eggs for starving teenagers, with a bored young Ronnie serving the guests through the specially built hatch, which also allowed Lizzie to keep an eye on things. If the noise became too loud or – every parent's nightmare – stopped altogether, she'd quietly peep in, just in case. The one memory she carries to this day is watching entranced as four or five girls, wearing roses in their hair, laughed and danced together.

Occasionally Ronnie would manage to sneak in and, for a little while, become part of his adored elder brothers' private lives. He learned to sit quietly and say nothing, merging into the background like a smiling mannequin, until someone wanted another sandwich or a cup of tea and he would be sent back to the kitchen. Years later people would still be remarking how the adult Ronnie always managed to merge into the background – especially when he'd done something wrong.

The front room was actually supposed to be Art and Ted's rehearsal room, for both had inherited their father's love of music. Art's instincts led to skiffle, blues and thence to R&B, while Ted was a jazz man through and through. So Ronnie's earliest musical influences were eclectic, to say the least. The age of four is the earliest he can remember making music with his brothers, or rather making one hell of a noise on Ted's drum kit, played with mad abandon by the three boys whenever their parents were out. These sessions inevitably resulted in massive arguments between Art and Ted – teenage musicians can be so sensitive – with fists flying and much rolling about on the floor. According to Ronnie, he was convinced that one of them would end up killing the other, which so upset him that he developed a nervous stutter. But either peace broke out or he learned not to take the free-for-alls so seriously, for the stuttering had gone by the time he was five.

The living room might have been turned over to Art and Ted to allow them to practise their music, but they had other ideas: they would try to sneak girls in, and then if a beady eye was watching through the hatch, upstairs. At which point, Art remembers, his father would usually shout out: 'Where do you think you are – on your father's yacht?' (Much later, when Ronnie bought a pub in Ireland, he called it Yer Father's Yacht. The sign shows Arthur in full naval uniform, and Ronnie painted it himself.) Neither Arthur nor Lizzie ever allowed adolescent fumbling to get out of hand. Their approach was to give their boys freedom, though never enough to let them make a serious mistake, until they were old enough to take responsibility for their actions.

But the biggest bar to Art and Ted's love-life was their little brother. As he freely admits, Ronnie learned both art and music from his elder siblings. It seemed only natural to learn about girls as well. Not everyone agreed with him. It's difficult to be amorous, even as a teenager, with a smiling child quietly lurking in the background, and on those rare occasions when both parents were out Ronnie would be given a few pennies and sent to the shops. Strangely, he never seems to have understood that the actual purchase was less important than the time taken in making it. To this day, all the brothers are convinced Ronnie would make it to and from the local shop in under two minutes – Ronnie with a sense of pride, the other two with remembered frustration.

The family dynamic changed for ever in 1955, when Art received his call-up papers. Two years' National Service beckoned, with the dubious distinction that Art was the nation's very last A1 conscript. The family dreaded a foreign posting, but in the event number 23267647, Private Wood, A, reported to the Army barracks in Devizes, Wiltshire, where he was issued with the regulation pick-axe handle and pledged to defend his country and the Dorset coast against anyone who might be impressed by a pick-axe handle. 'Still no sign of the dreaded Jap invaders,' Art would announce on his visits home, and Yiewsley would breathe a sigh of relief.

Ronnie was eight years old, and bereft. 'I was so close to my brothers. I was like a little lost sheep, without Art. Ted too was lost without him. In fact, when Art came home on leave towards the end of his Army career, Ted would happily donate his girlfriend to Art and vice versa.' Quite what the girls thought about the arrangement isn't recorded.

Even so, it couldn't have been a total waste of time at Devizes, for Art managed to found his own skiffle band, the Blue Kats.

Three years later Ronnie passed the all-important eleven-plus exam and went to the highly respected Ruislip Manor Grammar School. He'd originally been enrolled at St Martin's Secondary Modern in Yiewsley to continue his education, but good as it was, the school couldn't offer a final qualification in art. However, Mr Reesey – St Martin's sainted headmaster – realized that Ronnie would be wasting his time if he couldn't carry on painting. A transfer was arranged and Ronnie was enrolled in Ruislip Grammar's three-year art course. If all went to plan, he'd later follow his brothers to Ealing Art School.

Within a month of starting at Ruislip, Ronnie won an open art competition. The prize was presented by the famous band leader Victor Sylvester, and this was Ronnie's first and last brush with light music, as well as his first taste of fame. He began entering the 'Painting of the Week' competition set each Wednesday evening by artist Adrian Hill on the BBC's *Sketch Club*.

'He won it seven weeks in a row,' Art recalls today. 'He would get home from school, gulp down his tea and switch on the TV. Every bleedin' week it would be: "Yes, once again the winner this week is Ronnie Wood."'

Schoolboys can be quite bitchy when one of their number achieves fame, but this didn't happen with Ronnie. He still remembers the acclaim he received from his schoolmates with immense and touching pride, while typically playing down the cause: 'Yeah, well, I got a couple of pictures shown.'

Not so easy to play down was his appearance as Adrian Hill's special guest on *Sketch Club*, when it was staged live at St Albans Town Hall. Or the subsequent articles in the local newspapers, which were 'really encouraging to a young artist'. Growing up as the youngest of three brothers does teach you the value of modesty.

Very often the youngest brother in many families tends to go one of two ways: either he gives up, knowing he'll never be able to compete, or he becomes determined to excel, but quietly. Perhaps it all depends on how much love and encouragement he receives from his elder siblings, not just from his parents.

Tony Monroe was another new pupil at Ruislip. He and Ronnie discovered to their amazement that they were almost neighbours – going to different primary schools had managed to keep them apart, even though their parents knew each other. It was natural to travel to and from school together, ten miles each way, and in Tony's words, the two boys 'quickly became best mates on a number of levels'. Especially art and music.

Ruislip Grammar was one of those schools where teachers tirelessly encourage their pupils. It had its own choir, which staged regular recitals and entered most local competitions. The art department was equally committed, and altogether the school provided a perfect environment for children with an artistic gift or a competitive appetite. The atmosphere suited both Ronnie and Tony's hard-working attitude to their work: they wanted to learn, they wanted to succeed, and Ronnie at least desperately wanted to go on to Ealing.

Soon Tony's painting of a country scene became the winning entry of another television art programme, ITV's *Tuesday Rendezvous*. Remember that at this time, Ronnie more or less had the BBC sewn up via *Sketch Club*. That success earned Tony an article in the local newspaper – titled, with crashing unoriginality, 'A Rendezvous With Tony'.

Then another article, 'An Artistic Family' – the headline writer was pulling out all the stops now – featured all three Wood brothers, for by this time Art and Ted had a growing reputation as musicians. The article also mentioned that Ronnie had two paintings on show at a local CND exhibition (nothing to do with politics: artists will show anywhere); that he had enjoyed a record-breaking run on *Sketch Club*; and that he had just come second in a competition for a fire-prevention poster. The winner? Another local lad, one Tony Monroe.

'And that,' Tony reflects, 'was the start of our competitive rivalry. Although we always pretended not to be. If Ronnie went out with a girlfriend, I went out with her mate. If I entered a painting competition, so would Ron. We both felt we had to keep doing better by going one step further than the other. Ronnie, I remember, was never satisfied with what he'd achieved, and that continued right through from the art to the music. It's what would go on to give the group that edge later on.'

The Birds was the name of that group, which was to become one of Britain's top live R&B bands; and from which Tony was ultimately let go – by his best friend.

2
'All my ancestors lived on boats'

The baby Ronnie had been born into a music-mad family; the infant Ronnie grew up in a music-mad house. When he was five Ted had made him a drum out of the shell of an old banjo – if only to keep him away from his own drum kit. Art and Ted later clubbed together and bought Ronnie a guitar when he was ten. From Art he learned blues; from Ted he learned jazz. There was never any doubt that one day he would play in a group. Apart from anything else, both Art and Ted had their own bands and his father, Arthur, had one too.

'I was always fooling around with the instruments that Art and Ted kept stored in the backroom,' Ronnie remembers. 'Trumpets, banjos, kazoos, drums and, of course, washboards. But I knew the guitar was for me. When I saw someone playing I got an itch to pick one up, and believe me, I saw some great guitarists play with my brothers, especially Jim Willis and Lawrence Sheaf, and they helped me learn how to play. Jim showed me the fundamentals by writing out all the chords and finger techniques, while Lawrence showed me how to play all the great Big Bill Broonzy stuff. My first guitar was actually given to me by a guy named Chalkie White, but he took it back when he went into the Army. I was about ten years old then. Art and Ted felt bad about it, so they chipped in together and bought me a replacement, so I suppose that was my very first guitar.' In fact, Jim Willis spent hours painstakingly inking in finger positions on the guitar's neck, making allowances for the fact that young Ronnie didn't have the hand span of an adult. Talk to Ronnie Wood about Jim and Lawrence today, and you get the impression they were a combination of Hendrix, Clapton and Segovia – he still sees them in his mind's eye as he did when a child. But they undoubtedly were two young men who generously gave him a great deal of their time. It's one thing to be encouraged by your family – what else are families for? But it's quite another to be encouraged by your big brothers' mates. That really makes you feel important.

At that time Art was very much into Fats Domino and taught Ronnie

'Blue Monday' and 'I'm Walking'. But the record that made the greatest impact did so for tragic reasons. One day the brothers' cousin, Rex, arrived at the house in a state of great excitement. 'You have to hear this,' he told Ronnie's mother. 'I've bought it for Ronnie.' He then put 'Blueberry Hill' on the turntable. Ronnie loved it and immediately began learning the song.

The next day, 14 February, St Valentine's Day, Rex was killed in a car accident. He was just sixteen. It was the first time that Ronnie had been brought face to face with death. It wasn't to be the last, for his first girlfriend would also die in a car accident.

Yet Ronnie always seemed to be relatively untouched by tragedy. It isn't lack of feeling – only the total conviction that whatever happened, however bad things seemed, somehow he'd survive. 'I remember feeling that way as a little kid,' Ronnie will tell you, 'which is one reason why I never grew up worrying about money – I always knew that I'd be OK, I always felt emotionally secure. I guess it's to do with growing up in such a secure family.'

It is also because Ronnie has always had his music. He can pour all his emotions into his guitar-playing, and to a lesser extent into his painting. Threaten to take those outlets away from him and the security might well begin to crumble.

While Art was teaching Ronnie the finer points of the blues, Ted was teaching him about jazz. In fact, Tony Monroe always thought that Ted had the greater musical influence, for two reasons. First, because Art went into the Army for two years, when Ronnie was only eight, then left home altogether to marry his girlfriend Doreen in 1960, when Ronnie was thirteen. But at least Ronnie got to inherit the boxroom, much to Ted's relief. Second, because Art and Ronnie were effectively in competition with each other. Both played R&B, and no matter how great the affection, Ronnie at least wanted to go his own way.

'Ted was teaching me all about the music of Louis Armstrong, Bix Beiderbecke and Jelly Roll Morton,' Ronnie recalls. 'He was, and still is, a real jazz purist. He's got all those old 78s and jazz albums which he keeps in perfect condition in boxes. Meanwhile Art had crossed over to R&B with his group the Artwoods. Ted took me to my first live show, which was Duke Ellington supported by Chris Barber at Walthamstow Town Hall in 1959. I remember, in particular, Barber's drummer Carlo Little, who played a leopard-skin drum kit, a remnant from his days with Screaming Lord Sutch!'

It's often forgotten that Sutch was once a serious musician – well,-ish – who'd been at the forefront of the early R&B movement that would help revolutionize British music. He probably deserves to be an MP for that alone.

Nor was Ronnie a stranger to live performance. Back in the fifties many cinemas would feature groups during the intermission. Live music was an added attraction that also gave the audience time to buy their ice-creams, watered-down orange juice in an awkward square container, stale popcorn covered in sugar the colour of shit, monkey nuts, or frozen drinks-on-a-stick that always fell off into your lap.

Traditionally the live music used to be an organ, often rising magisterially out of the orchestra pit like a reverse Titanic. But this encouraged people to throw things, usually ice-cream wrappers, empty orange-squash containers and the favourite monkey nuts – horrible to eat but easy to score a hit with. Anyway, a medley of 'all-time favourites', invariably sounding like hymns on speed, didn't always sit well with Hollywood's latest offering. Until the Hammond helped kick R&B into the musical stratosphere, organs were something people mostly associated with church and the Blackpool Tower.

Art Wood played many interval gigs at the Regal in Uxbridge, often with his first group, the Art Wood Combo. Ted followed suit with his Original London Skiffle Group. Of course, when Art went into the Army, the music mantle of Bringing Up Ronnie had fallen on to Ted's shoulders. On this particular night in 1957, with Ted's band scheduled to knock 'em in the Regal aisles, word came that one of his musicians was ill. Luckily, Ronnie was free that night. In fact, he was free most nights – hardly surprising, since he was not yet ten. So it came to pass that Ronnie Wood's first live gig was playing washboard for the Original London Skiffle Group. They had to push him on, he was so scared. But once he'd got into the rhythm of it all, rumour has it they had to pull him off. The two films were *The Tommy Steele Story* and *Tommy The Toreador*, and in the interval the OLSG played the current Lonnie Donegan favourites 'Gambling Man' and 'Putting On The Style', which, given Ronnie's future career, were apt. Meanwhile Elvis Presley had a number one with 'All Shook Up'. And that was just as it should be.

Given Ronnie's background, and given that Tony Monroe was also music-crazy – the Everly Brothers and Buddy Holly – it was inevitable that the two boys would form a group. 'Our starting point was, of all things, classical,' Tony recollects. 'In fact, Ronnie and me would sing tenor and baritone duets together. Our school was renowned throughout the south of England because it had a seven-part choir, which helped us both later on in our performance, singing-wise. We were originally going to form an a cappella group using just voices instead of instruments, because we couldn't play any good enough! We came second in a competition around this time, in 1962. It was choir singing. We sang as a duet: a song-cum-hymn called "We Be The King's Men Hale And Hearty".'

The two boys began practising guitar whenever they could, and soon entered a local talent contest in Ruislip. They sang 'St Louis Woman', which was Ronnie's choice, and then an Everly Brothers number, both playing acoustic guitars. Unfortunately there was another group who'd modelled themselves on Shane Fenton and the Fentones. Not only that, but they had Fender electric guitars and, wonder of wonders, their own amps. To make matters worse, the group – neither Tony nor Ronnie can remember the name, perhaps understandably – also moved on stage like the Shadows. The group won the contest hands down. Tony remembers looking at Ronnie as they both realized: Uh-oh, so that's the next step. So let's go electric.

The great difference between Tony and Ronnie was that, musically speaking, Tony was always more easily satisfied. Not that he didn't love music, or that he didn't want to succeed. But music wasn't his mistress, his obsession, his life. That others felt very differently about it would be a tough lesson to learn for Tony, especially when he discovered that when pushed, Ronnie would always choose music before friendship. How could he do otherwise? Music was his life.

But that rejection was still some way in the future. During the early sixties Ronnie and Tony continued juggling their respective musical and artistic pursuits for a further two years at Ruislip Grammar. At sixteen they would take the O Levels necessary to land a place at Ealing School of Art, for at this point music was still just an absorbing sideline for Ronnie, who was pouring all his creative energies into painting. Too much so, for he neglected subjects like biology, chemistry, metal and woodwork. He was eventually caught cheating in his history exam after the particular dates he needed were discovered written up the length of his arm!

Meanwhile his musical education continued apace. In 1962 Art was singing with the great Alexis Korner's Blues Incorporated (featuring Chris Barber and Charlie Watts), while planning his first serious assault on the world of R&B with his own groups, the Art Wood Combo and ultimately the Artwoods with Jon Lord and Keef Hartley – accurate names for the groups, if not exactly inspired. Art was also taking Ronnie to the Railway Arms at Harrow and the Crawdaddy Club in Richmond, where bands like the Yardbirds and the Rolling Stones were just starting out. In fact, it was Art who first discovered, behind the ABC Bakery, the little beatnik drinking club, complete with old fisherman's nets and glass floats, which would soon become the famed Ealing Club. Both club and band names tended to be prosaic in those days, maybe to disguise the insanity within. And it was here that Brian Jones would first introduce himself to Mick Jagger and Keith Richards. The Ealing Club was originally known as the Moist Hoist, a name which referred to a practical necessity. Condensation poured down the walls and dripped incessantly from the ceiling when the club was full, threatening to electrocute musicians and audience alike. The answer was a tarpaulin, erected over the stage, which gave the place a certain coy ambience – even if it did play hell with the acoustics. Some fans were convinced that the tarpaulin was R&B's mocking comment on the obligatory fishing nets found decorating folk clubs and coffee bars. For British rhythm and blues was the new sound and the fans loved it for its hatred of bullshit and its raunchy lyrics.

R&B first surfaced in America during the forties, as a mix of blues and dance-band music – swinging, good dance-band music, that is. Don't think Victor Sylvester. Think Big Bill Broonzy and Duke Ellington. In the fifties, a watered-down version of R&B surfaced with banal lyrics and simple rhythms which was nicknamed rock 'n' roll – have you listened to Bill Haley recently? What the Brits did was take rock 'n' roll back to its R&B routes, add on skiffle (derived partly from bluegrass) for speed and then apply their own ideas. The irony was that they then exported the result back to White America, which took some time to realize that the whole thing had been started by mostly Black American musicians in the first place. And this is one reason why so many great Black American musicians began making what was almost a pilgrimage to Britain during the sixties: to jam with the groups that had kept their music alive. In fact, the Limey rascals had changed it almost out of all recognition, though it was still gratifying for men like Muddy Waters and Howling Wolf to be lionized by bands who were top of the charts on both sides of the Atlantic. Gratifyingly, the visiting musicians' concerts were invariably sold out, too.

Ronnie eventually managed to get two O Levels, in Geography and English Literature. But it was the A-Level pass in Art, taken two years early, which got him into Ealing School of Art, along with Tony Monroe – the only two Ruislip pupils who managed to pull it off that year. Once again, Ronnie made the local paper. He had achieved his dream, was about to follow in Art and Ted's footsteps – and the girls at Ealing were every bit as attractive as he remembered. But there was far more to it than that. First, Ronnie was well aware of the opportunities a college education offered. As he says, a little sourly, today: 'Working-class kids like me weren't expected to get any further education. We were supposed to leave school at sixteen and go straight to work in a factory. College was largely to do with the upper classes. I don't know if my parents thought it was a curse or a blessing that all three of their kids went to college rather than punch the clock.'

In fact, Ronnie's parents were always determined that all their sons would have every chance in life. And if society and the educational system expected certain standards from him, Ronnie was equally demanding. It was an unpleasant shock to discover that Ealing had changed dramatically since his brothers' time. He went there expecting that art would be taken seriously – not because it was to be his future profession, but simply because it deserved to be. In 1963 Ronnie found it a place of pretentious chaos.

Since its foundation in 1876, Ealing Art School – the institution's original name – had built up an enviable reputation as one of London's foremost colleges for fine art and associated technical subjects. In the sixties all that changed – along with the name – under the direction of Dr Orman Pickard. In effect, a bunch of second-rate academics were looking to make a name for themselves. They shared the then widespread belief that teachers and critics were just as – if not more – important as the artists themselves. Ealing's contribution to this new era of enlightenment would be the Ground Course, instigated by Roy Ascott, which 'combined science and behaviourism with artistic practice' and required the student to go through a period of acting out a different personality, in direct contrast to his or her usual one. The purpose of this 'experiment' was to enable students to realize their own potential. For example, Pete Townshend – who was at Ealing a few years before Ronnie Wood – had been required to assume a physical disability, using only a handmade trolley to manoeuvre himself around.

Not surprisingly, many Ealing students turned to music, which offered an essential discipline and sense of excellence. You can fake art, especially when it's anything anyone says it is, but you can't fake the ability to play the drums or a riff, to sing in tune or be truly original. Naturally, the academics loved the idea that art schools had become a breeding ground for rock and pop musicians, since it gave the impression that they themselves were at the forefront of popular culture.

When Ronnie Wood and Tony Monroe arrived at Ealing in 1963 they were disgusted by what they found. To Ronnie, in particular, it must have seemed like middle-class masturbation. His family remembers him coming home in the evening and complaining that 'they weren't doing serious art'. If this sounds a little po-faced, remember that all of Ronnie's musical heroes took their profession extremely seriously, and technique was just as important as the idea behind a composition. In fact, how could anyone ever hope to express himself musically without being able to play an instrument properly? Shouldn't the same apply to art? Especially as one of the new students was looking to a career in art to pay back his parents for the sacrifices they had made and the faith they had shown in him.

As it was, everything and anything at Ealing was open to artistic appreciation and expression. Shows with names such as 'Auto Destructive' and 'Flash Art' were put on, to a background of white noise or electric guitar feedback. Most of the students seemed to have given up any hope of becoming a professional artist in Ronnie's terms. In fact, most of them seemed to be forming or auditioning for the next big rock group to come out of Ealing. 'Almost everyone I knew in Ealing went on to be a professional musician,' Ronnie recalls. 'Even Art and Ted could have gone all the way, they were certainly good enough, but as Art says, he knew when to hang up his rocking boots!'

'We knew we had to get a band together,' says Ronnie. 'It was very obvious to us. I used to see Keith Moon around Ealing – he wasn't a student, but he lived nearby. I could see the fun he was having with Pete Townshend and the early days of the Who. He was a maniac even then, but the creativity impressed me. I also watched a girl named Linda Keith around school a lot. She was a student and really gorgeous and I was told she was going out with Keith Richards. I knew he was in the Rolling Stones. I'd seen their earliest publicity shots and I was really excited by them. Especially the pictures of them standing by the Thames with their long, straggly hair blowing in the wind. I looked up to them because they were a few years older than me. I'd seen them individually playing around the same club circuit as my brothers, with the likes of Alexis Korner. I thought, girls look at them differently. They want to go out with them. I simply realized that I'd do a lot better for myself, both socially and financially, by drawing people to gigs than drawing people on canvas!'

And so the deed was done. At least, it was decided that it should be done. Its realization would take a little longer. 'We had two real problems,' Tony remembers. 'One: who the fuck was going to be in it? And the other: what would we play? We realized very early on that our personal musical tastes were a bit at odds with each other. Ron was still very much influenced by his brothers, Ted in particular, because Art was that much older and had moved out to get married, so that left Ted at home, turning Ron on to jazz more and more. Art had just about got the

Artwoods up and running, who were quite jazzy too, so that was Ron's stable influence. But I was a rocker – Chuck Berry and Buddy Holly – so we didn't really know the answer, because there was just the two of us.'

They found the answer a few weeks later, at a gig by a local group called the Renegades. Actually, the Renegades were due to disband and the gig – at the nearby West Drayton US Air Force base – was to prove their last. 'We didn't have a clue who they were,' admits Tony. 'We were told by friends at Ealing Art School to check them out. We got talking to them after the gig and that's when we found out all was not well within. We wanted a bass player and drummer, so that was when it all sort of fell together. We left that night with their rhythm section. We got talking to their bass player Kim Gardner after the gig and he let slip that he thought the group weren't going anywhere. So we grabbed the chance and asked him to join Ron and me. Kim was so obviously the leader, so when he came on board so did Bob Langham, the drummer, and Robin Scrimshaw, their harp player.'

Originally, both Ronnie and Tony wanted Ali McKenzie, the Renegades' singer. They were knocked out by his stage performance, for he was a natural-born showman. But Ali, in the words of Kim Gardner – who would later form Ashton, Gardner and Dyke (Tony Ashton, keyboards; Kim Gardner, bass; Roy Dyke, drums), scoring big time with 'Resurrection Shuffle' – was feeling 'all deserted and played hard to get. Of course, when Ronnie and Tony realized Ali owned the PA system, Ali became even more important.'

This, after all, was the time when people were invited to join groups just because they owned an amp, PA system or had access to a van. Often, if the rest of the band improved and they didn't, they would end up as roadies or managers, because by then the group could afford its own equipment. Not cutthroat, merely practical. For example, Jimmy Winston had been invited to join the Small Faces, who were forming at around the same time in East London, simply because he owned a van. A fact he never quite understood until he showed up for a gig and found replacement Ian McLagan already performing with the group on stage. By then, the Small Faces could afford their own van. Naturally, Jimmy Winston sued the band, but not until 1969 – what kept him? – long after the Small Faces had achieved massive success, and, ironically, when the band could least afford it.

In one of those strange but true coincidences that crop up in Ronnie Wood's life, Kim Gardner, Ali McKenzie and Bob Langham all lived in or close to Whitethorn Avenue. Ali and Bob had grown up locally, while Kim had moved to the area from his native North Wales when he was nine. He had originally formed the Renegades with Ali when they were both attending St Martin's Secondary Modern. They were a typical after-school group of thirteen- and fourteen-year-olds, playing mostly Shadows stuff and a few covers of rare American R&B records they had heard at the USAF base in West Drayton – and occasionally managed to pilfer from the PX jukebox. It's a point worth making that the American bases in Britain, possibly without meaning to, played a definite part in developing British R&B. Maybe West Drayton should have a blue plaque.

The first solo Kim ever learned, 'Nivram', came from watching his hero, Jet Harris of the Shadows. 'I tried to look like Jet,' Kim admits, 'and our lead guitar player, when Ronnie heard us for the first and last time, had glasses like Hank Marvin. I remember we played James Ray's "If You've Got To Make A Fool Of Somebody", which I played for Ronnie and it knocked him out. He recorded it himself years later, on his first solo album.'

Ronnie called the first band meeting for the night after meeting the Renegades, and there he informed the new recruits that they would now go forth as the Rhythm & Blues Bohemians. The rehearsals began in earnest, taking place variously in the back room at Ronnie's when Ted wasn't around, on Wednesday evenings at the local Community Centre or, every Sunday morning, in the front window of the Rainbow Record Shop in Yiewsley High Street. The owner thought it would be good publicity, as did the group.

A month later the Rhythm & Blues Bohemians felt confident enough to perform live and threw open the Community Centre's doors to an invited audience of around 300 friends and family. 'We weren't very good,' remembers Tony. 'Only Kim and me had amps, so the PA went through Kim's along with the bass, and Ronnie and me both put our guitars through mine. Robin was singing and playing harp, which he wasn't very good at, and the whole thing sounded crap!'

It was fairly obvious that the Bohemians were destined to be a short-lived affair. Their lack of any real equipment and the need for a confident lead singer meant that their public exposure would be limited to the occasional gig in the Community Centre and their Sunday morning practice in the window of the record shop.

The answer to the Bohemians' problems appeared to lie with Ali McKenzie. But he was remaining defiantly stubborn, while acutely aware of the band's dilemma. 'He would even watch us rehearse,' Kim said, 'but he'd decided to keep his options open, hoping for a better offer.'

The better offer never came. Kim nagged constantly at his best friend. But the clincher came when Ali met a new girlfriend, Carol, who also lived in Whitethorn Avenue. At that point he consigned himself to the inevitable and joined the group. Robin politely stepped aside, but stayed on as the band's helper, often lugging to rehearsals the PA supplied by Ali. The new line-up was: Ali McKenzie, lead vocals; Ronnie Wood, lead guitar, harmonica and vocals; Tony Monroe, rhythm guitar and vocals; Kim Gardner, bass; and Bob Langham, drums.

Ronnie Wood playing harp? Since when? Since the day before, actually. His mother, Lizzie, tells the story: 'Ronnie picked everything up so fast, just like with his painting. He came home one night and he said, "Look, Mum, look what I've got" and he'd bought a mouth organ, a harmonica. He'd given a pound for it. I said, "What did you buy that for? You can't play it!" and he said, "I will." He took it upstairs to his bedroom on something like a Wednesday and started blowing it until he fell asleep with it, and in the morning he came down and said, "I've cracked it!" and that very night he was playing it on stage with the band.'

Art confirms the story – as a musician as well as a brother. 'He stayed up all night practically, and the next night people were going, "Great harp player!" and he'd only had it one day!'

At this point they decided to get rid of the vaguely beatnik-sounding Bohemians, a name never to be heard again in rock music until Queen recorded 'Bohemian Rhapsody'. But then, Freddie Mercury had been an art student at Ealing at the same time as Ronnie and Tony. At Ronnie's suggestion, they now called themselves the Thunderbirds, after the Chuck Berry song 'Jaguar And The Thunderbird'.

Local gigs followed, and the Thunderbirds won a Beat competition that netted them a permanent Saturday-night residency at the local Community Centre. Naturally, the group renamed their new venue the Nest.

Art Wood believes that this was the Thunderbirds' major step-up. They now had the security of a regular gig and the chance to develop their own sound. And it was not before time, because their individual preferences were all very different. Ronnie and Tony had become avid fans of the Yardbirds, in particular Eric Clapton. In truth, it was next to impossible to find any R&B musician who wasn't a Clapton fan. However, Ronnie and Tony couldn't agree about the Rolling Stones. To put it bluntly, Tony thought the Stones were a wishy-washy group who would be nothing without Mick Jagger, while Ronnie thought they were great. Ali agreed with Ronnie that the Stones had tremendous charisma, although they weren't his favourites. Kim liked anyone who turned him on. As for drummer Bob Langham, no one ever found out who he liked.

*

Soon all the local newspapers began publishing little stories about the band, where they were playing and what competitions they had entered. As witness the headline:

When The Thunderbirds Feather The Nest
NOW MODS AND ROCKERS RECKON THE DRAYTON SOUND

The same article went on to talk abut the 'West Drayton Beat' and reminded readers that the Beatles had also started as rank outsiders.

The Nest gave the Thunderbirds the first real money they ever earned, since they were allowed to charge people at the door and keep the takings. Not before time, either, for the group's instruments left a great deal to be desired. For example, Tony was still playing an old Hofner solid-body! Luckily Ronnie had managed to rent an elderly electric guitar, his first, for £25 from Terry Marshall, the owner of the Rainbow Record Shop. An early Thunderbirds fan, Terry allowed them to rehearse in the shop, as he had done the Bohemians, and even to use various items of equipment, on the strict understanding that nothing was 'borrowed' for a gig.

But at least they were sounding better now, largely because Tony's father had bought him a Vox amp for £130 the day after they won the competition – and this at a time when the average wage was less than £15 a week.

'Our family circumstances were different,' Tony explains. 'My parents were better-off and maybe that's where the competition started on Ronnie's side. Who was the best painter, who was the best basketball player, who was the most popular person – albeit we were great friends, or I thought we were. Like, when my Dad brought me that amp, I didn't think twice before giving it to Ronnie because he was the lead guitarist. I said to him, "Here, you have this and I'll make do with the old one," which was a tiny, fifteen-amp thing. It made a world of difference to his playing, because it was the first time we actually had a proper amp.'

Tony's father also helped with transport. None of the band was yet old enough to drive, so he made them two large wheelbarrows so that they could take the drums and amps from rehearsals to local gigs. If they ever played further afield, Tony's father or an older friend would drive them there. Pretty soon the band and their wheelbarrows became a familiar sight around Yiewsley and West Drayton – 'Turn your face to the wall, my darling, as the Thunderbirds go by' – but the barrows did at least make it easier and cheaper to get on to Eel Pie Island.

Like the Chislehurst Caves, Eel Pie Island, on the Thames at Twickenham, was to become one of London's legendary music venues. It was reached by a narrow bridge as symbolic as it was necessary, but the bridge's size meant that groups had to manhandle their equipment on to the island and then to the stage. That was the way it was done until an enterprising man realized that the bridge was just wide enough for a Mini-Moke and made himself a nice little sum taking across instruments and amps. But since they already owned two large wheelbarrows, the Thunderbirds could do it all themselves.

Eel Pie Island in particular became known as an R&B venue – Art Wood remembers fans of all ages flocking in at the weekend. 'That was one of the differences between now and then: there was no age limit to liking a particular type of music. I don't mean that everyone liked everything, but it wasn't strange to see kids, adults and even grandparents at the same gig. They'd be in their own little cliques, of course, but they were all there, all enjoying themselves.'

By contrast with America, where the pre-teen and the teenager had already been discovered and promoted, mostly as a way of selling anything from trainer bras to counselling, in the UK children were viewed as trainee adults. Those growing up in the fifties and early sixties were expected to be extremely responsible and to know how to take care of themselves from a comparatively early age. The great social divides based on age didn't really begin in the UK until the seventies.

Within a matter of months the Thunderbirds' tough, home-made brand of rhythm and blues had earned the band a large and extremely loyal following.

'Ronnie and I saw the Stones during this period,' Ali remembers, 'and they were obviously a big influence on any young R&B band at the time. Their sheer charisma . . . or whatever it was, they had it. But I can't honestly say they influenced the group at that point particularly, because, although we played the same sort of stuff, our roots in music were far more diverse to what we actually performed. Sam Cooke was my all-time favourite, alongside Marvin Gaye and later Dionne Warwick. Ron and Tony were into the Yardbirds . . . We were all into different things. So we took all these influences, Motown, R&B and rock 'n' roll and added our own extra ingredients. We were, after all, white English kids. There's no way we could have been just a Motown band, and sounded just one-dimensional like that – we just added our sound to this mish-mash.'

Ronnie remembers it differently. He was alone when he first saw the Stones – or if anyone else was there, family or his own band, he can't remember them.

'The first time I saw the Stones live was at the Richmond Jazz Festival in 1964. They were playing inside a tent that was bopping up and down, looking like an elephant with its big ass rocking and rolling from side to side. From the outside you could tell something good was happening in there. I went in and stood at the back, like this awkward kid totally intrigued by it all. I remember I was the last one to leave. Walking out, I kept on turning to watch the Stones haul their gear off-stage – and almost broke my leg walking into a tent pole. Then I went again to see them at the Windsor Cavern, when they were still wearing those uniforms. They were working pretty hard, doing about two shows a day. There was a long line of people zigzagging up the road, waiting to get in. I assumed the Stones were already backstage. Instead, this putrid orange van pulls up, packed with amps and human cattle. The driver – it must have been Ian Stewart – gets out and walks to the back door of the van and opens it. Five guys come pouring out like water over a broken dam and fall into the gutter, all in their wrinkled uniforms and sprawling in the dirt. And yes, I knew I belonged in that band. I've always been a believer in fate. I just counted on it happening, thought I'd be patient because it would fall in my lap someday. I just had to wait it out.' It would be a long wait. But it would be worth it.

Another musically significant event in the life of Ronnie during 1964 occurred when Ted left the family home to marry his long-term girl-friend, Gill. This meant that he could move into more spacious quarters – leaving the now famous boxroom empty. But not for long, as Art needed homes for his group. Keith Hartley, the drummer, was billeted with Art's mother-in-law, in his wife's old room, while keyboard player Jon Lord found himself the happy occupier of the Wood boxroom: £4 a week full board, washing and ironing included. This made Jon Lord the latest in a long line of musicians to teach Ronnie the finer points of their profession.

For Tony Monroe, the individual influences were what made the Thunderbirds, soon to be the Birds, so unique. 'The two-guitar set-up set us apart from a lot of groups. Ronnie and I were the R&B side of the group, whereas Kim was real rock 'n' roll and Ali was into Motown. Ronnie and me were very "arty-farty art school", so we were up on all the very rare R&B records like "St Louis Woman", Muddy Waters and all that sort of stuff. R&B was relatively innovative at that time, so we were very cool.'

Life was good for Ronnie. The band was beginning to develop its own sound. They had a regular gig and an ever-increasing group of regular fans. He was part of a musical and cultural explosion that would eventually infuriate so many people who were born too late for the sixties. It was truly bliss to be alive.

What could possibly go wrong?

The answer came on Sunday 31 May 1964, the day before Ronnie's seventeenth birthday. Stephanie de Court, whom he had been going out with for over a year, had been killed the evening before with three friends while travelling to a barbecue party in Henley-on-Thames. Apparently they had become lost, then been hit head-on by a drunken pilot driving home from Heathrow. The Thunderbirds had been playing to a packed house in Reading at the time, and Ronnie had been anxiously scouring the audience for her all night.

'She was my first true love,' he freely admits. 'I'd met her at Ruislip Grammar. I never fumbled with her, though. I was too awkward with girls then – sweaty palms and everything. I mean I simply idolized her. She would let me walk her home from school, carry her books and that was enough for me. I would run home from her house completely elated, clicking my heels in the air. The great thing was that she would come to the Nest to see us play, and even when we started to play other towns, she would drive up with a bunch of friends.'

The morning after the accident, Ronnie recalls, 'My father woke me up with the news. The subtle guy that he was: "Wake up, Ronnie. C'mon. Stephanie's been killed. Come downstairs and see her uncle." I was in a daze walking down the stairs and into the living room. There was her uncle, who said, "I'm afraid that Stephanie died in a car crash last night." Ah, I thought, that's why she never turned up.'

Stephanie's uncle also had with him the aftershave she'd bought for Ronnie's birthday, for she'd been expected to tea that same Sunday.

Tony Monroe heard about the accident by phone from Robin Scrimshaw, and they rushed round to console Ronnie by taking him to the local pub. 'It was the first time any of us had experienced death,' Tony said. 'We were all just kids, and here was someone who was not only dead but she was also our age. We didn't think about the other driver who died though, we were trying to cheer Ron up, which was obviously impossible. We weren't even old enough to drink legally and Robin, who was the tightest bloke around, gave Ron a pound for his birthday, which was a miracle in itself! But what sticks in my mind the most was Ronnie. He just sat there for ages, then looked up and said, "After all the money I've spent on her!" That was his reaction.'

Black humour used as an emotional release? Or one of those things that you say without knowing why, and then wishing to God you hadn't – probably because you can't quite come to terms with what happened?

One of those comments you remember years later and groan aloud with embarrassment and remorse, usually when you're waiting with a bunch of strangers for the bus. Or perhaps in that one throw-away comment – albeit caught by Tony Monroe, who is still wondering what he meant – Ronnie showed the 'been there, done that, time to move on' side to his nature that would characterize his professional career until he finally found his musical home with the Stones.

Ronnie went to the funeral and cremation with Tony and Diane Salmon, who had been Stephanie's best friend and had also been seeing Tony. He wore his new black jacket, tailored with a hint of Regency flair, white shirt, black tie, dark trousers and the square-toed shoes with two raised seams on the uppers. Still stunned, the three friends were quiet. For Ronnie, it was all a little unreal: there would be no grave to visit, nowhere to bring flowers. And the ceremony wasn't really about his Stephanie, but about the girl who had also belonged to her family and other friends.

A few days later, dressed more casually, he went alone to see where Stephanie had been killed: 'The tyre marks and everything. It happened on a strip called the Henley Fairmile. I just had the morbid need to go. There and then, after I'd seen it, I put it out of my head.'

It's not that Ronnie runs away from reality. It's just that he doesn't always notice it – especially when it threatens to interfere with his music.

3
Big in Cheshire

The Thunderbirds had reached a stage in their existence when they hovered uncertainly between local boys having fun and professional musicians. On the one hand they were developing a unique sound and an incredibly strong rapport with audiences. On the other, they were still trundling their equipment around in wheelbarrows or being driven to distant gigs by Tony's father or a family friend. Aside from being impractical, it was just so undignified.

Enter Leo de Klerk, a South African-born impresario who owned a string of nightclubs, including the Cavern clubs in Windsor and Reading. Leo was very typical of the type of pop businessman who began appearing in the sixties. He was young – in his early thirties – when he met the Thunderbirds, and always well dressed and charming. In addition to his nightclubs, Leo was also a bit-part actor, specializing as the smooth 'heavy' – he was also a body-builder – and would later appear in TV series like *The Professionals*. He also owned various nightclubs, acted whenever he could and was a genuine body-builder. But he was not South African – he was a South London cockney whose assumed name oscillated between de Clerck and de Klerk, and whose real first name was the not very hard-sounding Lionel. He ran his mini-empire with the help of two large West London brothers, Colin and Tony Farrell, also avid body-builders. Leo wasn't a gangster, but he was sharp, with a good eye for the main chance.

Leo had visited the Nest at the suggestion of a friend he was meeting nearby. According to Tony Monroe, Leo had been instantly impressed by the chemistry between the Thunderbirds and their audience. 'Leo, being an entrepreneur and with his club background, could see that here was a group he could put into his own clubs and save money while making money. By putting us on the road, he knew a good thing when he saw it.'

When he asked to see the group's leader, Leo was expecting to meet Ali. But a few minutes later he was a little surprised to find himself shaking hands with Ronnie Wood. In those days lead guitarists – no matter how good – simply didn't run bands. That role was always reserved for the singer, or lead vocalist. Which partly explains why today the rest of the Rolling Stones refer to Mick Jagger simply as 'LV' – even though he can play a pretty mean harp.

Leo made Ronnie an offer he simply couldn't refuse. He would manage the Thunderbirds on a professional basis and pay them each £10 a week – about £200 in today's terms. He would provide them with a van and pay for petrol and maintenance, as well as providing a road manager to drive them from gig to gig. Later there would be a clothes allowance and, in time, record deals and foreign tours. Leo effectively took a bunch of sixteen- and seventeen-year-olds up to a high place and offered them the world.

No one did their sums. No one realized that the Thunderbirds would be costing Leo at least £250 a week each in wages and expenses – roughly £1200 in modern money – and he would have to pay for the transport: a light-blue, second-hand Commer van. They would have to play an awful lot of gigs for Leo to show a profit – unless they became wildly popular. But if they did, they would still be stuck on £10 a week.

On the face of it, this was a career opportunity for which most aspiring groups would have sold their families into slavery, let alone themselves. And sell themselves into slavery is, of course, what the Thunderbirds did. On the one hand a bunch of naive, ambitious musicians. On the other, the archetypal smooth operator. Leo de Klerk had no idea how big the Thunderbirds could or would become. He wasn't exactly taking a chance – the group would repay the investment and then some, merely by appearing at his own clubs – but even so, it was generous slavery for the times. The only problem was that the deal never took into account the fact that bands and teenagers do often mature and begin asking awkward questions like 'What's really in this for us/me?' In truth, Leo began losing the Thunderbirds the moment he signed them.

For the present, all Ronnie knew was that the group had been together only a few months and yet here was the chance of regular work and a steady wage. Ronnie already knew what he wanted to do for the rest of his life. 'In the back of my head,' he recalls, 'I knew what choice I had to make. I knew I wanted to be a musician first and an artist second. My brothers would eventually choose art, but they'd still made good money out of music. The Artwoods had even played in Poland. The moment we started to make any fucking kind of money at the Nest, I knew the windfalls were soon to follow. I knew they would come in time. I mean, look at Elvis, he had to wait only a few years to sell a few million records, but Van Gogh sold only one painting during his whole life. The choice was easy. The rest of the band thought so, too.'

The choice may have been obvious to Ronnie, but whether Lizzie and Arthur could see it quite as plainly would prove a whole different matter.

'I had mixed feelings really,' Lizzie ruefully recalls. 'I wanted him to get on with his music. I didn't want him to stop doing his art, but I knew his heart was in his music. He was so good, I was very torn in between. A lot of people would have given their right arm to be at art school and he hadn't been there for even a year . . . But he had his mind made up and he had to go with his heart, not his art.'

Lizzie duly signed her son out of Ealing School of Art, but 'Mum was very upset about Ron,' Art Wood remembers. 'She really felt she'd ruined his career and she was frightened he'd fail. Ted and me were into our music, but we didn't drop out of art school to do it. There was never a choice for us, but Ron was giving up what looked like a real secure future to go off with that bunch of herberts the Thunderbirds. I was sure it didn't look like the right choice and Mum felt responsible. I got Ron a little job with my brother-in-law, Robert Colewell, who had a sign-writing company called Signcraft, and that calmed everything down a bit.'

Ronnie had also met the girl who would eventually become his first wife. Krissie Findlay was born on 11 February 1948, in Malta, where her father was stationed with the Royal Navy. Her mother was part Italian and part Swedish, her father pure Scots – an exotic mix that gave Krissie her captivating features: ash-blonde hair, blue eyes and high cheek-bones. But the first thing that Ronnie noticed was her bra.

'The first real memory I have of him is seeing him and Kim [Gardner] in the audience at the Crawdaddy, because they both had really long hair. The club had fluorescent blue lights, and I had a black blouse on with a white bra underneath so the fluorescent light lit up the white bra and all I can remember is Ronnie looking at my tits with this incredible great smile, and me thinking, who is this man? I just remember thinking what beautiful teeth he had 'cos it was fluorescent, and what a cheeky grin. Ronnie isn't what you'd consider handsome, but he was the most incredibly unusual-looking guy I'd ever seen, and I was instantly intrigued. Not exactly attracted sexually, but he did have an incredible impact on me. I just thought, yeah! I had no idea they were musicians until I saw Ronnie on stage with Eric later that evening.'

Krissie was sixteen, a year younger than Ronnie, but considerably more adult. As with many army children, her father's various postings at home and abroad had given her a maturity beyond her years. Constant travel, the need to be able to make new friends on a regular basis and the traditional self-reliance of Service families had given her an outgoing and vivacious personality. Very much part of the Ealing/West London social scene, whose central core of revellers included Pete Townshend and Richard 'Barney' Barnes, Krissie had become Eric Clapton's girlfriend and lover when she was only fourteen.

In those days the Crawdaddy Club was at the Richmond Athletic Ground. Krissie was naturally in the audience that night in early March 1964 when the Yardbirds' lead singer, Keith Relf – doubly impaired by severe asthma and having only one lung – was unsurprisingly taken ill in the smoky club. Eric Clapton asked the packed audience if anyone could play harmonica, and Ronnie, goaded on by Kim, hesitantly volunteered his services.

In the event, he more than held his own with musicians he had long considered his mentors. Art remembers: 'That was a real confidence boost for Ronnie. After that there was no holding him back. Now more than ever he knew what he wanted to be.'

The next time Krissie saw Ronnie was in April 1964 when he was playing with the Thunderbirds at Harrow Technical College: 'Pete and Barney had given me free tickets and I went with a friend of mine, Suzy [Cunningham]. I recognized Ronnie, but I remember standing in the audience thinking, I really, really like him but he's copying Eric – which he wasn't.'

And that was as far as it went, since at that time Krissie was still going out with Eric Clapton, and Ronnie with Stephanie de Court, so the question of any stronger attraction was purely academic. But by early June everything had changed. Stephanie was dead and Krissie's relationship with Eric Clapton was beginning to run its course, as first loves inevitably do. The Thunderbirds had turned professional and become the Birds, playing the occasional gig at the Station Hotel in Richmond. Krissie and Susie Cunningham went along one Saturday night and once again found themselves watching Ronnie perform on stage. That same night Leo de Klerk invited a few of the local gig-goers to a party to meet the group. Neither girl needed much persuading.

'Originally I was going to go for Kim, because that was the way Suzy and me planned it, like teenage girls do. But it didn't work out like that, because Suzy and Kim vanished into the garden and I saw Ronnie standing there by the fireplace. So we had a slow dance together and then we kissed . . . and then that was it, I knew I was in love. We seemed to spend every day together after that, which was very young to have such an intense relationship. I was living at home, he was living with his mum and dad, and he used to come to my place and we used to sit round the kitchen table and Ronnie would paint and I'd try and paint, because that was Ronnie's other passion. But our backgrounds were very different: I'd been bought up in a very proper, middle-class family, quite strict in its own way, and Ronnie was from this gypsy background . . . very free and easy, anything goes. He always lived for the now. When you were with him, he could make you feel like the most special person in the world.'

Shortly after he and Krissie began dating, Ronnie quit his apprenticeship as a sign-writer. Leo's plans for the group to go full-time and begin touring made a day job impossible. Perhaps equally important, sign-writing had proved creatively stifling, or 'totally fucking boring', as Ronnie succinctly sums it up today.

'My swansong was painting ads at the local football ground,' Ronnie recalls with a shudder. 'It had this steeply sloping corrugated iron roof over the stand that you could read from the other side of the field. It felt like fucking Everest and I was scared shitless going up there every day!' But then, that's what apprentices were meant to do, really: get scared shitless and so learn their place in the scheme of things.' Mind you, Ronnie did have the added distraction of a bikini-clad Krissie sunbathing on the centre-spot.

'That little job did give Ron a bit of security and a bit more money,' Art says, 'for as long as it lasted. Plus it was a bit "arty", which kept his hand in and enabled him to do his thing with the group too. But the main thing was, it had made Mum feel better. At least he kept it up until he turned pro.'

Nevertheless, it was the first and last time Ronnie ever worked outside the music industry. If he couldn't make any money by playing, he was prepared to starve – or at least go round to his mum's for his tea. Luckily Krissie also understood musicians and was prepared to support Ronnie in his dream. She knew how good he was, sensed he could be even greater, and embarked on a series of jobs, including temping in a solicitors' office and selling clothes for Zandra Rhodes, to help supplement his wages from the group. They were kids, it was all an adventure, all part of the new world the sixties were promising. They became inseparable, Ronnie already exhibiting his life-long need to have a strong and supportive woman with him.

When Ronnie turned professional in June 1964 he was still a minor, which meant any commercial contract had to be signed on his behalf by his parents. 'Leo came round our house one night,' Lizzie recalls, 'and gave me all these forms to fill in which I'd never seen or heard of, and he said I must sign here and here . . . He went on and on for so long about what he thought he was going to do that when I went to sign the form he said no, I couldn't use a ballpoint pen – it had to be in ink from a fountain pen, which I had to get from my neighbour Mr Pearce, who advised me to be careful, and to read the small print, which got me worried all over again.'

But she signed, if only because Ronnie had set his heart on turning professional. Besides, Leo was so well turned out and pleasant. He was South African, too, which somehow made him all the more believable.

Leo wasted little time in securing the signatures of Ali, Kim and Tony's parents. But it was with the fourth Thunderbird that he failed. 'Bob wouldn't turn pro,' Tony explains. 'He had this extremely over-powering mother who wouldn't let him turn professional. She thought we would all turn into "druggies"!'

The Thunderbirds needed a new drummer, and given the way they were originally formed, it was only natural to steal one. On 20 June 1964, a week after 300,000 screaming fans had greeted the Beatles in Australia, the Thunderbirds entered the 'Battle of the Bands' competition at the Uxbridge Blues Festival. The contest was a complete sell-out with over 400 people crammed into the West Drayton Women's Institute Hall (each competitor got a jar of home-made jam or a bean-bag frog. No. But they should have), and half as many turned away at the door. The Thunderbirds swept into first place and collected a trophy and £20 in prize money.

The *Uxbridge Weekly Post* ran an article announcing 'The Town's Biggest Swing Night Ever' and printed quotes from teenagers who declared the Thunderbirds were fab, wonderful and 'Yes! We want more of this!' Today Uxbridge, tomorrow the world.

The band also left the competition with a new drummer. Pete Hocking was from the Dissatisfied – which they definitely were when they saw one of the most naturally gifted and versatile drummers on the circuit vanishing fame-ward with Ronnie Wood and Co. Coincidentally, Jim Cregan, the lead guitarist of the Dissatisfied, would eventually join Rod Stewart on his *Atlantic Crossing* album, replacing Ronnie Wood and finally achieving his own fifteen minutes of fame.

Pete Hocking was twenty, and so up to four years older than the rest of the group. Ali was eighteen, Ron and Tony seventeen and Kim, who instantly renamed the drummer Pete Hockeystick, a mere sixteen.

'He hated being called that,' Kim remembers. 'He changed it eventually to McDaniels, said it sounded "bluesier".'

With Pete on board, the band could turn its mind to the next most pressing problem: a name-change. Chris Farlowe and the Thunderbirds had recently emerged as one of Britain's highest-profile R&B groups, and they could hardly accuse him of copying them. So the band plumped for the slightly more subtle the Birds, and Ronnie proudly painted it on the side of the not-quite-new Commer van supplied by Leo.

And so began a three-year odyssey that would see the Birds become one of the country's best-known R&B groups who never quite made it. They never got a record in the Top Ten, nor even the Top Twenty. Yet they brought R&B, great R&B, to the yearning masses from John o' Groats to Land's End – and, in the process, they had themselves one hell of a time.

'We were the biggest thing since sliced bread in Salisbury,' says Ronnie. 'We used to get mobbed, with girls actually wanting a piece of your hair – they'd actually rip it out or rip your clothes. It was our own little bit of Beatlemania. Birds-mania in Salisbury – now there's one that should have made the headlines. We were also pretty big in the West Country, up in Derby, Altrincham in Cheshire – we were fucking big in Cheshire!'

4
'A scruffy-looking lot, to say the least'

The van became legend, too. It was rarely, if ever, washed and certainly never repainted. In time even the group's name became barely distinguishable from the graffiti that fans – mostly female – wrote on the sides.

'We lived in that fucking van. Five days a week!' Ali fondly remembers. 'Bed and breakfast half a crown. All five of us in the same bed, and that was after travelling all night to get there! It was OK when we played locally or in Leo's clubs like the Zambezi in Hounslow, but it started to get a bit rough when we got a big following: then we had to really travel, and we travelled a fucking lot. There was only one motorway back then, the M1, so if, for instance, we had to play in South Wales, we would have to go via Ross-on-Wye, all the way round. It would take for ever to get anywhere. Six, seven, eight hours, maybe even longer. We'd get twenty quid and have to drive all the way back. Break down, spend the night in the van or nearly freeze to death!'

Hash and speed were the group's drugs of choice, often taken simply because the travelling was so boring. Nowadays even a struggling band would ask for quite a lot more, but in those days it was bliss to be merely young and alive and playing music.

Psychotherapist and gallery owner – and one-time avid Birds-watcher – Lindsay Wells, then a nineteen-year-old Mod, remembers the group well from this period. 'I used to go down to the 100 Club [in London's Oxford Street] when I was a student and they were absolutely fantastic. But they also had a real tension on stage – you could see that the guy who played rhythm guitar [Tony Monroe] often upset the other band members. He was always going off on his own, or trying to dominate everyone. And I remember Ronnie crouching down and playing his guitar around his ankles! . . . In my opinion, they were the band that got thousands of people hooked on R&B and really interested in good music. We never grew out of it.'

'We lived on sausages, egg and chips for three years,' is Tony's clearest memory. 'Leo got us an agency which got us bookings as far away as Scotland. We received our £10 a week and were now professional. I'll give you an idea of one typical week. On a Friday night we played Cleethorpes supporting Julie Driscoll and the Steampacket with Rod Stewart and Brian Auger. On Saturday we played with the Who on the west pier in Blackpool – that was after sleeping in the van and driving on these little country lanes. Then on the Sunday we played in Salisbury – completely the other end of the country! Then it would be two nights playing at Leo's clubs in and around Windsor and back up north by Wednesday. It didn't matter what the weather was like – snow, sleet or rain. It was a weird experience! We did one show in Scotland where we were on at 9 o'clock, then we had a midnight gig seventy miles away followed by a 3 o'clock performance a hundred miles further on. We had to live, crap and piss in that bleedin' van! We made a hole in the floor that we would piss through. It was like: "Can't stop, got too far to go, piss through the hole." The whole van was covered in lipstick where girls would scrawl messages to us, or scratch our names and theirs into the paintwork.'

But not all fans were quite so loving. Britain was still very parochial, and local boys in particular resented outsiders – especially long-haired ones from London – attracting and seducing their girlfriends, albeit with their music and stage presence, whenever they could. Except for Ronnie, who was still touchingly faithful to Krissie waiting at home for him in London. The rest of the band – especially Ali – seemed hell-bent on screwing their way around the country, and found the presence of a non-combatant in their midst just a little annoying. So it was that most of the group came to be occupied by two major concerns: how to avoid being attacked by jealous menfolk, and how to get Ronnie laid.

The little matter of Ronnie's reluctance to screw around was settled in the Altrincham Hotel, near Manchester. One of the Birds' groupies was determined, in her own picturesque phrase, 'to get Ronnie' and foolishly promised Kim and Tony that if they set it up for her, they could come and cat-call in the morning. Groupies do like their triumphs witnessed, and it was going to be such a jolly jape. In those days the guys used to share rooms on tour – Tony with Ali, Kim with Ron, Pete with the hapless roadie – and Kim duly promised that the girl would have Ron and the room to herself. The suspicion remains that she was either criminally naive, or driving on empty. She duly made her way to the promised land, and there, just back from the gig, was Ronnie, who in fact needed very little persuading. So she locked the door and things took their inevitable course, as things always will when there's a chance of embarrassment high on the Richter scale.

In this case it was occasioned by hysterical laughter, followed by three musicians bursting out of the walk-in closet. Still, at least they'd waited fifteen minutes. So as far as both Ronnie and the girl were concerned, it wasn't a total fiasco. Nevertheless, his colleagues were fascinated by the fact that Ronnie kept his socks on. Red socks. Either he was making a sartorial statement or he was very, very keen. Whatever the truth, he had just carried on regardless.

It was around this time that Mod was taking root. It began life in London as a street-level fashion statement. Small pockets were first spotted in Stoke Newington, Shepherd's Bush, Mile End and Bermondsey, apparently oblivious of one another's existence. 'Each part of London had its own little Mod scene,' Ronnie points out. 'There was the Birds in Yiewsley – even Art was riding a scooter – and the Who in West London and the Small Faces in the East, who were the first group to dress the same as the audience. For them it was natural, not like other bands who deliberately copied whatever the audience was wearing – and their dance steps, too.'

The roots of Mod lay in an appreciation of the ultra-cool, white American jazz look. But, being English, Mods looked beyond the obvious and realized that jazz had its roots firmly in Black American music. And that was just as well, because few Mods actually liked jazz, so instead they embraced Black Soul and idolized heroes like Otis Redding, Curtis Mayfield and Sam and Dave.

The Small Faces were the first real, home-grown Mod group. The Who, on the advice of their managers, also adapted a Mod look and later added a pop-art feel, in itself borrowed from Mark Four, who would become the Creation. The Birds fell somewhere in between: the Mods loved the hard, R&B sound but disliked the band's slightly feminine look. Overall, the favourite Mod groups were the Stones (Charlie Watts was definitely Mod, and the band looked hard), the Action, the Yardbirds, the Artwoods and John Mayall's Bluesbreakers. All these were an acceptable white alternative to Black American rhythm and blues.

Mod was also a working-class reaction against authority, a rebellion expressed by looking far smarter, harder and cleaner than your so-called betters. This first requirement was made possible by hire purchase, for Mods could now buy their clothes on the never-never. It was a clothes- and music-obsessed, intensely narcissistic movement, and in the begin-

ning, predominantly male. Mods had no time for sex, and given their
high-octane lifestyle, wouldn't have been very good at it anyway.

Nor was Mod violent to begin with – no one wanted to ruin their
clothes. Then the media rapidly got hold of the story. Within weeks Mod
was handed lock, stock and barrel to the High Street retailers as a
watered-down and pre-packed version of the real thing, and style wars
broke out in early 1964. The movement's elitist originators countered
the mass-market merchandising by constantly evolving – to which they
were prone anyway – as a speed-inspired lifestyle gave them the attention
span of a gnat on a bad day. They buzzed from venue to venue, shop to
shop, on their glittering Italian scooters, which had to be as dressy as
their owners. Scooter accessories came and went at the same alarming
rate as the latest thing in shirts. Mods' entire lives had been dedicated to
making a specific sartorial statement, which the High Street now wanted
to control.

The new pretenders, who never understood what Mod was really
about but liked the music, the drugs and the clothes, competed to be
Mod-er Than Thou. English tribalism asserted itself and the inevitable
violence broke out. Many people, including historians, assume that the
Mods only had one enemy: Rockers. In fact, they always tended to fight
more with one another than anyone else, until the media seized upon one
small incident. The subsequent publicity resulted in the notorious seaside
riots between Mods and Rockers in the spring of 1964. By the middle of
the year many groups popular with Mods were in the awkward position
of having to publicly distance themselves from their fans.

Inevitably, violence broke out during many of the Birds' live gigs,
helped by Leo's habit of booking the band into seaside venues favoured
by marauding Mods on Bank Holiday weekends. 'I remember we played
the Aquarium in Brighton, and just as we were packing the gear away,
all these Mods arrived on their scooters and for no reason started
attacking the van,' remembers Tony ruefully. 'They were just looking for
trouble. I laid out the first one so they all turned on us. Luckily we had
Colin [Farrell] with us, who was an out-and-out nutter, and Ali had a go
as well. The rest of them always did a runner – Kim and Ronnie and Pete
were never anywhere to be seen. I got my shirt ripped right off my back,
and then the flick-knives came out, and we had to do a runner ourselves.'

But the Birds raved on, becoming as wild if not wilder than their
audiences. Even so, there were sexual limits, as Ali remembers: 'We used
to go to the weirdest parties – not so much round our area but when we
were playing away. Kim used to say we've got an all-night party – do
you want to come to it? And I remember one particular one – we'd
played Oxford University – and we went to a party afterwards and a gay

bloke tried to get me. He grabbed hold of my arm and was trying to drag me away to fuck me, and Colin got hold of him and diced him down. And then you'd get invited to places where the mums and dads were there, mums and dads, and aunties and uncles, and you'd be invited, thinking it was a rave-up and they're all sort of drinking fucking sherry and a cup of tea!'

The obvious next step was to capture the group on vinyl to promote their sound to the media and gain record-company interest. Leo paid for an acetate – today's demo tape – of a Ronnie Wood composition, 'You're On My Mind', a steaming slice of powerful, British R&B driven along at high speed by Ronnie's wailing harmonica and Kim's thundering bass lines, to a series of agonizing breaks which flip the song on its head and change its direction. At several key points it showed a maturity in Ronnie's songwriting that was far beyond his years. On 24 June 1964 this number led to an appearance on ITV's *Ready Steady Win!*, a spin-off from *Ready Steady Go!* This was a weekly 'Battle of the Bands' contest, with a first prize of £1000 worth of musical instruments, held at the Associated-Rediffusion television studios in Wembley. The Birds' big break looked a certainty.

Ten million viewers tuned in to see the band open the show by performing 'You'll Be Mine', which compère Keith Fordyce – looking more like a vaguely disapproving headmaster than ever – described as 'a lively start!' But unfortunately it wasn't enough. The panel of judges included chart star Adam Faith and *Evening Standard* journalist Maureen Cleave. The Birds finished a demoralized fifth out of the six competing acts, the eventual winners being the very mod Bo Street Runners, featuring a young Mick Fleetwood on drums.

The fact was, mainstream music shows never really knew how to cope with hard-line R&B groups like the Birds. Nor did mainstream disc jockeys always understand them – or anything else, unless it sounded and looked like something Cliff Richard would be happy to take home to his mother. Too many British disc jockeys, journalists, record companies and programme makers believed that music was only pop/rock 'n' roll or classical or jazz. Blues was all very good in its way, but hey – didn't Frank Sinatra do that as well? So blues was either jazz or pop, right? Musicals like *My Fair Lady* or *West Side Story* were, of course, classic-pop, or pop-jazz. And heaven forfend that bands should look and sound dangerous. Why couldn't they be like that nice Herman and his Hermits, for gosh's sake? Now, they were really mass-market. Even the Beatles wore ties. Of course, an exception had to be made for the Rolling Stones, but it was generally felt that one bunch of nutters was enough –

until the Small Faces and the Who showed up. Even then an enormous amount of industry publicity insisted that the more extreme groups were deeply caring and responsible people, only prone to the occasional spot of high jinks, bless them. John Mayall's Bluesbreakers, probably one of the most influential R&B bands on either side of the Atlantic – that is, the world – never appeared on *Top Of The Pops*, despite line-ups that at various times included Eric Clapton, Ginger Baker, Peter Green, John McVie and Mick Taylor, and whose debut album was one of Decca's all-time bestsellers. But if you didn't appear on *TOTP*, then you didn't really exist.

Leo de Klerk expressed his and the group's disappointment in the local press, but promised that the Birds would still 'fly higher', adding: 'I still have faith in the boys, they really have something and I know they will get to the top!' Meanwhile the *Hillingdon Mirror* was less complimentary and delighted in declaring 'Beat Birds Beaten' and repeating that Maureen Cleave 'hated their long hair'. How the press love to destroy the talented. Or perhaps she felt unable to mother them. On the other hand, Sir Francis Chichester had just set a new record for a single-handed Atlantic crossing, and Cilla Black had a number one with "You're My World", so perhaps Maureen Cleave had just been swept up in a tide of well-groomed jingoism.

But at least the Birds were beginning to be noticed. On 19 August they took part in BBC1's *ABC Of Britain*. With their usual immaculate timing, the band competed for the media spotlight with Great Train Robber Charlie Wilson, who'd just escaped from prison, and three women who'd been found guilty of indecency for wearing topless dresses. Musically, they were up against the latest Beatles album, *A Hard Day's Night*. It must have seemed to the group that you had to be a criminal, or supremely gifted, or female and naked to make any sort of impression on the general public. What else was new?

Undeterred, the Birds continued their round of club dates and in October 1964 secured a Monday-night residency at London's prestigious 100 Club. One of the supporting Monday-night bands, who used to play when the Birds were taking a break, was the Tridents, featuring a certain young guitarist named Jeff Beck, who would never like playing second fiddle to Ronnie Wood. Another group with a regular spot was the legendary Pretty Things, whose drummer, Viv Prince, always liked to sit in with other groups. Given that he was a) usually stoned out of his mind, and b) one of the great hard-man drummers of the time, he got to play a lot with the Birds. But then Pete was also invariably stoned out of his mind, and didn't always notice.

*

Meanwhile Leo, armed with the now well-worn acetate of 'You're On My Mind', capitalized on the Birds' brief, bleak TV exposures and managed to see Decca's Dick Rowe, still head of A&R despite being more famous for turning down the Beatles than eventually signing the Rolling Stones. (And then only because a merciful George Harrison had recommended them.) Dick Rowe passed the Birds on to his assistant, Franklin Boyd, who duly signed them up. The Birds entered Decca's recording studios for the first time in October 1964 to record their first single as professional musicians, an accomplished version of 'You're On My Mind'.

Most of the band hated this first studio experience. They preferred to play live on stage, and naively viewed record-making as a tedious chore; especially Ali, who needed an audience in order to perform. By contrast, Ronnie's background had given him an insight into how the music business really worked and to him the recording studio felt like home.

The B side was a treatment of 'You Don't Love Me' which owed a great deal to both the Pretty Things and the Stones. Both tracks are a perfect example of how British R&B groups could take the original sound from the States and bully it into something new and very exciting. The record was released in November to wild acclaim in West Drayton, Salisbury and Cheshire but nowhere else. It simply wasn't mass-market enough – there was some industry doubt as to whether it was even pop – and got very little air-time, either. For this was before DJs like John Peel or the sainted Kenny Everett were allowed to introduce weird and wonderful music on their shows. Britain's radio stations lacked the musical variety enjoyed by Americans, and if the record company wasn't totally behind a new release, forget it.

That was the problem with the music industry in the early sixties: everyone knew that musical tastes had changed, that evolution if not revolution was in the air; but the industry itself was ill-equipped to handle it. For every George Martin or Glyn Johns there were a thousand confused souls wondering what the hell to make of these latest sounds. Naturally it was a situation ripe for the hustler selling reassurance and specialist knowledge. If you think the sixties groups are interesting, you should look at the period's managers, promoters and musical con artists, who burst on to the music industry like pirates boarding a rich, fat, stately Spanish galleon.

But at least the Birds had a record out. And that meant you were really professional, that your fellow musicians would start taking you seriously. It also impressed club owners and agents, and venues throughout the land would soon begin advertising the imminent arrival of Decca's newest recording sensation. Getting a record out also meant that the band would be auditioned for BBC radio. Two audition reports from 1965 survive to make interesting reading. The first, recorded on Friday 12 February, was heard by the Talent Selection Group (whoever said the BBC has suddenly become bureaucratic?) on Monday 15 February. The Birds – Leader: Ronald Wood – performed 'I Ain't Got You', 'Bring it to Jerome' and 'Leaving Here'. All things considered, it was not the best of times to have auditioned. The day before, America had bombed North Vietnam, raising the spectre of world war. Cigarette commercials had just been banned from television. Enter a hard-drinking, hard-smoking, hard pill-popping and extremely aggressive group that played American-based R&B.

Seven people sat on that Talent Selection Group. Comments included: 'A scruffy-looking lot, to say the least'; 'their numbers were very monotonous . . . lacking in entertainment value'; 'ordinary . . . not of broadcasting standard'; 'ponderous, unoriginal styling'; 'A difficult medium to deal with and this group is not outstanding enough'; 'musically and rhythmically unexciting'; and 'A rather dreary R&B group . . . vocally unexciting'. Roger Fusey gave the Birds an unenthusiastic pass; his was the only one.

But as for the comment 'A scruffy-looking lot, to say the least' – this is a little strange, because Ali, for one, was addicted to clothes and Ronnie was developing his own Art School/Regency/Mod style. Ali was also notorious for arriving at the start of a tour with enough clothes to dress the entire band. He'd always be the last one to be picked up, would insist on hanging everything, fresh from the dry cleaners, all along the inside of the van. And as The Birds wended their merry way to Scotland, Cornwall, Wales or Cheshire, Ai's voice could be heard imploring his mates to 'mind me trousers' . . . 'watch out for me shirts' . . . and 'hey, that's a new jacket.'

Certainly the Birds' publicity photos show a neatly if interestingly dressed group. The famous checkered belts, by the way, couldn't be bought. The Birds made them themselves, using that checkered metallic tape used to decorate cars. 'Go-faster' tape it used to be called, and courtesy of their drummer's step-mother, the Birds were no strangers to speed.

In April 1965 the Birds released their second single, a cover of a slightly obscure Eddie Holland number, 'Leaving Here'. Originally the song had followed that winning Motown formula which could be relied on to transform even the most boring run-of-the-mill composition into something special. But, subjected to the Birds' full-on, twin-guitar assault, it became the group's personal property. Moreover, it looked set to inch its way up the charts, purely on its own merits, especially as they had enough fans to guarantee a Top Fifty entry. The B side was 'Next In Line', a second composition by Ronnie Wood. Years later avid Birds fan Lemmy would take the Birds' version of 'Leaving Here' a stage further and make it one of Motorhead's biggest-selling singles.

'Leaving Here' also led to the Birds' infamous appearance on ITV's *Thank Your Lucky Stars* when they were lowered on stage with wires – and yanked off the same way. For Kim, the real sickener was that their new shirts – dark blue with light-blue collars and cuffs, from Star Clothes – were ripped open to take the wires. As it was, Pete landed backwards on top of his drum-kit, unable to face the audience, and Kim was briefly dumped on to an old lady's lap before being swung back on to the stage and finishing the set still suspended a few inches above the floor.

In early 1965, Krissie's parents moved to the Midlands. But Krissie, exerting her formidable independence, refused point-blank to leave London and Ronnie. After some discussion, it was agreed that she could stay on in the family's flat in Ealing until her parents were settled. When that time came, the flat would have to be sold and Krissie would either have to join her parents or find somewhere new to live. With understandable trepidation, the Findlays left London. Their fears were soon justified, for Ronnie effectively moved in.

Krissie was still seventeen when she discovered she was pregnant. The sixties might have been swinging, but illegitimacy still carried a terrible social stigma. 'I kept it all to myself and never told Ronnie,' she recalls. 'We were so poor, and couldn't afford to bring a baby into the world living as we did. I couldn't tell my parents, either. Everyone I really loved would have wanted me to keep the baby, but none more so than Ronnie. But I knew – or thought I knew – that would be the finish of his career because we were too young to cope. Nowadays it must seem mad, because kids seem to think nothing of being a young single mum. And there isn't the same sort of shame attached to it any more. What made it even more difficult was that I'd been brought up a Catholic to believe abortion was wrong.'

Ronnie and Krissie had recently met Rod Stewart and his girlfriend, Jenny Rowlands, daughter of Rod's manager, John. Rod had just released his first solo single, 'Good Morning Little Schoolgirl', and Ronnie and Krissie had been regulars at the Thursday-night residency at the Marquee Club in Wardour Street of Rod and his group the Soul Agents.

The four had got on well together. Ronnie looked up to Rod, who although only a couple of years older, seemed vastly more experienced. Krissie felt the same way about Jenny and turned to her older friend for advice. Not to help her make a decision, though: Krissie had already made up her mind, and all she needed was an address. Jenny supplied it.

At that time abortions were as medically safe as one could afford. Krissie couldn't afford very much, and a couple of days later was rushed to hospital, where she nearly died from complications and an infection. Ronnie was away touring with the band. Krissie left a message with Lizzie to say that she was going to visit her family, and then another to say she was going on holiday to Malta, whereas in fact she'd been sent there to recuperate.

'My parents tried to break us up, which was why I was sent to stay with family friends. They liked Ronnie, really loved him, but they didn't think he was right for me. They hoped I'd forget him in Malta.'

While Krissie was away, her parents arranged for the sale of the flat in Edge Hill Road. This had always been the plan, but now there was the possibility that without the flat, Krissie would come and live with them for a while.

When Krissie returned to England, it was to 8 Whitethorn Avenue, to be reunited with her lover in his own family home. They stayed there for only a few months, Ronnie sharing a bedroom with Jon Lord, who'd been promoted from the boxroom so that Krissie could move in. 'Ronnie used to creep in in the early morning for a snuggle,' Krissie laughs. 'Until one time we both fell asleep and his dad caught us when he got up for work. He came in to ask if I wanted a cup of tea . . . which was when I first heard his famous line: "Where do you think you are, then – on yer father's yacht?" We were both really scared, but then he said: "I suppose I'd better bring two cups up, then." He was such a lovely man.'

Meanwhile the Birds were flying high with 'Leaving Here'. Four girls had even set up the official Birds' Fan Club, based in Hillingdon, Middlesex, and sent out thousands of postcards specially prepared by Leo and the Harold Davison Agency, which was now enthusiastically booking the band nationwide. All the signs were good. 'This is the one that's going to do it, boys,' Leo enthused – especially after the agency reported live interest in the group from all over Europe. Decca gave them thousands upon thousands of little pink stickers that announced 'The Birds Are Leaving Here' and gave the record's catalogue number. These they happily stuck on any available surface, including equipment belonging to other groups.

Ronnie was so sure that the song would be a hit that he had his first guitar custom-made at Marshalls' of Ealing: a solid Fender Telecaster body fitted with a Danelectro twelve-string neck and finished in lime-green, which he named a Danecaster.

Tony answered the fan letters.
Kim got drunk.
Pete got stoned and Ali got a new suit.
The record was selling well and everyone was happy . . . for a month.

5
'All I really want to do . . .'

In May 1965 a flurry of angry letters began arriving at the Birds' Fan Club. It seemed that the single the fans thought they'd ordered wasn't the one they finally received. Instead, they'd been given a jingly-jangly cover version of a Bob Dylan song.

The American Byrds had landed – spelt with a 'y' but pronounced 'serious trouble' for the British group – and were racing past 'Leaving Here' in the charts with 'Mr Tambourine Man'.

'All the fans were saying that they ordered the Birds' latest record from the local shop,' Ronnie remembers, 'but they'd been given just fucking folky rubbish instead.' By June, 'Tambourine Man' – already an American number one – was sitting on top of the British pile and still selling, while 'Leaving Here' had simply left.

Columbia, who'd released 'Tambourine Man', launched the biggest campaign that Britain had seen in years. The Byrds were billed as America's answer to the Beatles – never mind that they didn't write their own songs yet. But they were under the protective wing of ex-Beatles press officer Derek Taylor and had been invited to England in August by Mervyn Conn and Joe Collins, father of Joan and Jackie.

Neither Conn nor Collins was a rock promoter; both had more of a showbiz impresario background. They had been caught up in the hyping of the group by an American media desperate to regain the rock 'n' roll crown. It wasn't just pride – money was at stake, too.

In the sixties, British and American groups played each other's countries on a one-for-one basis. Visiting US performers could play in the UK only if a British act could be found to replace them back home, and vice versa. Panic set in when a suitable British group couldn't be found to accommodate the Musicians' Union ruling. However, at the last minute the Dave Clark Five nobly volunteered – the Byrds were also a five-piece band – and were duly booked to play Stateside.

Excitement mounted as touchdown approached. As usual, journalists

were caught up in the frenzied anticipation as much as any impression-
able fan. Headlines proclaimed: 'BYRDS BIGGEST CRAZE SINCE
BEATLES!' and 'Byrds: America's biggest group ever!' Even the jingoistic
New Musical Express predicted 'Byrd Mania'. Mervyn Conn started a
massive poster campaign that simply announced: 'The Byrds Is Coming',
stealing the (ungrammatical) idea from the 1964 poster campaign that
promoted Hitchcock's film *The Birds*. Ironically, the movie had once
given the British Birds a small amount of unintended publicity. Conn's
posters covered London. The Birds took one look at them and threw
their little pink stickers in the back of the van. They were never to
become collector's items.

Then, on 2 August, Leo struck back. 'It was in the early hours, on
a Monday morning,' Ronnie recalls. 'We'd just finished a gig up north
and I'd only just got to bed. Leo called and told me to get myself down
to the airport, which was only a few miles away. When I got there at
eight o'clock the place was full of screaming girls and the Birds were
all moaning about having to get up so early – except Leo, who was
fuming and saying that he was going to "teach them fucking Yanks
a lesson".'

Leo's tactic was to produce seven writs which claimed infringement
on the Birds' registered name and sued for damages and loss of earnings.

It was a cold day in August when the Byrds landed at Heathrow. Derek
Taylor should have warned them about the British weather and to pack
something warm. Instead, they trooped shivering in their thin, Californian finery through Immigration, through Customs and into the Arrivals
Hall, to be greeted by hundreds of shrieking girls plus a group of pissed-
off British R&B musicians armed with writs.

'It was Leo and the Farrell brothers who actually served the writs,'
Kim remembers. 'One for each Byrd, and obviously two for luck. They
shoved them in their hands and the cameras were going crazy. We sort
of shuffled around and looked at our feet for a bit, then sloped off and
waited for the pubs to open.'

In fact, the other two writs were served on Mervyn Conn and Joe
Collins.

When the Byrds' leader, Roger McGuinn, was asked for his reactions,
he dreamily quoted a Dylan lyric: 'I don't want to compete with you . . .
all I really want to do is be friends with you.'

For his part, Leo had been completely serious. Columbia's legal
department swatted the writs aside as if they were arthritic flies. Even if
Conn was right when he said, claiming to be utterly appalled, that it was
'just a nasty publicity stunt', it hadn't been a very good one. The British

media had invested so much in Byrd Mania that no other band could be allowed a look-in.

The fans felt differently. British audiences weren't ready for a permanently stoned Californian group composed of pampered, petulant and overprivileged Hollywood brats who modelled their entire image on Brian Jones. As usual, those same journalists who had so brilliantly elevated the Byrds to God-like status now turned on them. It began well enough with a series of successful press conferences, then meeting the Beatles, courtesy of Taylor, and tripping around Carnaby Street boutiques. It started going wrong when the TV show *Ready Steady Go!* was turned over to them and they failed to deliver live their expertly recorded sound, even if the studio audience did swoon on cue. This was followed by a string of disastrous live shows in wholly unsuitable venues, including Mod clubs like the Flamingo, where the Byrds' ultra-cool demeanour annoyed audiences used to being fully entertained. At the Pontiac Club in Putney the band was heckled all through the first set, and not only by British Birds fans. The biggest cheer of the night came when DJ Rick Gunnell announced that records would be played until Geno Washington and the Ram Jam Band (also American, and Mod favourites) returned, replacing the Byrds' second set.

The ill-fated tour limped painfully on, with Conn adding more and more dates in an attempt to regain that loving feeling – and get some of his money back. But before long the Byrds really regretted not packing something warm, when the first of them, bass player Chris Hillman, collapsed in the dressing room with an asthma-related chest infection. He was closely followed by McGuinn, who collapsed with a temperature of 103°F and then drummer Michael Clarke – who only got the job because he looked like Brian Jones – went down with the flu. Gigs were cancelled and the press speculated that the Byrds had simply had enough. A final kick when they were comatose was delivered by no less than the *NME*'s Keith Altham, who wrote snootily that: 'They were simply pretenders to the Beatles' crown.' Even Derek Taylor turned on his charges: 'Take them out of Hollywood . . . put them in the real world . . . and they couldn't handle it.' A trifle harsh, perhaps, considering that Conn had expected them to play thirteen gigs in six days.

And so the dejected Byrds flew home, vowing never to return until the time was right. And it never was – except for McGuinn, who since 1967 has brought several different Byrds line-ups to the UK.

The Byrds' first experience of England was sourly immortalized in their song 'Eight Miles High'. Everyone assumed it was about drugs, but the Byrds insisted it was a merely a reference to landing at Heathrow. The band's hatred for England wasn't totally xenophobic. It was one of the wettest summers on record and many English patriots were also dreaming of warmer, sunnier climes. Mods, too, had been an eye-opener and the line: 'In places small faces abound' was a reference to DJs continually playing the diminutive Mod group's records at every club where the Byrds suffered. Probably the most scathing crack was made at the expense of the British Birds: 'No warmth can be found from those afraid of losing their ground.'

In a final twist to the tale, when the Byrds returned to the States they recorded the same Dylan song McGuinn had quoted at Heathrow, 'All I Really Want To Do', and it became Columbia's best-selling single in the UK.

In August, when this further Dylan cover version was released, Ronnie and the Birds were once again auditioning for the BBC. This time only four people sat on the Talent Selection Group. One of them remembered the Birds from the previous time, and saw: 'A marked improvement from their last audition. An R&B group providing a good sound, all being adequate instrumentally and vocally. The lead singer has a good, rough R&B type voice and his performance is now up to standard.' By contrast, one of the panel said: 'Most unattractive lead voice.' Another comment was: 'Poor equipment giving guitar distortion of the worst quality . . . uninspired arrangements causing a bad attack of Listener's Monotony.' 'A very dreary R&B group,' was a further assessment.

Maybe the Birds weren't as good as they and their fans thought they were. But their records, even today, do have a certain something. The guys could certainly play. But there is a valid reason for resurrecting these audition reports. Because what comes over loud and strong is that the Birds were a group who really needed the buzz from an audience to come alive. It's also worth noting that they'd been woefully under-rehearsed, as no one had ever taught them how to play live in a studio. Finally, the 'experts' were judging all R&B groups by the Rolling Stones. What the band desperately needed was some serious tuition and the type of publicity that stops an expert dead in his tracks.

Andrew Loog Oldham did the publicity bit for the Stones – and quite brilliantly. Who can forget when they were voted the group that parents would least like to see their daughters going out with? Or the rumour that they were all dying of leukaemia? Or all the scurrilous stories about their sexual contests? The Stones were quickly established as mad, bad and dangerous to know. Even if they hadn't been consummate musicians and performers, they would have succeeded for a brief time at least.

No one did the same for the Birds. In fact, there was only one DJ who regularly mentioned the group in his column: Jimmy Saville, who'd actually heard them play and liked the sound. For all his clowning around, Saville was one of the few DJs who both knew and really cared about music and musicians. But he could never quite fix it for the Birds.

Unaffected by their second BBC rejection – except, that is, for Ronnie, who took it personally – in October the Birds recorded their third and last single for Decca, 'No Good Without You, Baby'. This was an attempt to further develop the formula sound of 'Leaving Here': recording an obscure American soul number in their own aggressive style. It had looked like working with 'Leaving Here,' and the Birds were convinced they were on to a winner. It was backed by a Wood original, 'How Can It Be,' a double-tracked crescendo of pent-up angst – possibly the best recorded example of how powerful the Birds' sound could be.

It flopped. Even so, there was no shortage of live gigs. It seemed that their heavy workload was unaffected by two and a half successive flops. They even landed a respectable spot on the programme at the Glad Rag Ball – above Geno Washington but below Ted Heath And His Music – at the Empire Pool Wembley in November. At an event at which Donovan headlined and the main supporting acts were the Kinks, the Hollies and the Who, the Birds' inclusion effectively established them as one of the top twenty live acts in Britain.

So who needed a record in the charts anyway? Ronnie did. He could imagine growing old with the band, still touring the same faded venues until his gnarled fingers could play no more.

6
'Stiggy-poo wasn't fussy'

Ali always liked Leo de Klerk and to this day thinks that the Birds were wrong to fire him. But as Leo paid the group a clothing allowance and Ali could have used a second van just to carry his dry-cleaning, the singer would feel that. Actually, the truth is a little more complex. Leo looked after the boys very well, but they were his boys and they did what he said. This was fine by Ali, who liked being looked after, but not so fine with the rest of the band, who felt they should be making some of the decisions. All except Pete McDaniels, by now so permanently spaced out on drugs that he found it hard to decide whether it was light night or dark day.

Specifically, Ronnie, Tony and Kim thought they should be making more money. But at the same time career tensions were beginning to surface, particularly between Tony and Ron. Not that Tony noticed them at first, although he did think Ronnie should have credited him with more of a creative input into the songs they developed together. He remembers Jon Lord – still lodging *chez* Wood – pulling Ronnie to one side, in a brotherly sort of way, and telling him as much: 'I think that was a catalyst with Ron. After that he saw me as a threat. I'll always remember coming back from a gig one night, after we'd sacked Leo, and there was this heated conversation going on, like there always is when you're still all fired up, the adrenalin's still pumping and it takes a hell of a long time to unwind. And suddenly Ron, who's been saying fuck-all, turns to me and says: "You'll be good at whatever you do, but you're not doing it in music." It was like bells being struck, and I thought, oh, all right, I know where this is going.'

Of course, Ronnie's remark might have had something to do with Tony's increasing habit of snapping back at interviewers that he wasn't simply a rhythm guitarist, but a second lead. There was no question but that the two boyhood friends were becoming increasingly disgruntled with each other.

In part the problem was one of ambition. Ronnie came from a

professional music background and knew exactly where he wanted his career to go. The others, represented by Tony, were reasonably happy to carry on the way they were, although more money would have been nice. The trouble they were having with Leo encapsulated all the tensions, all the niggling doubts and disagreements that had built up within the group over the past three years.

It all came to a head on 31 December 1965. They had been playing a New Year's Eve gig at the Starlight Ballroom in Sudbury, but at the end of the night neither Leo nor the Farrell brothers were there to collect Leo's share of the door money. Big mistake. Peter Lindsay, the Starlight's manager, handed over a large amount of cash to Tony, asking him to give it to 'your boss'.

'I couldn't believe it,' Tony remembers. 'I was looking at nearly a thousand quid! And we were costing Leo – what? – maybe five hundred a week, tops. We were working flat out and had to be earning Leo a fucking fortune. I called the rest of the band over and showed them. Ali wasn't too worried, said maybe we should ask for a rise. I don't think Pete even heard what I said. But Ronnie and Kim were really pissed. We felt so stupid, you know? Like we were little kids who'd been ripped off by this big bad adult. The fact that Peter Lindsay called Leo our "boss" didn't help, either.'

When Leo finally showed up to collect the takings he was met by a quietly amused Lindsay, who had a message for him. 'I've already given the money to that Tony,' Lindsay explained. 'And by the way, I think they're giving you the sack.'

Leo arrived at Tony's house at around two-thirty in the morning, accompanied by Colin Farrell. Tony's mother eventually opened the door. Leo was as polite as usual – and just as insistent. Could he see Tony? It was really terribly important. Tony's mother was equally firm. No, he couldn't. Tony wasn't there.

Leo and Colin Farrell left, apologizing.

Tony sat in his bedroom, clutching a large amount of cash and wondering what the hell the band was going to do next.

No such misgivings troubled Ronnie. He'd gone home and to bed secure in the knowledge that whatever happened would be for the best.

Kim knew that whatever Tony and Ronnie decided would be OK by him.

Pete had nodded off wondering what year it was.

And Ali was dreaming fitfully about a new shirt that was missing its buttons.

*

Naturally, Leo was piqued, but was generously inclined to overlook this single act of mutiny. After all, he had just announced to the press that the Birds were 'flying high into '66' with a proposed tour of Ireland and Scandinavia and another single due for release at the end of January. The group could keep the money from the Starlight; Leo had his eyes firmly set on a far bigger pay-day. Yet he must have seen the writing on the wall. All that was left to him was to make as much money as he possibly could from the Birds before they migrated to another manager.

Playing at the Glad Rag Ball had raised the band's profile sufficiently for Leo to wangle them a part in the cult B movie *The Deadly Bees*, a limp thriller starring Suzannah Leigh as a shagged-out pop singer seeking rest and relaxation on a quiet island somewhere off the British coast, not a million miles from Ealing Studios. Unfortunately the brochure never mentioned that the island was inhabited by a swarm of killer bees and various homicidal maniacs. The Birds were intended to represent Mod as they lip-synched to 'That's All That I Need You For', another composition by Ronnie and Tony and one of three new songs recorded on 12 January. Despite a script by *Psycho* writer Robert Bloch and director Freddie Francis's best efforts, the movie was underfunded and it showed.

The Birds went to the film studio on the 14th, straight from an all-night gig, still sweaty, unshaven and exhausted. Even so, they managed to project their sharp Mod aggression and cool, despite being plastered with heavy make-up. But the episode was one more nail in the coffin of Leo's management of the group.

As was the fate of their fourth single, 'What Hit Me?' Another Wood/ Monroe composition, this was recorded on 18 March. It was meant to be the hit record that Leo had so proudly announced two months beforehand. But it was never released – mainly because Decca decided to drop the band, not wanting to go another bloody fifteen rounds with CBS and the American Byrds. All of which was naturally Leo's fault. His response was to introduce the group to a new record label called Reaction, formed that same month.

What follows is affected by selective memory loss. The former Birds can remember what happened, but not exactly in what order. Or who was ultimately responsible for getting them involved with one of London's most infamous crime families.

It all began one night in March 1966. The group had been playing at a club in Catford and as they were packing up their equipment, a tall, dark stranger approached them. He was a powerful-looking man in his mid-thirties, well-dressed and with a certain air about him, who said how much he'd enjoyed the gig.

Above: Sketch Club Champ

Left: Ron and Buster

Art, Ron and Ted with Lawrence Sheaf

Ron at Whitethorn Avenue

Ron with his first electric guitar

Dapper Wood. 'My friends called me Cleopatra.'

Whitethorn Avenue

The Birds – 1965 and big in Cheshire

Ali and Ron

Above: The Birds live at Windsor in 1965

Right: Ron on the up

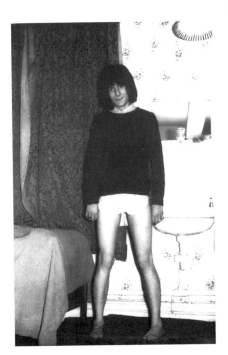

Cleopatra on tour

Tony Monroe, Ron and Ali McKenzie

The Birds – the Next Big Thing, 1964

Above: The Birds – Woolwich
Barracks, 1965

Right: customised Mods, 1965

Transport courtesy of Leo, circa 1965

Above: Getaway vehicle supplied by the Richardson brothers

Below: The Birds – Woolwich Barracks

The Creation: Jack Jones, Kenny Pickett, Ron and Kim Gardner

Ron, Jeff Beck, Mickey Waller, Rod Stewart

The Faces: Ian McLagan, Ron, Ron Lane, Rod and Kenney Jones

They got talking. One of the Birds mentioned they were having management problems. How sad, said their new friend, how shocking. Had the band thought about taking on a new manager? They were thinking about little else. Well, maybe their new friend could help. Funnily enough, he'd been a fan for some time, ever since he'd seen them at a club in Bromley. Interestingly enough, he had an involvement with several clubs himself, had been thinking of getting more closely involved in the music scene for some time. He also had a very good solicitor in Mayfair. Maybe they should all meet up in a few days' time. Why not? the band said.

There was no great mystery as to why Charlie and Eddie Richardson would want to take over the Birds. They did indeed have interests in many clubs, and knew how many fans the group brought in. Besides it was the sixties and even traditional villains were branching out – although the Richardsons were far from traditional.

If the Kray twins epitomized the public face of villainy in that era, the Richardson brothers represented a far more skilful and imaginative approach to criminal activity. Based in Bermondsey and Rotherhithe, they followed a tradition of organized crime that was old when the East End was nothing more than a stew-pot of pickpockets, muggers and diseased whores. Whereas the Krays were criminals who went into business, the Richardsons were primarily businessmen who went into crime.

For example, it was the Richardsons who developed the 'long-firm' fraud [the practise of setting up a trading company which establishes a good credit rating, orders large amounts of goods on credit, sells them off cheaply and disappears] to near-poetic flights of fancy, but always those that made money. They relied as much on intelligence as they did on muscle – although they were never short of the latter. Frankie Fraser, of the gold-plated pliers and an interest in amateur dentistry, worked for the Richardsons, and the man was truly fearsome. Not very tall, but with a brooding stillness about him that made even strangers look the other way. But then anyone who'd spent so much time in solitary confinement would probably look pretty damn thoughtful too.

The Richardsons had firmly avoided the celebrity circuit, unlike the Krays, whose egos would prove as fatal as their actual crimes – just because they supplied rent-boys to the gentry didn't mean they belonged, the upstarts. That was the Krays' biggest crime: not knowing their place. Although shooting people in front of witnesses didn't help much, either. The great myth, of course, was that the Krays only ever harmed their own – unless the word 'own' refers to anyone who had something the Krays wanted.

At least one of the Birds must have known that their new friend – and soon, new friends – were a little 'heavy'. But then so was Leo, and the band had spent the past two years playing the club circuit, where few if any club owners or managers were known for their shy, retiring natures.

In fact, the normally shy and retiring Richardson brothers had achieved a certain notoriety in early March. For a while London was talking about little else – except the missing World Cup, the twelve-inch-high, solid-gold Jules Rimet trophy, stolen from its display case in Westminster. Which does have some relevance here, because Pete Mc-Daniels was actually arrested for the theft. He'd been walking to a Birds gig at the 100 Club from his flat in Westbourne Grove when he'd been stopped by an increasingly frantic police force – the World Cup itself was only a few months away – on the grounds that here was a suspicious-looking character carrying a big leather holdall that chinked suggestively. As indeed it did: Pete was taking his cymbals to work. Of course, those were more innocent times, when a thief could be expected to walk the streets of London carrying a solid-gold statuette that had been stolen several days previously.

Matters weren't helped when Pete refused to let the police look inside. How could he? He was carrying the group's supply of blues, purple hearts and black bombers, and had more drugs on him than the average chemist's. Luckily the police were only interested in the Jules Rimet trophy. When he eventually did agree to open his bag, they took one look, saw the cymbals, realized they weren't gold but brass and told him to go. By which time, he'd missed the gig. The trophy was eventually found by a dog called Pickles under a bush in South London on 27 March. The band should have seen the episode as an awful warning. They didn't.

On 8 March Eddie Richardson and 'Mad' Frankie Fraser had been shot at Mr Smith's nightclub in Catford, in a protection-racket take-over, and taken to hospital under police guard. This means that either Charlie or one of his associates had originally approached the group in Catford, for none of the Birds remembers their original contact being bandaged. Or even walking with a brave limp.

At the first meeting the Birds handed over their contracts with Leo to an individual introduced as their new friend's solicitor. In exchange, the Richardsons suggested that all future live engagements could be handled by their good mate Roy Tempest, whose agency offices were in Wardour Street, Soho. This would obviously mean leaving the Harold Davison Agency – assuming the contracts with Leo could be legally broken.

Somehow the Birds were left in no doubt that the contracts would be legally broken. If not, something else would be. Throughout April they kept contact with Leo to the bare minimum, and kept their new friends to themselves. Meanwhile news articles in both the *NME* and *Melody Maker* reported that the Birds would be signing with the Reaction label, in order to release their fifth single, 'Say Those Magic Words', another Wood/Monroe original. Reaction was the label set up by Robert Stigwood in order to help the Who's managers exclude record producer Shel Talmy from any royalties.

Then, in May, came a more formal meeting at the Richardsons' Park Lane headquarters, to which Leo was invited. There was a large, impressive, polished wood table in a large, impressive room. The Birds sat on one side, opposite their new friends, who, needless to say, were also large and impressive. At the far end sat Leo and his solicitor, flanked by the Farrell brothers. To a casual onlooker it might have looked like a trial, with Leo as the accused.

'The contract's illegal,' the Richardsons' solicitor began. 'The boys are underage.'

'No it's not,' Leo said, a trifle smugly. 'I got their parents to sign. Every one of them.' How right Lizzie had been to worry about the small print.

'It's still fucking illegal.'

'Oh yeah? Why?'

'Because you forgot the education clause,' the Richardsons' solicitor explained gently. 'You have to provide a certain number of hours' tuition every week in the case of minors. You didn't. So what have you got to say about that?'

Leo looked at his own, increasingly nervous solicitor, who'd drawn up the original, flawed contracts, and spat out: 'You cunt!' Then he got up, pushed back his chair and stormed out, leaving his copies of the contracts on the table. The Farrells followed, leaving behind the now terrified solicitor watching as his original work was torn to shreds before his eyes.

That night there was a party at a large, impressive house in Bromley, south-east London's version of a stockbroker belt, where all upwardly mobile south-east London villains aspired to live. Large, impressive drinks were shoved into the Birds' hands as their cigarettes were lit with sold-gold lighters. Brightly dressed women with beehives and curves tut-tutted at how thin the boys were, and force-fed them with salmon and roast beef. Meaty hands clasped the Birds' shoulders and large, impressive promises were made. Phrases like 'All right, my son?' and 'Now we'll get you a proper record deal' filled the air. The future looked good. In a few weeks they'd sign new contracts. The Birds felt that they'd grown up. They went home to West Drayton knowing that their luck had finally changed.

But they were still just a little concerned about Leo. Not to worry – their new friends, who were interested in assuming the managerial role, had already thought of that. A company was formed called Popgressive, with the Richardsons' solicitor appointed as Chairman. The new deal was loyally reported, as normal, by the West London newspapers. One headline announced: 'Break-aways in Beat Street' above a story saying that the Birds had flown away from their manager to warble their pop tunes on their own.

The interviews were given by Tony Monroe, who'd apparently appointed himself the band's spokesman and business adviser – yet another source of friction with Ronnie. Tony was quoted as saying: 'We broke away about a week ago because of a certain unrest which has been going on for some time.' Straight-faced, the reporter added that to protect themselves against any possibilities of legal action the group had their own protection in the form of a company called Popgressive. Of course, what Tony never realized was that the group's dynamic had long changed. The group was now being run by Ronnie and Kim.

The article also mentioned that Leo had taken back the group's van. Quite what he'd do with a clapped-out, scratched and lipstick-smeared elderly Commer, complete with a hole in the floor that stank, is anyone's guess. One can only hope that whatever he did was mercifully swift and with full R&B honours.

Leo still has connections with clubs in the Windsor area and in 1983 gained some small revenge when he barred an inebriated Ronnie and Mick Jagger from one of his establishments, and was heard to say: 'I've waited years to get one over on that fucking Ronnie Wood.' For Leo knew what others had only suspected. While Tony Monroe had become the Birds' spokesman in getting rid of Leo, the move had been orchestrated by Ronnie. The fact was, Leo had never given them a hit record. Worse, his publicity stunt with the American Byrds had made the real Birds look silly.

The Birds' transport problem was solved at a meeting held at Kim's parents' house between Ronnie, Kim, his father and the Richardsons. Kim laughs about the memory now. 'We did it my house because my Dad had got concerned about who we'd got involved with. He wanted to secretly record the meeting because we hadn't signed any contracts. We hid a tape-recorder under the table, covered with a tablecloth and taped the whole conversation with the Torture Boys. Ronnie and I were giggling and kicking each other under the table, going "This is fucking great!" I wish I had that fucking tape now!'

The meeting ended with enough cash handed over to purchase a new, long-wheelbase Ford Transit minibus, worth about £15,000 today, and just like the one Art Wood had bought for his band. The rest of the Birds never discovered how Ronnie and Kim had come up with the money, but one thing became abundantly clear: he who pays for the transport, calls the tune. Now more than ever, Ronnie and Kim were firmly in the driving seat.

And, as well as a new van, the group now had a new agent, Roy Tempest; new personal management, Popgressive; and a new record label, Stigwood's Reaction. What was more, Ronnie and Krissie had a new home: a small flat in Benbow Road, Shepherd's Bush, partly financed by Krissie's new job working for a solicitor. They could even allow themselves the occasional luxury of eating at a nearby Mexican restaurant, where they both tasted steak and bitter chocolate sauce for the very first time. Everything seemed to be working out fine.

Robert Stigwood was an enterprising gay Australian who'd arrived in London in 1957. Initially he'd worked as a clerical assistant in the social services before setting up his own theatrical agency. By March 1966 he had his own label, Reaction, which was licensed to Polydor, formed solely to release the Who's single, 'Substitute'. He also controlled Cream and the Bee Gees.

It was during this period that Ronnie first met Jimmy Page, or rather Jimmy's guitar. The musician came later. As Kim remembers it: 'Jimmy was a top session man then. Anyway, he was working in the studio next door, had gone out and left his guitar behind. It was truly fucking amazing, some sort of weird Japanese thing with this fucking great sound, and Ronnie went in and pinched it for the track we were recording. And he's halfway through a solo when Jimmy Page comes back looking for it. Ronnie was really fucking embarrassed, says: "Oh, is this yours?" Jimmy was all right about it, and told us he was just about to join the Yardbirds in place of Clapton, which was a fucking good gig to get. I remember Ronnie being well pissed off because we loved the Yardbirds. He went out the next day and bought the very same guitar.'

A few years later Jimmy Page would 'borrow' Krissie, then Ronnie's wife, for a year. That's the problem with rock musicians – they're always misplacing things.

*

Recording sessions for Reaction finally began in June 1966. 'Say Those Magic Words' was cut on the 5th; 'Daddy, Daddy' on the 15th; and on the 20th a cover of a French song entitled 'The Doll Who Said No' – a great song, but a pretentious title to the Birds, who retitled it 'Good Times'. The memory is still painful for Tony Monroe. 'It was fabulous! We got the disc from France and had it translated. It was a really beautiful song – very unusual and very original. Ronnie and I thought it was fabulous. Ali said it was our finest moment. We wanted it to be the next single, and even said so in *Melody Maker* [which listed the release date as 29 July], but Stigwood was still sticking with "Magic Words". He called the shots, deciding what was and wasn't to be released – and that wasn't. Instead, he would have us in recording and re-recording stuff and we thought, oh, so this is going to be the next release, then. But nothing ever was and it went on like this for months.'

What none of the band realized was that Stigwood was distracted, locked as he was into a major legal drama of his own making with record producer Shel Talmy and Decca. It was not a good time to be around him. He was also nurturing a fledgeling Cream, then known simply as Eric Clapton, Jack Bruce and Ginger Baker, who played their first gig on 30 July.

What Stigwood did do, for some inexplicable reason, just possibly contractual, was rename the group Birds Birds and, for more logical reasons, market them as London's first gangster group. He produced a three-page, fold-out promotional brochure for which the band had their hair cut short – except for Ronnie's, which was only lightly trimmed – and posed for photos wearing double-breasted suits complete with carnations . . . while carrying sub-machine guns . . . in front of Roaring Twenties limousines with gangster-friendly running boards and spare wheel. Either Stigwood knew about the Richardson link, or he really did have exceptional foresight, for within twelve months Hollywood-inspired gangster chic would be all the rage.

By now Krissie was working as a receptionist for manager Don Arden in his Carnaby Street office, where she witnessed at first hand some of the problems another band was having. The Small Faces, despite a number one with 'All or Nothing', seemed to be permanently broke. She introduced their lead singer, Steve Marriott, to Ronnie: 'Because I felt both Steve and Ronnie were very similar. It was funny, but I had no idea the Birds ever had any problems – Ronnie kept everything like that from me. I thought he could possibly help Steve with the problems the Small Faces were having – and I knew how much Ronnie loved the band. It was a bad time. Don Arden had stopped taking their calls for some reason, and

Steve and Ronnie Lane blocked up every line on the switchboard, so that no one else could get through and Don would have to talk to them. He was really angry and came and shouted at me as if it was my fault. Towards the end the Small Faces got really scared about Don. I heard that soon after they moved to that cottage in Marlow, a car pulled up and someone shot at the house. I remember telling Ronnie [Wood] about it, and saying how lucky we were not to have those sorts of problems. And he just laughed.'

Ronnie and Steve remained close friends until the latter's tragic death in a house fire in 1991. Hanging in Steve's kitchen there had been a big print of Keith Richards done by Ronnie, and Steve would good-naturedly point it out to guests, asking if they'd noticed 'Ronnie Wood's tracing'.

Stigwood might not have been ignoring the Birds' phone calls, but Ronnie was less than enamoured with the group's new name, or the way that Stigwood was trying to repackage them. The brochure announcing the Robert Stigwood Organisation's sole representation for Birds Birds, as opposed to the Birds, gloats lovingly that: 'Birds Birds is paradoxically one of those rare groups elevated to "hit parade" status without ever having had a Top Twenty record. The group members describe their music as aggressive, scientific wildness and regimented excitement, and see each performance as an environment in which the senses and music are integrated and in which the audience is hypnotically made to respond. They believe in basing their performance on a combination of art, science and music and personify the science of life rather than that of destruction.'

Just the sort of quasi-intellectual bullshit that had helped drive Ronnie away from Ealing School of Art. But Stigwood's pretentious spiel gets even worse: 'That Birds Birds is a happy group is exemplified by the fact that there have been no personnel changes since the band was formed as "The Birds" in 1964. At that time, Tony, Ron, Ali, Kim and Pete had no group experience and just decided to play together as an enjoyable experience. Little did they foresee that Birds Birds would ultimately resolve their futures as that they would be acclaimed as one of the major Ballroom and club attractions in Great Britain.'

Inaccurate, misleading and indescribably mimsy, too. It went on: 'This is a group of musicians influenced by no external musical strains, but willing to adapt any suitable melodies or to create their own where none exist. Here is a group unafraid to use a discord where it is meaningful – five musicians eager to perform for sheer fun and the satisfaction of achievement.'

It is a truth universally acknowledged that the first sign of serious trouble with any organization is often heralded by fulsome publicity. It's as if the PR people use bullshit to disguise their own lack of belief, instead of trying to fool some of the people long enough to make a profit.

One thing Stigwood did get right was his description of, and prediction for, Ronnie. 'Ron Wood (Guitar/Harmonica/Vocals),' he wrote, 'lives for his music. With him playing is more than a way of earning money. He is one of our finest guitarists and harmonica players who excels in the Blues. At nineteen, Ron can be assured of an outstanding musical career ahead.'

After much deliberation on Stigwood's part, 'Say Those Magic Words' was finally released in September, the Reaction label's fifth single. It was yet another cover version, this time of a McCoys album track. As usual, Ronnie and Tony were relegated to the B side with their composition 'Daddy, Daddy', then considered to be a far-reaching, experimental example of auto-destructive Modism. In hindsight, 'Daddy, Daddy' was just a bit of a racket, but typical of 1966. Once again the Birds/Birds Birds were spared any chart action, and spent all their free time practising in the Regent Sound studios waiting for Robert Stigwood to show up. He rarely did.

It slowly began to dawn on the group that Stigwood's long-term interests lay elsewhere. Rumour had it that the Beatles' erstwhile boss Brian Epstein was on the lookout for a partner in his NEMS organization, and Stigwood was going all out to impress. In a calculated move, he invited American soul stars the Four Tops to London and arranged a date for them at Epstein's Saville Theatre. Epstein was easily lured and snared by Stigwood's enterprise and, with his eyes set firmly on a piece of the Cream's action, offered him the deal Stigwood had always known he'd get.

At the same time, certain rumours begin to surface about the Richardson brothers. Nothing too serious – something about large-scale fraud, armed robbery and nailing a police informer to the floor – but enough to make the band worry just a little. Even more so when they read about mock trials held by criminals in a large, impressive boardroom furnished with a large, impressive table at an equally impressive Mayfair address. The very same room, in fact, where Leo had been given what some would say was his lucky break. When they tried to call their new friends, no one answered.

Ronnie and Krissie had been forced to leave Benbow Road when they could no longer afford the rent. The couple moved to a cheaper flat in

Edens Court, close to the Uxbridge Road – their fourth address in little over a year.

Suddenly the group was directionless, riding around in a van bought with money borrowed from real gangsters. Naturally enough, they turned on each other. Specifically, they turned on Tony, who, aside from the escalating musical differences with Ronnie, had assumed responsibility for the band's business affairs. As Stigwood's brochure had pointed out: 'Tony helps with the group's administration.' They needed someone to blame, and Tony had put himself well into the frame.

Tony partly blames the falling out on the fact that he was doing a job that everyone else had refused to do. 'I was the most vociferous member of the group and used to do most of the organizing because no one else was interested – particularly Ronnie. Anything that involved organizing went right over his head. He didn't give a shit as long as he got to play. I mean, he was such a natural musician that the logistics of being in a group – bearing in mind we were practically managing ourselves – were way above him, he wouldn't get involved in that at all. I thought I was the catalyst of the group, I'd keep things together, often sit in as mediator if people were falling out. But I also think it was because we were getting paid a lot more for gigs, with Leo gone, and they thought: "We can do without Tony and we can split it four ways instead of five." Although Ali and Kim and me made friends again afterwards, I haven't spoken to Ronnie to this day.'

More to the point, Krissie and Tony's girlfriend, Susan, disliked each other – but then Krissie and Tony had never been the best of friends themselves. She'd never forgiven him for telling Ronnie she was just another hanger-on, when they'd all first met. Nor for the way Tony had spoken out when she was briefly double-dating Ronnie and Eric Clapton in those early days, and had told Ronnie to 'Fucking dump her!'

Friendships between men may survive conflicting girlfriends, but never a conflicting wife. As Ronnie says: 'Girls get in the way and it's, "Oh, don't say that about my husband", sort of thing. It was the same vibes with the Faces, with Jan Jones against Sandy McLagan and Krissie Wood against Dee Harrington [Rod Stewart's girlfriend]. But in the Birds' days it was Krissie against Susan. Whoever the girls were, they always got in the way and they'd set their husbands up against each other, or off in the wrong direction, and that would ultimately finish the band. That's probably why we were called the Birds' Birds towards the end, because we were all bossed around by the birds – the Birds' birds bossed the Birds around.'

The conflict finally came to a head with the group's last weary tangle with Mod violence. They'd been playing at an East London club and at the end of the gig the familiar jealousy of the band surfaced. They were now being road-managed by ex-Thunderbird Robin Scrimshaw, who'd had the good sense to be away that night, leaving the driving and humping duties to another old school friend, Roger Jeggo. Actually, Jeggo had really gone along for the ride and was totally unprepared for a violent stage invasion. One minute the audience was cheering, the next it turned into a horde of pill-crazed Mods intent on beating the Birds to a pulp. Jeggo bravely decided to intervene. Tony went to help him, as the rest of the group were hurriedly unplugging.

'I was the only one who went to help him, and the boys didn't like it, claiming I'd jeopardized the equipment. By the time the police arrived Roger was in a terrible mess, all his teeth were hanging out and he needed stitches. I turned to the others and said: "You bastards! You ran away again!" I got Roger to hospital and stayed with him all the night while they sewed him up.'

The following day Tony turned up for a band meeting at Ronnie's flat, where Krissie told him that they'd all gone to see Stigwood. Still a little annoyed by the previous night, Tony went home to catch up on his sleep, only to be woken by a call from Stigwood himself, who informed him that he'd been sacked – but not to worry, the group might change their minds, and if they didn't he had another band Tony could join.

'I was completely brain-shot,' Tony said, 'and I asked Stigwood who was instigating it but he wouldn't tell me because he was trying to talk them out of it, but they seemed quite adamant. So eventually Kim and Ali came round to tell me personally.'

A devastated Tony, tears streaming down his face, sprang at Ali screaming that Ali was his mate, why were they doing this to him – and why wasn't Ronnie there? The one ray of hope in his mind was that Ronnie and Pete were staying neutral – or didn't even agree – and could clear up the whole mess.

'Well, not exactly,' Kim explains. 'It was all Ronnie's idea to begin with.'

Et tu, Ron.

A still shell-shocked Tony took up Stigwood's offer of joining his latest infatuation – a new group called the Gods, featuring a promising young guitarist called Mick Taylor.

'It was like starting all over again,' Tony recollects. 'I was a lot older and they were just starting out and playing the same shit-holes we played two years ago. My heart wasn't in it, I was totally embittered by the whole thing, so I just gave it all up and tried to adapt to Civvy Street, like coming out the Army. I went on a building site, got married and didn't listen to music for years. But what still hurts is Ronnie's actions. We'd been like brothers and it disappeared over night. I'd known him for seven years and we'd learned to write songs together. We'd taught each other guitar, gone to school with each other, shared conflicting girlfriends together. We had so many things in common, we were both artists. There'd always been rivalry, but now it was replaced by animosity. "Those Magic Words" turned out to be "Fuck off, you're sacked."'

Stigwood infiltrated NEMS in December and the band – now a four-piece and calling themselves the Birds again – recorded yet more songs to add to their growing mountain of unreleased records. One of Stigwood's parting shots, acting on Kim's confidential advice, was to hire the Tornados' drummer, Clem Cattini, for the recording sessions that would prove to be the group's last. The track was 'Granny Rides Again', a solo Ronnie composition, and Pete, probably sensing that he was next in line for the chop, simply stopped going to the studio whether he was needed or not. And that was the last anyone has ever seen or heard of him, except for one strange meeting two years later. Tony was coming out of a sports centre in West London, after playing in a basketball match alongside Robin Scrimshaw – who'd finally discovered a use for his height.

'I saw this figure sitting on a bench. He looked familiar, so I walked over and found myself staring at Pete. I was so happy to see him, until I realized he looked down and out, like a tramp. I went up to him and said, "Pete, it's me, Tony! How are you? What are you doing?" And he just stared blankly at me, said, "My name's not Pete and I don't know who you are." And I said, "Don't be stupid, of course you know who I am!" And Pete just got up and shuffled off. I stood there, watching him until he disappeared, wondering whether I'd really seen him. It was so weird. But it was Pete – you don't spend three years with a bloke without knowing him.'

With Tony gone, there was no one to find work for a group that was now effectively a three-piece combo. No one to liaise with an agent, no one to tell them where to be and when. Stigwood was too busy with his new job to look after a band that already had the smell of yesterday's men about them. That's the nature of the business – not the death of a thousand cuts, but a thousand unreturned phone calls. Not that anyone thought to tell Ali, who still kept on showing up at Regent Sound.

'I thought it was a bit odd. I was up there most nights, overdubbing vocals, always on my own, overdubbing, overdubbing and overdubbing the overdubs. But it was Christmas and I thought everyone was out doing their shopping.'

Eventually even Ali realized it was over. He went to the studio one last time, spent a half-hearted half an hour overdubbing, then walked out, leaving a note: 'GONE FISHING'.

7
'I never wanted to mention Jeff's spots'

And where had Ronnie and Kim been while Ali was overdubbing himself into a stupor? They'd been working with elder brother Art and Artwoods keyboard player Jon Lord, plus the Pink Fairies' drummer John 'Twink' Adler in a new group provisionally titled the ArtBirds. Ronnie and Art had both realized that their respective bands were no longer contenders, and decided to pool the best of their resources. There would be no room for Ali, since Art would obviously be lead vocalist, as he had been with his own group.

Ronnie always felt a little guilty about Ali, left on his own in a recording studio, laying down tracks for a record which would never be released by a group that had ceased to exist. By way of making amends, in 1975 he coaxed Ali to come and record at his home studio in Richmond. Ronnie put together a studio band comprising himself, Kenney Jones, Ronnie Lane and Mick Jagger (who played rhythm guitar). Nothing came of it, however, and Ali is still waiting to hear the tapes – last rumoured to have been buried at a lonesome crossroads at full moon, with a stake through the centre spool.

The Artbirds could well have taken off. They had the talent, experience and individual reputations. Unfortunately, there was a slight age disparity – not one that affected musical appreciation or ability, but one concerned with creature comforts.

Art was beginning to enjoy a comfortable home life with his wife, Doreen. Ronnie and Ali were talking excitedly about touring Germany and Poland, countries which Art already knew well. One day he went on his own to look at the Ford Transit that would be his new touring home, and shuddered: 'Fuck that for a game of soldiers!'

Going up and down the M1 as an unknown band, after all this time, would have been a gig too far. But that hardly explains the Artwoods' bizarre transformation less than a year later into the St Valentine's Day

Massacre – a lame attempt to cash in on the Bonnie and Clyde craze then sweeping London. Art still winces when asked about the episode that ruined the group's credibility and hastened their ignominious end. He would eventually work with brother Ted's graphic design company, but he never completely hung up his rocking boots – Quiet Melon was still to come and even today he still plays and produces. Even so, he'd said goodbye to any thoughts of stardom. He'd been at the forefront of the R&B boom in Britain, had played with Alexis Korner, fostered the careers of Keef Hartley and Jon Lord, and had been instrumental in turning the Moist Hoist drinking den into the famous Ealing Club. If anyone had deserved chart success, it was Art. He hadn't got it. Time to go home, but with no regrets. Besides: 'Me and Ted were always happy that at least one of us made it. And Ronnie made it big enough for all three.'

The ArtBirds renamed themselves Santa Barbara Machine Head. 'We wanted to have a West Coast progressive name,' Ronnie says, 'like Big Brother and the Holding Company, Strawberry Alarm Clock or the Chocolate Watch Band. Only our name sounded hard.'

SBMH (aka the Head) did in fact record three tracks, all written by Jon Lord, who was still living in Arthur and Lizzie Wood's boxroom. 'Porcupine Juice', 'Albert' and 'Rubber Monkey' are three songs that can legitimately lay claim to being the embryonic strains of Deep Purple; or, as we like to refer to them, the Boxroom Tapes. Certainly it was enough for Lord to go off, reinvent himself and found Deep Purple, the world's first classically influenced and extremely loud, heavy rock band.

On 21 December 1966 Ronnie, Krissie and Kim went to Blaises nightclub in South Kensington in order to catch one of Jimi Hendrix's early London gigs with the Experience. There they ran into Jeff Beck, who was the guest of Hendrix's manager, Chas Chandler, the former bass player with the Animals. News had just broken that Beck had been sacked from the Yardbirds. As manager Simon Napier Bell put it in *Melody Maker*: 'Due to Jeff's ill-health on two American tours, it has become obvious that he is not up to intensive touring. Reluctantly, the Yardbirds will carry on as a four-piece.'

This only weeks before Beck was about to embark on the most exhaustive period of concentrated live work in his career. The truth was, his grandstanding and ill-health had given the Yardbirds the excuse they'd been looking for. Even so, it wasn't all one-sided – Beck had, after all, seen his old friend, Jimmy Page, brought in as competition for him, which wasn't nice.

Beck mentioned that he was thinking of setting up his own group. The next day he got a call from Ronnie asking for a job. If the Birds, ArtBirds and Santa Barbara Machine Head weren't all already dead beforehand, they were now.

'I'd known Jeff since his Trident days and obviously from watching the Yardbirds,' says Ronnie, 'so I felt confident enough to ring him up and offer my services along with Kim's.'

Just like that.

In fact, Ronnie had also been present at the Marquee Club when Beck had auditioned for the Yardbirds. Art Wood had already booked the club to audition for drummers, following the departure of the Artwoods' drummer, Reg Dunnage. Art charitably allowed the Yardbirds to double up and audition for a guitarist to replace Clapton, who'd left because the Yardbirds weren't playing pure blues; he'd objected to the commercial success of 'For Your Love'. Art remembers seeing this nervous and very spotty young bloke sitting all by himself with a guitar between his knees.

'I went up to him,' said Art, 'because he was the first one there. He was literally shaking, he was so scared, said he'd come to audition for the Yardbirds but didn't think he was good enough. There was a line of other guitar-players waiting outside the club, but no fucking drummers for me, and it was meant to be our fucking audition! And I told him, "Don't worry, it'll be fine, just do your best, son, and you'll be all right." Which he was, because they didn't bother to audition anyone else after him. Oh, and we did get one drummer Keef Hartley, who'd originally replaced Ringo Starr with Rory Storm and the Hurricanes.'

Then, it had been a little galling for Ronnie to see a former support guitarist join the group who, next to the Stones, were his idols. But now, aside from the delicate problem of who would be lead guitarist, Ronnie relished the opportunity of working with him. Beck was high-profile, and therefore Ronnie's next logical move. It also suited his and Kim's firm resolve to maintain their musical partnership – Kim had replaced Tony as Ron's creative sparring partner long before Tony had finally been given the push.

So it was that Ronnie and Kim began 1967 by dropping in on Jeff's first audition/rehearsal sessions at a studio in Goodge Street. Beck's first choice of a rhythm section had been the ill-advised pairing of ex-Pretty Thing Viv Prince, and the one-time mean and moody ex-Shadow Jet Harris.

It hadn't worked: Viv just wasn't user-friendly, and Jet was mostly drunk – ostensibly just one more rock 'n' roll tragedy, but in fact a man who was arguably one of the greatest bass guitarists Britain has ever produced. A well-publicized affair with the bottle had already cost him two successful careers and earned him the tag of being unemployable.

Which makes one wonder why Beck had ever considered him in the first instance – maybe he was desperate, a bad judge of character or just didn't want people around who might outshine him.

Kim for one was shattered to see how far his hero had fallen. As Ronnie remembers: 'Jet was, like, shot to pieces. I think he turned up a couple of times to rehearsals but was obviously out of the game, which was a shame.' Note that Kim and Harris had been asked to the same rehearsal. In effect, they were both auditioning for the same job. In the event, Harris stopped showing up and disappeared into near obscurity. Ronnie always reckoned that if only he'd hung around long enough, Jet could have joined the Faces, where his behaviour would have been understood and even positively encouraged. In this assessment he is perhaps missing the point that whereas the Faces behaved badly because they wanted to, Harris no longer had any choice. Viv Prince was next to go, replaced by Beck's old Tridents band-mate, Ray Cook.

Beck did have one major asset in his choice of vocalist Rod Stewart, who at twenty-two years of age was already established as a veteran of the British rock circuit.

Rod and Ronnie had originally met in October 1965, the day when Rod had performed his début solo single, 'Good Morning Little School-girl', on *Ready Steady Go!* It was not actually in the studio, but later that evening when he'd been accosted by the enthusiastic eighteen-year-old Ronnie in a pub. It was to be the start of a lifelong friendship and a shared hairstyle.

Beck had moved from Balham to Sutton in mid-January, following the final split from his wife, Patricia.

'He had this big penthouse place,' Ronnie remembers. 'So we started going over there to rehearse, me and Kim. Or Jeff would sometimes come and see us, driving this Stingray with an Afghan hound in the back. Neighbours loved it. But after a while Kim was asked politely to sort of "Would you not play bass?" Jeff said to me, "I don't think Kim's going to cut it on bass, would you tell him?" And I said yeah, but I like Kim, I don't want to throw him out. And Jeff said, 'Well, I'm not going to throw him out, he's still going to be a friend, but he's not going to work in this project – do you think he could live with that?" So I had to say to Kim, "Look, this is how Jeff wants it." I said, "I'm really sorry, I don't quite understand it, or why, but he wants you not to play bass, he wants to try someone else: me." And Kim said, "Oh, no, that's cool, you got my blessing, you go on ahead and I'll go and do something else." He did really! He was really fair about it, didn't get all mean and moody and say, "Oh, I've been thrown out." The good thing for me was I had reached saturation point on the guitar at that point, I was sort of losing interest in it. Then when Jeff said, "Would you consider playing bass?" I thought yeah, why not?'

See how well musicians organize things when they're left to their own devices, without managers getting in the way. The point is that musicians only want a chance to play and nothing, or no one, is allowed to get in the way. And that Ronnie was still moving through life almost as in a dream, convinced that ultimately, everything would happen for the best in the best of all possible worlds. Like Voltaire's Candide, Ronnie always possessed that awful innocence which can destroy far wiser and even more cynical people who get too close.

Rehearsals for Beck's new group now moved to Studio 19 in Soho's Gerrard Street. There was only one problem: Ronnie didn't own a bass guitar and hadn't got the money to buy one. So he stole it.

'I got it from Sound City on Wardour Street, right by the big Durex sign. Me and Kim had stood on the corner for about two hours, pretending to say goodnight, but sizing up a bass. I chose a Fender Jazz because it was nearest the door. So I went and grabbed it off the wall and ran up a Chinese alley. A few years later, when I was with the Faces and had made a few bob, I went back in and said, "Hello, I'm the bloke who nicked your bass years ago and I'm here to pay for it" – and they were delighted because they [bass guitars] were so much dearer by then!'

February 1967 began interestingly. The Musicians' Union banned the Rolling Stones from singing 'Let's Spend The Night Together' on the *Eamonn Andrews Show*. On the other hand, the films *Alfie* and *Georgy Girl* – which both featured a high quota of nights spent together – did well at New York's Golden Globe Awards. Petula Clark, with 'This Is My Song', was fighting it out with the Monkees' 'I'm A Believer' for Top Ten honours.

And *Melody Maker* announced the arrival of Jeff Beck's new group, booked to support Roy Orbison on a nationwide tour also featuring the Ryan Twins and the Small Faces. Ronnie was also quoted as saying: 'I don't mind playing bass with Jeff. He's a very good blues guitarist and I expect we will be playing blues – with a difference.'

How right he was.

No one in their right mind ever toured with the Small Faces.

But Beck's new, though only fifty-percent manager, Peter Grant, and record producer Mickie Most, were desperate to get Jeff Beck launched on the road to pop – not R&B – stardom, and as a solo artist. 'Hi Ho

Silver Lining' was due to be released on 10 March. It all made solid commercial sense.

The tour kicked of at the Astoria, in North London's Finsbury Park, on 3 March 1967. True, Jeff Beck's group was under-rehearsed. On the other hand, who could have foreseen that their amplifiers would break down in mid-act? The Small Faces' Steve Marriott for one, as he'd happily sabotaged them in the first instance. Why? Well, it was all a bit of a laugh, really. Later on during the tour, Marriott would 'borrow' Orbison's guitar just before every performance, while the rest of the Small Faces chatted to the great man, and retune it to an even higher pitch, forcing Orbison to reach for notes previously thought impossible except for castrati. Orbison – handicapped by poor eyesight – never realized why the Faces were so friendly before each performance. But he did spend a great deal of time on stage squinting mournfully into the wings, where his new best friends were collapsed in hysterics.

Krissie Wood's memories of Ronnie's early days with Jeff Beck are still clear. 'I remember the first rehearsals with Jeff and it was in a – not dingy – but an underground studio in Soho, in Gerrard Street, but I remember it very clearly 'cos I liked it, it was really good. And I think Jimmy Page walked in at that point. Everybody played together but it wasn't jamming, everybody just wanted to play. But the Finsbury Park Astoria was truly weird . . . they all had to wear yellow suits, which I found really extraordinary. And all of a sudden the power went off [thanks to Steve Marriott], leaving Rod and Ronnie looking silly in these yellow suits and black collars, that didn't quite fit. Jeff was quite moody that night, too. I hated "Hi Ho Silver Lining". The song was OK, but with a vocalist like Rod, why have Jeff singing it?'

According to Krissie, the switch to bass caused no problem for Ronnie, although she maintains her suspicions about why Jeff wanted it done. 'Ronnie loved playing bass, he was a great bass player. But I don't think Jeff was being very honest about why he wouldn't let Ronnie play guitar. OK, Ron is a guitarist and played bass like a guitarist, so the sound was really unique. But at the same time Jeff seemed unable to let him pick up a guitar and I felt that was jealousy.'

Jeff Beck's début had not been a success. The music press savaged the shows – and Beck personally – in the way that British journalists have made their very own: 'Jeff seemed to have difficulty even playing a good solo'; 'Jeff sounded diabolical, it's hard to believe he's a guitarist praised to the heavens'; 'gimmick and stack of noise.'

Beck immediately quit the tour, replaced by P.P. Arnold, former backing singer for Ike and Tina Turner, and Marriott's current squeeze. 'A lot of reasons contributed to me calling off the tour,' Beck told *Melody Maker*, desperate to find an excuse. 'All these things seemed to come to a head on opening night. It's not worth appearing on a bill starring such names as Roy Orbison and Small Faces. Frankly, I would never tour with such artists again. I'd rather top a ballroom tour.'

Which was a bit unfair on Roy Orbison.

The trouble was, so many people were unable to resist being unkind to Jeff Beck. He took himself extremely seriously, unlike Ronnie or Steve Marriott. They took the music seriously, but life still had to retain an element of fun. Which is perhaps why they were viewed as never quite growing up. Beck never seemed to be comfortable with musicians as talented as he was. It was as though his insecurities only allowed for one star per group, and it had to be him. He did make an allowance for Rod Stewart, though.

The first to suffer was drummer Ray Cook, who was also made the official scapegoat for the Finsbury Park Début Disaster. He was unceremoniously sacked, and that after being assured that his position was permanent, to the extent of being urged to buy a brand-new drum kit costing £400 – say at least £2000 at today's prices.

Ronnie's new rhythm section partner was Mickey Waller, an old friend of Rod's from his Soul Agents days, who'd also previously drummed with Georgie Fame and Brian Auger's Trinity.

'I feel I'm entitled to one mistake,' Beck was quoted as saying in *Melody Maker*, when once again asked about the Finsbury Park fiasco. 'People who like music and know I've got Rod Stewart and Mickey Waller with me will know I have a good group now. I challenge any group to compete with us in a group battle!'

Notice that he didn't mention Ronnie Wood.

Praising Waller turned out to be a little premature. In two and a half years the Jeff Beck group went through six drummers – Viv Prince, Roger Cook, Mickey Waller (twice), Rod Coombes and Aynsley Dunbar. And by the end of March 1967, Waller quit – for the first time – to join the Walker Brothers (none of whom were actually related), replacing Gary Leeds.

Waller was replaced by Rod Coombes, another friend of Rod's. If it seems that Rod was becoming something of a foreman, he was; but only from the best of motives: precisely the ones that had led him to join Jeff Beck in the first instance: 'We thought we'd better help him out . . . I mean, for a guitar player like that to come out with "Hi Ho Silver Lining" was a crime.'

Rod also brought in ex-Shotgun Express member Dave Ambrose to play bass, so that Ronnie could play second guitar. In early April the new five-man line-up were summoned to plush offices at 155 Oxford Street, where they were told by Peter Grant that he had bought out Simon Napier Bell's fifty-percent share in Jeff Beck; and that together with Mickie Most, he had set up RAK Management; and that an agency deal with NEMS was in the offing; and that the other four members of the band would have to negotiate their wages separately. Luckily for Rod, he had his own manager to do this for him. The others didn't, and it was made clear that day that Grant regarded them as nothing more than hired help.

'It was like the Oxford Street Mafia up there,' Ronnie says, 'with the Andrew Oldhams, your Peter Grant etc, all them wheelers and dealers. They used to have two of them on either side of the office and I'd go in with Rod and they'd say, "No, not you, we just want to see Rod", and they'd talk money, then say, "Oh, you can come in now Ronnie", and that's how it used to be. They were just bullying Jeff all the time, which was a fucking shame.'

Beck's new five-piece band was now being billed as the Jeff Beck Group, as opposed to simply Jeff Beck. They opened at the Marquee on 11 April 1967. With Ronnie back in his old familiar role – in a two-lead-guitar line-up, just like the Birds – the Group set about restoring Beck's slightly tarnished reputation.

Art had gone along to support his little brother, taking Jon Lord with him. Both men 'Thought it sounded great,' Art still enthuses, 'with Ronnie and Jeff playing, they used to be great for each other. Ronnie would go dah-dah and Jeff would go wah-wah and then they'd both go bah! and the crowd loved it, you know, it was really exciting guitar battles. Afterwards Jon Lord went up to Jeff and said it was the best band he'd ever seen.'

Great for the crowd, great for Ronnie – but not so great for Beck. According to Ronnie: 'Jeff fucking hated it. He wanted to be the only guitarist in the band. So Dave Ambrose had to go and I was back on bass. Jeff's management treated me, Rod and the rest of the guys like second-class citizens both musically and financially. People would just come and go. Not that Rod seemed to mind – but then again, he was happy being around anyone that breathed, seeing as how his last job had been a gravedigger! But Rod was pretty shrewd when it came to money. Come to think of it, everyone did a lot better than me. I just struggled on the best I could.'

Sure enough, the next to go was drummer Rod Coombes, replaced by Aynsley Dunbar, ex-Mojo and John Mayall's Bluesbreakers, who could be said to know a thing or two about percussion and the blues. Indeed, Dunbar stayed for four full months.

'That's how it used to be,' Ronnie says ruefully. 'It was all them cunts up in Oxford Street going, "The band will be much more popular, sell more records if you get this guy in and that guy out." But all it did was fuck everyone off – the band and the fans. When they asked me to play bass again, I just went, "OK, you want me to play bass, I'll play bass, it's your fucking band, mate." He was being paid the princely sum of £15 a week, a fraction of what he'd been making with the Birds and there were few options open to him.

The great British wedding-reception favourite 'Hi Ho Silver Lining' had been released on 24 March with Rod Stewart on backing vocals. It had a fourteen-week run in the charts, predictably peaking at number fourteen when the band appeared on *Top Of The Pops* on 27 April. In fact, it was only Jeff Beck who was actually seen. Ronnie, Rod and Mickey Waller had to stand watching from behind the cameras as Beck, in close-up, mimed his way through an excruciatingly bad singalong number as unrepresentative of his style as it is possible to imagine. Even though it was his first official non-appearance on *Top Of The Pops*, Ronnie was happy to sit out of shot, as was Rod – especially as the Who were also guesting that evening. They had their pride, and even Jeff Beck could see the absurdity of the situation: 'I quit the Yardbirds to concentrate on playing the guitar, which was why I had a really great vocalist like Rod Stewart and a rhythm section with Ronnie and Mickey with me. You have to remember that around this time Cream had released "I Feel Free" and Hendrix had "Purple Haze". And all I had was "Hi Ho fucking Silver Lining".'

Ronnie also remembers how much Beck hated the song. When they played live gigs, he often used to persuade Rod to announce: 'And now our guitarist is going to sing our hit, "Hi Ho, Hi Ho!"' At which point Beck would shout across the stage: 'No, I fucking ain't!' So much for Mickie Most's dream of bubble-gum pop stardom. It was obvious that the Oxford Street Mafia planned to take the Jeff Beck premium brand downmarket for short-term profits. And the more money Beck made personally, the larger Peter Grant's own percentage. Which meant that the other band members – except for Rod – were not on a retainer, but only paid on a gig-by-gig basis. Which meant that session musicians were used for recordings. Did it matter that the sound was a little different than when the group played live? Not a bit. Jeff Beck himself was the money-making, solo, star, and the rest of the group simply had to learn their place.

It was a time of deep frustration for Rod Stewart: 'There was this guy

[Ray Cook] who got sacked just after he'd bought these drums on hire purchase. Then after the Finsbury Astoria nonsense, nothing happened for a while until Aynsley Dunbar came in as drummer ... beautiful drummer, really got the band together. But a blues purist, who left because he didn't think we were playing real blues. One night we did a gig at the Saville and Ronnie and me came on dressed in flowers and caftans – it was the time of flower power – just to take the piss, but Aynsley took it really bad and quit that night. So we got Mickey Waller back, and he and Ronnie played great together. But then Beck started recording without crediting us, like "Tally Man" and the group's anthem, "Rock My Plimsoul". And with crap like "Love Is Blue" he didn't even use us, and we'd all have to stand in the wings while Beck did it live on stage. You ever see those two Beck albums? There was never a picture of the band on them, only Beck by himself. I guess his ego got inflated – but he was usually OK with me. Aside from the crap going out on singles, the problems were mostly to do with the money. None of us, except for Beck, ever earned a great deal. And all the line-up changes, of course. Like after the second American tour, when Beck decided to sack Ronnie and Mickey, which had to be one of the best rhythm sections going at the time. The band was never the same after Ronnie left.'

In fact, Rod got it wrong: Dunbar didn't leave the group until August. But being faced by two freaked-out hippies on stage really had made his mind up. Dunbar left to form his own true blues band, the Retaliation, which went on to absolutely nowhere. Finally, faced with the reality of authenticity – which usually meant starving to death – Dunbar returned to the pop world in 1973 wearing stack-heeled boots and a spaceman's outfit, as one of Ziggy Stardust's Spiders From Mars.

On 11 May 1967 the Jeff Beck Group featured on *Top Of The Pops* for the second time – or rather, Jeff Beck featured as a solo artist singing 'Hi Ho Silver Lining'. Once again Ronnie and Rod watched from behind the camera – doubly embarrassing because the show included Jimi Hendrix, who was promoting 'The Wind Cries Mary'.

However, a better gig occurred on 2 July, when the group supported Cream at the Saville Theatre. Also present were John Mayall's Blues-breakers, plus Jimmy Powell and the Dimensions. It was rather like a school reunion: Eric Clapton and Jack Bruce of Cream had served their apprenticeship with John Mayall, as had Beck's drummer Aynsley Dunbar. Mayall's current drummer was none other than Mickey Waller. Rod Stewart had played harmonica with Jimmy Powell. Jeff Beck and Eric Clapton had both played with the Yardbirds. Before she met Ronnie,

Krissie had been Clapton's girlfriend. Of course what no one could possibly have known was that Mayall's then lead guitarist, Mick Taylor – late of the Gods, with ex-Bird Tony Monroe – would be replaced by Ronnie Wood as lead guitarist in the Rolling Stones eight years later.

It was at this gig that Ronnie first met George Harrison – at an aftershow party at the Speakeasy – who was to become a lifelong friend. So much so that when, in the early seventies, it's alleged that Krissie Wood had an affair with George, while Patti Harrison did the same with Ronnie, the two men are said to have greeted each other with a cheery 'How's my wife?'

The next night, Krissie and Ronnie returned to the Speakeasy, where a celebration party was being held for the Monkees, who'd just achieved three sell-out nights at Wembley, and who were America's latest, manufactured, mass-market answer to the Beatles. Socially, Ronnie had arrived for he was part of a guest list that included all the Beatles and their wives; Lulu; Brian Jones, who was always at everything; Dusty Springfield; and Krissie's old flame, Eric Clapton. Mick Jagger and Keith Richards would have been there, but they were currently spending a night in jail following the drug bust at Richards's Sussex farmhouse, Redlands – which was why the Monkees had performed that night's gig wearing black armbands. Both Mick and Keith were later released without charge.

On 7 July Jeff Beck released the single 'Tally Man', which didn't credit Ronnie Wood even though – along with the rest of the group – he played on both sides. On 24 August Beck made another solo appearance, on *Top Of The Pops*. Ronnie went along, if only for the performers' free bar, and once again met Jimi Hendrix. The two got on well, as always, although Hendrix had yet to see Ronnie play live.

By now, Ronnie was beginning to get the message and after doing a handful of gigs over the next few months, finally went AWOL in early October, just after he'd sat in as a guitarist with the Crazy World Of Arthur Brown for a BBC Radio 1 session, broadcast on the 8th. Aside from this, the high point of his summer and autumn had been when Jeff Beck played at a festival called The Summer of Love at Woburn – 'arranged by kind permission of His Grace, the Duke of Bedford' – and the Small Faces' set had to be cut short when the tent mysteriously burned down. But what really hastened his departure was the arrival of a group called Vanilla Fudge from America. Jeff Beck saw them at the Astoria on 4 October and was deeply impressed by bassist Tim Bogert and drummer Carmen Appice. Word got back to Ronnie of quite how impressed Beck was: 'I heard he was sniffing around, had his eye on 'em, and knew he wanted to get them in the band. So I just thought, fuck it, I'm not hanging around to get sacked. It wasn't as if we were doing much, anyway. I mean, Jeff only used to show up for a gig if he felt like it, and that wasn't very fucking often. We must have cancelled more than we fucking played!'

Rick Cunningham, a lifelong friend of Ronnie, remembers turning up a concert and going backstage before the gig to see Ronnie, Rod and Mickey Waller tucking in to the hospitality food and drink. They were getting extremely drunk. Cunningham asked where Jeff Beck was, and why the band wasn't getting ready for the gig.

'He hasn't shown up – again,' Ronnie said.

Cunningham couldn't believe it. The place was packed and the fans had begun chanting for their idol. 'What are you going to do?' he asked. 'What about Jeff?'

'Fuck him,' Ronnie replied shortly. 'It ain't my name on the front.'

Not only the group, but the fans too, had to learn their place.

By September 1967 Ronnie was more than a little restless. 'I'd spent a year with Jeff Beck and I was still struggling.' He needed a job and a sense of direction. Krissie was still temping and they were short of money. Still, Ronnie wasn't too worried. Something would turn up – it always did.

8
'I created on and off for a year'

Flashback to January 1967. When Kim Gardner had been let go – before he'd actually started – by Jeff Beck, he'd asked his old friend Robert Stigwood for advice.

As Tony Ashton remembers: 'Kim always played up to Stigwood because he knew Stigwood fancied him rotten. He used to get whatever he wanted just by leading him on. It was maybe a bit out of order, but you couldn't help laughing.'

Stigwood had already helped Ronnie and Kim by clearing up the debt still owed on the van by buying it for the Bee Gees – who never did discover that it had originally been financed by one of London's most feared criminal families.

He also introduced Kim to the Arthur Howes Agency, the most powerful booking organization in London. Howes had been one of the first to take a chance on the Beatles back in 1962. Their first performances for him – as support to chart-topper Frank Ifield – had left audiences lukewarm. But Howes, a shrewd judge of talent, had recognized their huge potential and secured an option to promote further shows by the Beatles, despite their being virtual unknowns, as and when he chose. The deal paid off handsomely within a few months and Howes found himself with a major financial grip on Beatlemania. In 1966 he teamed up with record producer Shel Talmy (see 'A Nasty Reaction', pages XX–XX) and formed Planet Records. This was a small independent label whose priority was the Pop-Art, demi-Mod sensation, the Creation, then at their gimmicky height following two massive European hit singles, 'Making Time' and the German number one (and a much later irritation by Boney M), 'Painter Man'. It's often forgotten, like the band itself, that Boney M were a German group, and that covering 'Painter Man' was a tribute to a band who had been legendary in Germany but almost unknown in Britain.

There was only one problem: the Creation were both totally neurotic and terminally paranoid about each other. Every now and then two of them would gang up on a third, with the fourth keeping well out of it, and fire him. Or one of them would quit before he could be fired. Or they'd just fire each other *en masse*. Which was really OK, because then they would happily re-form since there wasn't anyone officially left in the group to say who could or couldn't join. On the other hand, the Creation were one of the most innovative and exciting bands Britain ever produced, with the Who, for example, copying their anarchic stage act. Although for the Creation it wasn't an act, but all too frighteningly real.

After two brilliant singles, drummer Jack Jones had been fired by bass player Bob Garner in favour of an unknown Liverpool drummer and friend of Garner's called Dave Preston, only to be embarrassingly rehired less than three weeks later by lead vocalist Kenny Pickett, who then effectively fired himself and was replaced by Kim Gardner.

'That was strange,' recalls Jones. 'Kenny had got it into his head that we were going to fire him, which was rubbish, and he sort of confronted us all with it, saying, "I know you want to get rid of me, total paranoia, so I'm fucking leaving." So he did, and no one wanted him to. Anyway, about this time Eddie [Phillips, lead guitarist] said he'd heard that Kim Gardner from the Birds was looking for a job, via the Arthur Howes Agency. No one had heard that the Birds had finished, we just assumed they were always firing each other like us, so we set up a meeting.'

The rest of the group showed up at the agency on 10 February 1967, to find Kim sitting in reception with Phillips, who told them Kim would be at rehearsals the next day. Just like that. But that was OK for Bob Garner at least, because Kim showed up with Ronnie Wood and for a wild moment he wondered about firing Eddie and getting Ronnie in his place. No one had been fired for at least a week and the band members were getting restless.

However, Ronnie's motives were totally honourable: 'I'd always thought Eddie Phillips was cool and I'd heard about how great a guitar player he was. I'd heard he played with a violin bow and fucking hacksaws, which was way ahead of Jimmy Page, so I went along with Kim to watch.'

By all accounts it was the rehearsal to end all rehearsals, even by the Creation's weird standards. Bob Garner switched to lead vocals, in order to accommodate Kim's more versatile bass playing. Then there was John Dalton, who later joined the Kinks, who also played bass. While the recently self-fired Kenny Pickett arrived just as the rest of the group was plugging in.

'He was storming about,' recalls Kim, 'calling everyone cunts, and I didn't actually know who he was, because the Creation mostly played on the Continent. So I'm standing there, and Ronnie's sitting on the amps watching all this, and I turn to Jack [Jones, the recently re-hired drummer] and said, "Who's that bloke?" and he goes, "Oh, that's the singer" and I'm like, "I thought Bob's the singer" and Jack says, "Well, he is, but he was the bass player" and then I look over to John [Dalton – bass, yet to be fired] and say, "Well, who's he?" and Jack goes, "He's the bass player too" . . . and I said, "What the fuck! How many fucking bass players does this band need!" And Ronnie just cracked up.'

The Creation's fragile, ever-changing alliances may have helped give it that hard-edged brilliance which so illuminated their live performances, but they also destroyed the group's stability. Kim could see that the group was ultimately doomed to implode; but with nothing else in the offing, and since 'the fucking wages were good', Kim got Created.

His first jaunt with the Creation began the following month when the band gave the Rolling Stones a serious run for their money as support group on a short tour of Germany, beginning on 29 March. 'Acid was quite new then. I remember we had our drinks spiked on the very first show . . . we did the whole show on acid, which was absolutely brilliant.' With an electrifying stage act, manager Tony Stratton-Smith's dogged determination and Shel Talmy's masterful production expertise, the Creation had all the ingredients needed to become a world-class act.

Sadly, by late 1967 the incessant in-fighting had totally decimated the group, to the point that the pioneering Eddie Phillips suddenly quit under threat of divorce from his wife. He was briefly replaced by the unknown Tony Ollard – who actually remained that way. Bob Garner had also quit, leaving Jack Jones and Kim Gardner. However, a rhythm section on its own does not a band make.

'Thing was,' Kim explained, 'we'd had a single due out in January 1968. But Bob had gone back to Warrington, and Eddie had gone home to try and save his marriage, because he'd got the ultimatum from his missus: me or the band. Which was bollocks, because she left him anyway and he ended up playing bass for P.P. Arnold – which Ronnie could identify with. Anyway, me and Jack thought there was still a lot of money to be made off the Creation name in Germany alone, and Jack was talking to Kenny Pickett because they'd remained friendly, and it was agreed to give it one more go round the block. I went and found Ron and he was skint and pissed off with Jeff Beck, and I said, "Do you want to make some real fucking money? Come on, let's milk this." We had tours lined up with Holland, Spain and, of course, Germany – and Ronnie only had a few gigs lined up with Jeff Beck towards the end of the year.'

*

Ronnie and Krissie were renting a flat above the Little Pink Pig estate agency in Lower Sloane Street, together with Peanuts and Butch the goldfish and Beano the cat. Not all estate agents are bad – Perry Press, who owned the Little Pink Pig allowed them to live there rent-free, for courtesy of Jeff Beck's management, money was extremely tight. Krissie had taken yet another a job, this time selling on Harvey Goldsmith's Big O poster stand in Kensington Market. The couple were poor but happy; even so, a little more money was always welcome. And it was into this scene that Kim Gardner suddenly arrived one mid-October morning, with a suitcase stuffed with cash.

'The Creation basically lived in Germany eight months of the year,' Kim explains, 'so we didn't have to pay British tax. But we did used to come back to do TV gigs and stuff. And triple gigs – like one at five p.m., make the next town and set up by eight, and the last one by eleven. We made a lot of money – I used to have to come to England just to spend it! But I couldn't spend it all – used to stay in Bridal Suites, and still couldn't fucking spend it. I made £13,000 just in gig money. Jack Jones used to be an accountant, so he just split the cash four ways.'

Kim took Ronnie and Krissie out in his new Jaguar to explain the Creation's set-up. And, harking back to his earlier acid experiences, offered to impart his slightly superior knowledge of the drug. 'Ronnie was learning to drive at the time, so I let him drive my Jag on acid. He was driving and tripping and suddenly he can't find the steering-wheel. He's trying to pass this big truck, and I'm seeing all these red flashes, and suddenly he goes, "The steering-wheel's gone! It's fucking gone!" and he can't really drive anyway, but he's laughing his head off and the truck's getting closer and closer. Just then he cuts in front of it, and the truck hits us and we spin around and around like a merry-go-round. And we're both grinning at each other, tripping in a car spinning out of control, and screaming "Whaaaaaaa!" '

Suitcases full of cash. New Jaguars. Multicoloured driving lessons. What ambitious professional musician wouldn't jump at the chance to join a two-man band? There were still a few commitments with Jeff Beck – including a session on *Top Gear*, genius DJ John Peel's influential Radio 1 show. Aside from John Peel, the only real buzz Ronnie had got from playing with the Jeff Beck for the past four months was his first date outside the UK: at Ghent, in Belgium, on 13 October. But then Ronnie learned that Beck had fleshed out the group with pianist Nicky Hopkins and singer Madeleine Bell – another Mickie Most inspiration – for recording sessions for a new single, 'Love is Blue', in December. Both the recording session and single were news to Ronnie – as was the unofficial discovery that Jeff planned to play bass himself. He could sense the 'Not Wanted On Voyage' label was about to be tied around his neck. Bearing in mind that Ronnie and Jeff had been friends since 1965, Jeff's behaviour was a little cavalier, to say the least.

Ronnie began 1968 as a full-time member of the Creation (Version IV) and part-time member of the Jeff Beck Group (who's counting?). He flitted between both bands during January and February, playing a handful of gigs to promote Beck's new single 'Love Is Blue' – which he doesn't actually play on – while rehearsing with the Creation. Ironically, 'Love Is Blue' only reached number twenty-three on the Hit Parade, beaten out of the Top Ten by Frenchman Paul Mauriat's version of the same song, which also made it into the US charts. Beck was reduced to making slighting remarks about the record: 'We rushed into the studio and the whole thing was finished in a couple of days,' he told *Disc & Music Echo*, 'and the fantastic thing is I really like the melody.' Rushed into the studio? Which just happened to have been booked at least a month earlier? No one had forced Beck to go along with Mickie Most's dreams of bubble-gum pop stardom. The least he could have done was put on a brave face about a record that left many critics and fans totally bemused. Instead, he went to announce that he'd changed the group's name to Jeff Beck's Million Dollar Bash. Given how little most of the other musicians were earning, the name was little more than a bad joke. Nor did it ever catch on.

Even Rod Stewart was beginning to become disillusioned with Beck and his management. In the true musical tradition of making a bad situation worse, Stewart signed an ill-fated solo deal with Andrew Loog Oldham's Immediate Records and produced the single 'Little Miss Understood', which died of general neglect.

In March Ronnie told Rod he was leaving Jeff Beck to concentrate on the more lucrative opportunities offered by the Creation's European bookings. He didn't bother to tell Beck himself; after all, Beck had hardly been communicative over the past year.

The first item on Ronnie's new musical menu was an April tour with the Creation to Germany and Spain. The recollections of Roman Salicki will give some of the flavour of the tour. A Polish refugee who'd been a top fashion photographer in London during the mid-sixties, he'd originally learned his trade with Michael Cooper, famous for his work with the Rolling Stones and the album cover for *Sergeant Pepper*. By 1967, Salicki was burned out and bumming around the South of France, where he ran into Shel Talmy. The two men got on well, so much so that Talmy persuaded Salicki to work as his personal assistant.

'One of the bands he [Talmy] was recording was the Creation and

Shel asked me take them out on the road, which meant Germany . . . Everything was fine for a while, but with the Creation you never knew what they'd get up to next. And driving through East Germany was especially scary, because they had watch-towers and tanks all up and down the autobahn. We had to go through Checkpoint Charlie when we left West Berlin – me, the roadie and five long-haired idiots stoned out of their minds, and who didn't give a damn about anything even when they were straight. The American guards said, "Listen, guys, we don't advise you to go through. If you do, it's at your own risk." But we did and crossed over to the Eastern checkpoint, where there were all these stony-faced guards. And the band were making faces at them, and making all these disparaging remarks, but after we'd been grilled for about an hour and a half they finally let us go. And as we went through, the boys stuck their naked arses against the van windows, which somewhat worried me.

'We eventually got back into West Germany, checked into a hotel and the first thing the boys wanted to do was go out and get drunk. Which was nothing new, because every night they were absolutely stoned and drunk out of their minds. They'd bust up hotel rooms, insult people, cause riots – anything to make my life miserable. I seemed to have spent the entire time placating hotel managers, cops, club owners, Border Guards . . . generally, keeping the band out of prison. Especially Ronnie and Kim – I was sure I was only going to come back with Jack and Kenny, leaving the other two banged up in some jail, probably in the East.

'But when the band went on stage, they were very professional. They did the job they were supposed to do and they did it well. It was really like a Beatles scene: total sold-out chaos at the concerts, people stacked up against each other, and the boys playing with the audience. It got to the point where I'd be up on stage trying to slap the girls away, except one time Kim Gardner put his boot in my back and pushed me into the audience, but that was OK because I was an honorary band member, so I wasn't mauled too badly.

'I finally got back to London totally exhausted. I enjoyed the band, they were a great bunch of guys, but there comes a point where you say, "I don't want any more of this. I want to go home." '

In May Ronnie was one of the many musicians asked to play on Beck's ground-breaking album *Truth*. It finally looked as if Mickie Most had learned his lesson, for the album was unashamedly adult rock. The same month also saw the release of the Creation's new single, 'Midway Down', recorded in January, with Ronnie playing lead guitar.

Talmy's own label, Planet, had folded in the aftermath of the Great

Payola Scandal in late 1966. He'd moved his operation to Polydor, who allowed the group to record whenever the opportunity arose, but without any real commitment. The Creation had laid down six tracks, the first of which, 'Midway Down', ironically turned out to be the band's swansong. Written by a little-known German composer, the song, with its circus theme, owes a great deal to the Beatles' 'Being For The Benefit Of Mister Kite'. It was also a priceless slice of sixties psychedelia, with the lines 'Ten foot giant finds it tough to lift a feather', and 'Three foot midget hopes he won't be small for ever'. The song descends into a la-la-la singalong in the finest pub tradition. It was backed by the group composition, 'The Girls Are Naked' – a closer approximation to the Eddie Phillips sound on early Creation recordings – and released simultaneously in Britain and Germany. These were excellent, well-structured pop songs, every bit as instant as anything the group's contemporaries were producing. But without any real record company push it sank without trace, even though the Eddie Phillips reprise earned it a respectful airplay on German radio. Always important, respectability in Germany – but it won't pay the rent in England, where the indifference continued.

Two further releases were lined up for German consumption only: a cover of 'Boni Maroni', backed by 'Mercy, Mercy, Mercy', and 'For All That I Am', backed by the group composition 'Uncle Bert' – credited to Garwood Picton, which was an amalgamation of their surnames. 'For All That I Am' was probably the band's finest hour, with Ronnie's full-on fuzz guitar shaping the song.

'The Girls Are Naked' was inspired by the signs above shadowy doorways that the band used to read in the backstreets of Soho, *en route* to playing at the Marquee in Wardour Street. The recording demonstrates how much at ease Ronnie and Kim were with each other's playing: it begins with a mighty Gardner bass line that builds the song for an excellent lead guitar intro.

But underneath all this, the Creation had troubles, best explained by Shel Talmy: 'They [the original line-up] hated each other. They couldn't put aside their personal enmities for the good of the band, or the good of themselves. So instead of becoming extremely rich superstars, they've all become very working/middle-class nobodies. Not Ronnie Wood or Kim Gardner, of course – but Kenny had basically done nothing before he died, and Eddie unfortunately was a bus driver for years, which is like "what a waste!" And Bob – I have no idea what happened to Bob. It was like he was born with three chips on his shoulder, a totally disruptive personality, I think is the nicest thing I can say about him. Jack was cool, fine with the whole thing, and of course when Ronnie Wood came in he was great. But Bob thought he "deserved", quote unquote, to have more notice than he did. Certainly more than Kenny or Eddie. which was wrong – he wasn't even in the same league. Maybe it's because people from up north, like Warrington, have this fucking attitude!'

Talmy still talks of the Creation as being the greatest of all the groups that never made it – and this from the man who knew a thing or two. 'I was still determined to push the Creation even after the original band broke up – just as they were about to explode in England in 1966. They managed to carry on, and regained the lost ground very quickly with Kim. England had lagged behind when it came to the Creation, which was fine because I had my eyes firmly set on the States, that was their obvious market, they could have gone on for thirty years because they were as good as the Kinks or the Who, maybe even the Stones. But the main players couldn't even stand to be in the same country as each other, never mind the same band. Ronnie was a good choice but I always felt he was brought in by Kim when it was all over. Kenny had a presence, he had a real attitude, he really looked the part and for a little while he was the lead singer. He was the first one to my knowledge to initiate Action-Art painting live on stage – and of course they almost burned a theatre down in Germany, because they would ignite the paintings afterwards using aerosol spray-paint cans like little flame-throwers. That got them some great publicity – this was before Jimi Hendrix had set fire to anything and it got them the number one record in Germany. Unfortunately Eddie was the rest of the band; there were very few guitar players around who played as well as Eddie could. Ronnie was good, but he wasn't anywhere near Eddie, who was certainly a more interesting player. I never gave up hope of getting him back in the group, and this is no disrespect to Ronnie, because Ronnie is a wonderful guitarist. It just wasn't the Creation. But I still went across in order to get them a big American deal, hoping it would reunite them. Which I got. A five-album deal with United Artists worth millions of dollars. But when I got back here there wasn't a band in any shape or form. There wasn't a band at all. Here I was with this huge fucking deal and it was all over in the meantime! The original guys were all to blame because each and everyone of them contributed to the gradual erosion of the band. What a fucking waste! Those guys were the biggest regret of my career when I think of what they could have been and what they would have been, too!'

On 20 May 1968 a now dying Creation left for a short tour of Germany and Holland. Ronnie's place in the Jeff Beck Group was taken by Junior Wood from Tomorrow – a group only notable because guitarist Steve Howe went on to join Yes. What proved to be the Creation's last gig was performed at the John Lewis department store's theatre in Oxford Street in early June. Although according to Jack Jones's diary, the band did play one more time. Unfortunately, no can remember where, or anything at all about it.

Former Creation lead singer Kenny Pickett died on 10 January 1997 – shortly before he was to be interviewed for this book. Luckily Mike Stax, editor of the brilliant *Ugly Things*, the magazine specializing in obscure R&B and garage bands, has allowed exclusive use of an earlier interview where Pickett remembered Ronnie in the Creation's line-up: 'I think Ron was with the band on and off for about nine months. It was well after the Birds. He was our lead guitarist, a good lad, good fun, yeah. He wasn't a particularly good guitarist, but he turned the band round in a different direction, leaning more towards B.B. King, R&B, that sort of stuff, because that's what Ronnie was into. So we almost reverted back to when the Creation was the Mark Four, doing cover versions and stuff. It was full circle, which felt really weird, like I'd come back in at the very beginning. Ron was still with Jeff Beck at the time, but I don't think it was happening, so Ronnie came on board – but he left us when he got the chance to go to America with Beck. But that was fine, because the Creation was just about dying by then. That last band was a good band, but it wasn't the Creation as people knew the Creation to be.'

On the Friday he died, Kenny Pickett had just guested with a friend's band at his local pub in North London. After leaving the stage he went to the bar and ordered a pint. Someone walked up behind him and tapped him on the shoulder to congratulate him on his performance. Whereupon the Creation's former lead singer fell to the floor dead.

Following three autopsies the authorities were still unable to determine the exact cause of death. Pickett had managed to remain an enigma right to the very end.

The Jeff Beck Group began an eight-week tour of the States on 14 June, without Junior Woods but with Ronnie. The lure of America had proved too strong for him: goodbye Creation, hello New York. Especially, hello Bill Graham's famed Fillmore East, where the group was to support the Grateful Dead.

'I only went back with Beck because I wanted to go to America,' Ronnie admitted years later.

Or as Kim said: 'Ronnie joined the Creation to get him into Europe, and rejoined Beck to get to America. In the same way I joined the Creation for Europe, and formed Ashton, Gardner and Dyke to get to the States, which had always been our goal, right from the Birds days. America was our aim, and it was more important than money.'

Originally, and at Tony Stratton-Smith's suggestion, Ashton, Gardner and Dyke was to be called Charisma. But as Tony Ashton later said, 'We didn't even know what charisma meant, let alone spell it, so we just used our surnames, the way Clapton, Bruce and Baker did before they became the Cream, and later you had Crosby, Still, Nash & Young. So Tony took the name for his own record company, and that's how you got Charisma Records.'

If there'd ever been any doubt how Jeff Beck and his management viewed the rest of the band, that first tour to America quickly confirmed it: with contempt. While Jeff and Peter Grant stayed at the Hilton, Ronnie, Rod, Mickey Waller and Nicky Hopkins were crammed into one room in the Goreham – and kept short of money.

'We were so desperate, one time we had to go down to the automat and steal eggs,' Ronnie admits. 'The Goreham wasn't too bad in theory – real rock and roll hotel, all the bands used to stay there – Cream, Sly and the Family Stone and Hendrix – but they had their own rooms, and we were all together. Still, the place had real energy – in fact, Rod and I passed by there a few years ago and they still had the same staff.'

The group played Fillmore East for the first time on 14 June. It was a resounding success – so many encores were demanded and given that the Grateful Dead had to cut short their set. Beck and Peter Grant went back to the Hilton, and the rest of the band to their one room at the Goreham.

It should have been a resounding personal triumph for Beck, for the Yardbirds had played their last gig on the 5th, and here he was setting New York ablaze. But there was a spectre at the feast. Jimmy Page had stayed on after the Yardbirds' last American tour and had been invited to join – as observer – the Jeff Beck tour by manager Peter Grant. Every night he stood in the wings, gauging the audience's reaction to the way the group played. And he was staying at the same hotel. Beck could tell himself that his old mate had simply come to support him.

'Aggravation and unfriendliness developed very early with that band,' Rod Stewart remember. 'Especially as Jeff would stay at a top-class hotel, and the others would be at Hotel Third-On-The-Bill round the corner. In the two and a half years I was with Beck, I never once looked him in the eye. I always looked at his shirt, or something like that.'

Page had been flown out not to support Beck, but to emulate him – although it could be argued that Beck had taken his own stage act from the Yardbirds, and modelled his playing in part on Eric Clapton. All the same, you have to admire Peter Grant's chutzpah. There he was, launching Beck in America with one hand, while nurturing Page and Led Zeppelin with the other. Peter Green's judgement would turn out to be correct, however: Jeff Beck was doomed to be remembered for 'Hi Ho Silver Lining', while Led Zeppelin would become rock gods.

Following the Fillmore East shows, Beck was asked by Jimi Hendrix to play a benefit gig at the Reality House Rehabilitation Center on Staten Island.

'Jeff said, "Do you fancy doing a gig with Jimi Hendrix? and we said yeah!' Ronnie reminisces. 'And when we were playing, Jimi came up and guested with us, starting bossing us about. He was the first person who ever gave me great credibility in the band. He'd stop the music and say: "Jeff, why don't you shut up and give the bass player a chance?" And Jeff's face just sort of crumpled up. Jimi used to give me solos, at Staten Island and later at the Scene Club [at the Daytop Music Festival], he used to recognize my guitar playing through the bass. When we got back to England he even gave me a dog! But Jeff really hated me getting that kind of recognition. I mean, here was Jimi, the world's greatest fucking guitarist, telling Jeff to shut the fuck up and let the bass player have a go!'

Hendrix showed up every night of the group's five-night residency at the Scene Club, guesting with them on each occasion, and giving greater and greater prominence to Ronnie's bass playing. To make matters worse, New York was hit by a week-long torrential downpour, and the humidity played hell with Beck's spots.

Beck had always been extremely sensitive about his complexion. Going on stage looking like a survivor of the Black Death, with Jimmy Page taking notes from the wings, and Jimi Hendrix liable to turn up any moment and insist that the bass player be given solos, did nothing for his peace of mind.

Even when the tour became a sell-out success, and the band became the darlings of the American music media, Beck's misgivings grew and grew. Especially when that very success helped Rod Stewart get a solo deal with Mercury Records, after being seen at the Shrine Auditorium in Los Angeles by producer Lou Reizener. True, Peter Grant did ensure that Beck's album, *Truth*, was rush-released in the States. But that hardly helped with Beck's nagging suspicions that some band members had their own fans – one reason, perhaps, why the album cover only mentioned Jeff Beck. You had to read the sleeve notes to discover that he was supported by the same group who'd helped that first tour become such a success. The album entered the charts at number 163 and quickly rose to fifteenth place by October, when the band was sent back to America in order to promote it – this time with tour manager Richard Cole, who would go on to become tour manager for Led Zeppelin. Ironically, Cole would appoint an assistant roadie called Kenny Pickett.

The first tour lasted until 24 August, and when Ronnie returned home it was to find an offer waiting: would he like to join Jimmy Page and Chris Dreja in a group to be called the New Yardbirds, with a ten-day tour of Scandinavia? The original Yardbirds had broken up in July; both Page and Grant were eager to try out the ideas gleaned from watching the Jeff Beck Group. Ronnie declined. That Scandinavian tour, plus the next tour of America with Beck, would have meant that he'd be away from home for well over six months, and he was badly missing Krissie. Besides, for all his misgivings about Beck and his management, the group was one of the hottest in America and staying where he was would give Ronnie the chance to really make his name in the Land of the Free.

Chris Dreja would eventually leave the New Yardbirds and become a photographer. The group hired John Paul Jones as bass player in Ronnie's place, and Robert Plant as lead vocalist. Ronnie Wood had turned down the chance to join the band that would go on to sell over forty million records worldwide.

On the other hand, he did go on to become a Rolling Stone. Which was all he'd ever wanted.

When the Jeff Beck Group returned from their second American tour, they played a welcome-home gig at London's psychedelic hot-spot, the Middle Earth Club, at the Roundhouse, Chalk Farm, North London: Rhythm and Blues meets the Hobbit, unthinkable only a year or so before. Beck was confident enough to refuse a follow-up series of American dates that Peter Grant had provisionally booked over Christmas. No problem – Grant simply sent Jimmy Page and the New Yardbirds instead. After all, Page had spent a long time studying Beck's stage act and knew he could do better. The band wasn't called the New Yardbirds any more, courtesy of a crack by Keith Moon. 'You'll go down in the States like a lead Zeppelin,' he joked – and the name stuck.

Beck wasn't worried about his old mate taking over the tour. Why, he'd even heard that Page was actually employing the same stage antics as former Creation lead guitarist Eddie Phillips – using a violin bow, for example – and look what happened to him: nothing. Besides, Beck was busy buying himself a new house, in true rock-star fashion, a secluded mansion in the heart of the countryside, into which he would move with current girlfriend, the *Truth* album cover star, fashionable model and, later, friend to cats, Celia Hammond.

Meanwhile Ronnie and Krissie were also on the move again, this time to the Gloucester Place (W1) flat belonging to Ten Years After guitarist Alvin Lee, who was off with his group to improve their profile in the States.

'Kim knew Alvin's girlfriend, Lorraine, very well,' Krissie recollects, 'so really it was Kim who got everything sorted. It took a lot of the pressure off. Ronnie was due to go back to America with Jeff soon, and we wouldn't have to worry about rent money, which became a problem every time Ronnie went away.'

Even given that Ronnie had always been a free-spender, the lesson was plain. Jeff Beck was living the rock star lifestyle, while Ronnie was relying on hand-outs. Nor were the rest of the band much better off, except for Rod Stewart, whose manager had negotiated a separate contract and who, in any event, was due to issue his first solo album.

When they moved into Gloucester Place Ronnie and Krissie looked like a Romany Dr Dolittle and a pagan, blonde high priestess, for they took with them a small menagerie, and Krissie had embraced New Age fashion with a vengeance – especially when it came to beaded headbands and flowing silks.

The band reunited on 14 January 1969 for a single gig at the Marquee, before beginning sessions for the follow-up album to *Truth*, and their third American tour. Chris Welch, in *Melody Maker*, described the gig as 'a little rough' but went on to say that the group was happily different and unpretentious, and once they developed a head of steam, could blow many a group off stage. Following which, Beck, displaying his customary loyalty and tact, stated that the whole band 'are lazy bastards' – except for Beck, naturally – and blamed the rustiness on the Christmas lay-off: 'You'll never find the Jeff Beck Band rehearsing.' It never seemed to have occurred to him that if true, this was as much a comment on his leadership and Peter Grant's management, as on musicians who should have been grateful for the mere opportunity to play with such a maestro.

Early in February, a day or so after a relatively low-key gig intended to be as much for practice as anything else, at the Tally Ho Pub at Tolworth, the group entered the Kingsway Recording Studios to begin sessions on the album to be called *Beck-Ola*, produced by Mickie Most. But it was too soon for post-modern irony, and the title merely sounded naff – which was as it should be, because the album was destined to be one of those truly awful records that only the most convinced fan can listen to without laughing. A cover version of Presley's 'Jailhouse Rock', for example? Or was that an example of Most-modern irony? Another track was 'All Shook Up' – delusions of grandeur, or total lack of imagination? This, combined with 'Ol' Man River' from the *Truth* album and the perennial 'Hi Ho Silver Lining', could easily have sent Beck to the end-of-the-pier cabaret circuit.

On 11 February, a few days before the band were due to fly to America, Krissie's twenty-first birthday party was in full swing when the phone rang. Not the neighbours complaining about the noise, but Peter Grant wanting to speak to Ronnie. 'We won't be needing you for the American tour,' Grant informed Ronnie casually. 'You and Mickey Waller have been sacked.'

As Beck later explained to the music press, he'd noticed that Ronnie and Mickey's playing had deteriorated over the last couple of gigs. But hadn't he called *all* the band 'lazy bastards'?

Krissie remembers that night very clearly. 'Ronnie was standing talking to Rod after the phone call, except he was so shocked he hardly could talk – especially so soon after turning down Jimmy Page's offer to join Led Zeppelin.'

One of the things that Ronnie found hard to understand is why Beck would fire the rhythm section on the same day. 'I still feel now, as I did then, total disbelief. But I just smiled when I got the news, and thought, thanks very much for Krissie's present, Jeff. But firing both Mickey and me on the same day? I remember saying to Mickey, "You're a great drummer. I don't give a fuck if they fire me, but if they've got rid of us both, something's seriously wrong.' Actually, I think it was more Jeff's management, although Rod reckoned it was down to Jeff that I got the sack, and Nicky Hopkins who got rid of Mickey. Thing was, Jeff never liked me and Rod together because he couldn't understand our sense of humour, he always felt left out, and thought we were always taking the piss out of him because of he had these hideous yellow spots. Which we weren't. Well, not all the time anyway. I mean, he always thought we were talking about him behind his back, so they got rid of me. All Grant and Most liked doing was wheeling and dealing and keeping Jeff happy. You can just see them saying, "OK, Jeff, let's get another rhythm section, Jeff, anything you fucking want, Jeff, you're the fucking star." But it didn't work and they had to come crawling back a few weeks later, going, "Oh, Ronnie, ple-e-e-ase, we need you, please can you come back?' Cunts!"

Waller was a little less bothered by Beck or Hopkins or the Oxford Street boys than Ronnie. 'I couldn't have cared less. I'd already played with a lot better musicians and a lot better bands than Beck. I'd only joined so I could tour the States. And I've never missed Beck, he was always too weird. I do remember Ronnie was very upset, but I always thought Krissie was upset a whole lot more. She liked Ronnie playing with that band, she always liked high-profile musicians, she was a bit of a groupie really.'

Ronnie's replacement was Douglas Blake, an unknown bass player from New Zealand whose only claim to fame was that he played with gloves on. Maybe he came from the North Island, and felt the cold. Maybe he was just pretentious. But at least he was an unknown, and therefore, no possible threat to Beck.

Waller was replaced by Tony Newman from Sounds Incorporated. He could play pretty well and wasn't disliked by Nicky Hopkins, who could be an arch-troublemaker at times – especially in the company of someone with an ego like Beck's. But the new line-up obviously needed to rehearse, so Beck's first five US dates were cancelled. This would give the group a full week to practise before picking up the tour in Boston.

Meanwhile a somewhat disillusioned Ronnie managed to pick up a couple of sessions with the new Apple Records signing, the Iveys, who went on to become Bad Finger. He did toy with the idea of joining up with Mickey Waller, who'd wasted no time in forming a new band called the Silver Meteors with guitarist Leigh Stevens, formerly with Blue Cheer.

'Leigh had moved from LA to live in England,' Mickey explains, 'and we'd become good mates when I'd gone to California. So one night I took him and his girlfriend, Liz, over to meet Krissie and Ron. They got on really well, we all spent a lot of time hanging out together, but Ronnie never asked to join, so eventually I got Pete Sears in on bass and a singer called Harry Reynolds.'

Mickey Waller also took Ronnie and Krissie to see Ronnie Lane at a cottage the Small Faces bassist had just rented. 'Ronnie didn't know Lane very well, but in those days everyone sort of knew everyone else, at least well enough to just turn up. Lane was rehearsing with the other Small Faces, but without Steve Marriott, who'd just left.'

Lane for one was totally unaware quite how fateful that meeting would be. 'I didn't really know Ronnie. I'd seen him around Steve's [Marriott] now and then – he always had this big smile on his face, and I always remembered him as the Smiling Head.'

Ronnie knew that Marriott had ignominiously left the Small Faces, stating publicly that he 'wanted to play with real musicians who played real music', which Ronnie thought a little mean. He was also intrigued to learn that Lane, McLagan and Jones were determined to stay together, and moreover were thinking of it as a fresh start – they'd even joked about calling the new group Slim Chance.

'When Steve left,' Lane remembered shortly before Marriott's death, 'I thought the hardest thing in the world would be to assemble a group of guys who would get on well together musically and socially. So why break up a friendship with the others, that had grown really strong after working together for five years? And we decided to stick with each other and hunt around for a guitar player.'

That day, courtesy of Mickey Waller, the three remaining Small Faces found one. Only they didn't know it yet.

As it was, Ronnie returned to London with the comforting knowledge that at least he wasn't the only one starting afresh. Over the next few days he was equally comforted by a series of postcards from Rod Stewart in America, saying how miserable the band was without him and that Beck had already fallen out with Douggie Blake. But the icing on the cake came a few days later, with the news that after only one try-out gig in Virginia, Blake had been sacked. This resulted in yet more shows being cancelled, including Boston. With a contracted tour stretching into April, Beck and Grant were faced with the mother of all lawsuits: they'd have to pay dear for the privilege of losing their own appearance money.

Grant called Ronnie again. 'That was great,' Ronnie recalls. 'I dictated my own terms, I'll never forget it. They were really fucked and the tour was on the line. So I said, "I want two fucking grand a gig." You could hear him swallowing on the other end of the phone.'

Grant had no choice: Ronnie knew the repertoire and, perhaps more importantly, knew how to play with Beck. The fact that he already had his own group of fans – one reason, perhaps, why Beck appeared to resent him – would have to be endured. For however much the two men disliked each other, once they were on stage and playing they could lose themselves in the music – enough, at least, to satisfy the average fan. And it's average fans who buy the most tickets.

Ronnie flew out on the first available flight and joined the tour party for two shows at the Psychedelia Ballroom in Chicago, on 14 and 15 March. He wasn't exactly welcomed with open arms. The management were openly resentful.

'Vibes were decidedly hostile,' Rod Stewart remembers, 'and Ronnie was well pissed off with it – you could tell he was just using the group as a filler while he looked for another band.'

Even so, the tour was a commercial success – and Ronnie managed to meet up with his wandering landlord, Alvin Lee, when the group played alongside Ten Years After and the Moody Blues at the Shrine auditorium in Los Angeles. But then came the infamous San Diego Pop Festival in April, when, playing alongside Brit bands Savoy Brown and the legendary John Mayall's Bluesbreakers, the Jeff Beck Group watched the chaos caused by massive overcrowding, with police helicopters buzzing angrily overhead, and police on horseback trying to corral the crowd.

Beck cancelled the rest of the tour, promising to return in May and so make amends to various angry promoters and disappointed fans. He was later quoted as saying that the cancellation was necessary in order to concentrate on developing material for the new album, *Beck-Ola*. Tour insiders put it down mainly to the escalating ill feeling between Beck and Ronnie – whose £2000 per gig (about £8000 in today's money) came directly out of Beck's own cut – and to Beck's knee-jerk reaction to a typical American riot. That said, the new album did need work – but not by Beck. When *Beck-Ola* was finally released (in June 1969 in America and December in Britain), the five original tracks (of seven) credited Ronnie Wood and Nicky Hopkins four times; Rod Stewart three times; and Jeff Beck and Tony Newman (the drummer) once. In other words, Beck hadn't contributed a great deal in words or music. Arrangements and brilliant guitar work, yes, but always with Mickie Most having the final say. This suggests another reason why Beck and Grant were prepared to pay Ronnie £2000 a gig: they needed his songwriting ability. Incidentally, this would be the first time that Ronnie and Rod Stewart would write songs together, a partnership that would ultimately result in such classics as 'Gasoline Alley', 'Every Picture Tells A Story' and 'Stay With Me'.

Back in London, the band trouped into the Kingsway Recording Studios again. A studio full of serious-minded Swedes shooting a documentary about the genius of Mickie Most gave Ronnie the excuse to duck out of recording and spend time jamming with Lane, McLagan and Jones again. But there was no real discussion about Ronnie joining them. 'We jammed together and we weren't very good,' Ronnie Lane was to later recall. 'Ronnie was all right, not brilliant, but we thought why not? We never expected him to turn out as brilliant as he is now. He'd been mainly playing bass and to be honest we wondered if he was the man for the job. But we thought that none of us was brilliant, so we'd work at it together.'

The album was finally finished at the end of April and released with the revised name *Cosa Nostra Beck-Ola*. The first name was bad enough – actually, a nickname that Peter Grant had given his then star client – but this one, a sad attempt to cash-in on mobster-mania, sounded just a little too desperate. Grant and Most were now trying to package Beck as the charismatic hard man of British pop.

Ronnie played live with Beck on 25 April, when the group headlined at the Lyceum Ballroom in London. On 2 May they returned to the States, still with Ronnie, to make good their promise to play all their cancelled gigs. It was the fourth time the band had gone to the States in less than a year, and Krissie was feeling lonely. Nevertheless, the extra money Ronnie had been earning had certainly helped her feel more secure. They'd made a deal: the first big money Ronnie made would buy a Revox reel-to-reel tape recorder, and the next would go towards a deposit for a house. And he'd made sure she was OK financially before he left.

In the four years they'd been together, Krissie had become used to being Ronnie's Old Lady. She'd become used to being in a partnership, the loyal woman who went out to work to help her lover's career. Suddenly she was no longer quite so equal. It's a problem that faces many rock wives or live-in girlfriends at some time or another: everything is wonderful and romantic when they're both struggling, but when fame and fortune arrives for one of them, everything changes. Krissie had to face up to the fact that Ronnie's accelerating success was now due more to his talent than her support, a transition that has made many another woman insecure.

But Krissie, whose childhood had taught her independence, reacted slightly differently. The closest she could get to Ronnie's whirlwind existence, except on the rare occasions he was home, was to meet their mutual friends at clubs like the Speakeasy – which she could now afford to visit often, since for the first time Ronnie's wage packet matched his profile. There she could always meet someone who'd just seen him on tour, and the gossip would help fill in the gaps between his letters. There, too, she could feel part of a scene in which Ronnie was becoming a major player. She could mix with older stars, like the Beatles and Stones, who now accepted Ronnie – and by association, her too – as one of their own. And to all intents and purposes she was. After all, she had grown up with people like Pete Townshend and other Ealing Art School alumni like Richard Barnes, who'd renamed the High Numbers the Who. She'd known Jeff Beck when he was support band to the Birds. Krissie was flying. Lonely, but still flying high.

One evening towards the end of May, Krissie was at the Speakeasy with her long-time friend Susie Cunningham. They were sitting alone at a table when a familiar figure walked up.

'Hi – do you remember me?' It was a slightly silly question, given the circumstances.

Krissie looked up at Eric Clapton. 'Of course I do.'

Clapton stayed and chatted. Susie went home alone. Krissie went home with her first lover.

'It was a spur of the moment thing,' Krissie was to say many years later. 'But to this day I don't know why I did it. I had no reason to believe that Ronnie had ever been unfaithful to me. Maybe it was just this thing of the first real boyfriend, someone who was there at the right time. Except it was the wrong time, I suppose. But what you have to understand is how different things were in those days. Everyone was just sort of floating around, feeling that freedom was all that mattered.'

Nineteen sixty-seven had been the Summer of Love, and people had swallowed the hippie myth hook, line and sinker. If it felt good, it did you good. Spontaneity was god. As, of course, was Clapton, according to London graffiti. So who could blame the girl?

Such digressions are always best kept to oneself, and Krissie had the sense never to tell Ronnie. But that episode established a pattern that would eventually destroy their relationship.

9
'I would have kept the band together just to play Woodstock'

With all contractual dates covered, the Jeff Beck Group returned home in early May with a clean slate. They'd been supported by Joe Cocker and the Grease Band for four nights at the Fillmore East, and by the Nice for the remainder of the tour. In America, at least, they could do no wrong.

The group played at a home-coming party at the Marquee, which also celebrated the America-only release of a single, 'Plynth (Water Down The Drain)'. And it was here that Mickie Most enlisted their help in boosting the American profile of another of his acts.

Singer-songwriter Donovan had done well on the British circuit. However, Americans tended to see him as an English Dylan and Most was trying to harden up Donovan's image by pushing for a 'rockier' approach. It was a route Donovan was more than happy to follow, having tired of his own whimsical, lightweight pop profile. Eager to reach America's growing Adult Orientated Rock market, he jumped at the chance of joining up with Beck.

'It was totally Mickie's idea,' Donovan charitably remembers. 'And it turned into the most extraordinary session I ever did.'

Donovan duly reported to Advision Studios, where he was surprised to find that Mickey Waller had taken the session-player's shilling, instead of Tony Newman. Actually, any student of the era knows that Waller turned up absolutely everywhere, mainly because he was simply the best drummer for hire. This made Beck and Grant's sacking of him all the more suspicious.

'He was giving the skins a fair old wallop of a drum groove, and it suited the song perfectly,' Donovan recalls. 'I said, "Hey, Mickey, how ya doin'? Ya heard the song, then?" And he replied, "Haven't heard a bloody thing." And I said, "But that's the drum pattern for the song." And Mickey said, "Well, you're all right, then." Nicky Hopkins was the next to show, a thin and waif-like character. He asked me to sing the song while he read a Silver Surfer comic book. There were only two chords, and Nicky got my funky groove down and he liked the jazz, and never said another word after that, the whole session.'

Of course, Donovan had no way of knowing that Hopkins had been instrumental in ousting the easygoing Waller from the Beck band touring line-up. Or about any of the other politics that had so bedevilled the group's existence.

'Woody arrived next with Rod Stewart. It was the first time I'd ever met Ron. Mickie Most had laid on these little snacks and fine wines, but they both looked hung-over from the night before. I thought it was funny how a lot of great guitar players had taken on the bass part in bands over the years – there's always too many pickers to go around. I remember Beck's guitar was locked in the van, so Most rented him one, and Jeff asked for any old Fender. When Jeff cut into a riff for the intro it just left me breathless. Then the whole band just followed on two phrases and the arrangement and it was all there. Madeleine Bell and Lesley Duncan sang back-up vocals and the whole thing came together as easy as that. I wrote most of the song on the spot and the whole thing was done in six hours. The absolute cool of Ron Wood moved the song along – powerful but controlled madness. The final track was christened "Goo-Goo Barabajagal", which summed up the song's on-the-spot spontaneity perfectly. It was a fact that wasn't lost on Beck, either, when he said, "Let's be fair, a song with a title like that isn't something you sit at home playing for six weeks." True – but it was a quirky little masterpiece, dominated by Woody's fluid bass lines and Mickey Waller's voodoo drumming. I recorded another three tracks with Woody, one called "The Stromberg Twins", which was about carburettors, hot-rod cars and two Jewish twin-girl fans that Ronnie knew. Jeff was into hot-rods and I guess the song was about him. The other tracks were "Trudi (Bed With Me)" and "Home-sickness". Ronnie was this Artful Dodger character, always was, always will be. He epitomizes that street-urchin grin of British rock. His playing is superb. He's able to change from rhythm to lead in the classic style that Brian Jones taught to Keith Richards.'

'Goo-Goo Barabajagal' was a unique – and extremely successful – example of Hippie meets Rock. Could it be that Mickie Most really did have a feel for music? Or was he just hoping for a miracle? Perhaps the truth is that he rarely let good taste get in the way of money. But when he wanted to, Most could be an inspired producer.

One of the era's great unanswered questions is why Beck and Donovan never recorded a follow-up, as this one record was to prove, for both them, their last flirtation with the singles chart. The other slight mystery is that, according to the record's label copy, Tony Newman played drums. So either Donovan was totally mistaken or Waller's playing was later wiped.

But the experience had whetted Donovan's appetite for playing with rock groups. He duly looked around and decided on the Small Faces, whose lead singer and co-founder, Steve Marriott, had just walked out. Would they like to become his backing band?

The point about Donovan is that he really was and is a genuinely nice man. Far too nice to have ever become involved with three strutting little Mods from the East End. Luckily, they must have felt the same way. Or as Ronnie Lane so succinctly put it: 'Why don't you fuck off?'

Apollo 10 splashed safely down in the Pacific on 26 May, the same month that the Fab Four had fittingly released 'Get Back (To Where You Belong)' – a title that also summed up Ronnie Wood's mood. He knew it was only a matter of time before he was fired again, and he wanted to play lead guitar. What isn't always realized is that behind that street-urchin grin, Ronnie can be single-minded to the point of ruthlessness when it comes to the furtherence of his own career – especially when he could combine an interesting career move with helping out his older brother, Art.

Life had not been good to Art recently. Basically, he was bored. It hadn't been quite as easy to settle down as he'd hoped, and the music was still calling to him.

'The Artwoods had long since broken up. But for some unfathomable reason Fontana had still kept an option on me which I thought I'd exercise. They gave me free rein of a studio and said, "Come up with some new stuff." But I didn't have a band any more. so I asked little Ron if he'd help out. And he said he knew that Ronnie Lane and the other Little Faces weren't doing anything, and that he'd ring them up and ask if they'd help, too. And they did, bless them. I remember Ronnie Lane turning up on his bicycle and hanging his clips on the studio hatstand. Rod came along with Ronnie and we made up these songs on the spot: "Engine 4444" and "Diamond Joe". More songs about trains, because everyone sung about trains, that's what you did then. Rod and me did this call-and-response vocal and Ronnie made up the tune. It was very close to how the Faces ended up sounding – obviously because it was the same players, but they didn't know it was going to be the Faces at the time, if you know what I mean. All it did for me was show how much a better singer Rod was than me, which was not a good idea when you're doing your own demos. It was like: "That's very nice, Art – but who's the other bloke singing? He's good, you're crap." We recorded another two songs, "Right Around The Thumb" and "Two Steps To Mother" and I called the group Art Wood's Quiet Melon. I took the demos to Fontana and they hated all of us, saying they were uncommercial and unreleasable, and you can't have any more studio time. I said, "Well, I've done my bit, it's not my fault you hate them." '

One of the main drives behind Quiet Melon was the fact that both Ronnie and Rod Stewart were fed up with the Jeff Beck situation. Quiet Melon provided some much-needed light relief as well as helping Ronnie cement his relationship with the three remaining Small Faces. Whether or not Lane, McLagan and Jones knew it yet, Ronnie was intent on pulling them all together in a new group.

There was no record deal in the offing, but Quiet Melon had all got on well together and decided to look for some live gigs. Easier said than done – throughout London they could only find one agent who was remotely interested in them. But at least Rufus Manning managed to find them work at the Oxford and Cambridge May Balls. At the latter they were supposed to support P.P. Arnold, with Kim Gardner replacing an absent Ronnie Lane.

'We were on two hundred quid for the night,' Art reminisces, 'which was good money. We played for three-quarters of an hour, doing mainly standards plus a few of our own songs, a lot of blues numbers, and then came off stage, ready for a beer and to go home. Which actually meant everyone having more than a few drinks and throwing these strawberry pies at each other. Then the promoter came up and said that P.P. Arnold wasn't going to play, and would we mind going back on for another £250? We were back up there the moment he said it. Afterwards, Kenney came up to me and said, "Thanks, Art, that's the first time me fruit bowl's going to be full in weeks!" '

That initial camaraderie survived into the Faces, becoming one of their biggest on-stage assets. But the Quiet Melon experiment soon petered out. It lasted long enough for the official announcement of the group's formation in *New Musical Express*, plus a flurry of press ads, not to mention the business cards. At which point Art decided: 'Sod this for a living' and packed it in, going to join his younger brother Ted in his graphic design business, which Ted ran in conjunction with his jazz career – including a long stint as singer/drummer with the Temperance Seven. Today Art can still be coaxed out to play the occasional set – just try stopping him – with a revamped Quiet Melon Two, which also features ex-Kinks drummer Mick Avory. Ted now plays full-time with Bob Kerr's Whoopee Band.

*

Of the two singles that the Jeff Beck Group released that year, the first was their own 'Plynth (Water Down The Drain)', written by Hopkins, Stewart and Wood, backed by the inexplicable cover version of 'Jailhouse Rock'. It didn't even get a UK release date and flopped in America – prompting Nicky Hopkins to throw an artistic tantrum and relocate to California, where he would carve out a respectable career as a session musician before joining Quicksilver Messenger Service.

On the other hand, 'Goo-Goo Barabajagal' made it to number twelve in the UK and thirty-six in America. Which was good, if only because 'Hi Ho Silver Lining' only made it to number fourteen in the British charts. None of which worried Ronnie one jot, as he was spending a good deal of time rehearsing with Lane, McLagan and Jones and had effectively dismissed the Jeff Beck Group from his future plans – once they'd finished the next US tour. At £2000 an American gig, the Group still did have its uses.

Beck managed to pull together the remaining member of his Group – without Hopkins, and so once again a quartet – together for one last, weary American tour. They left on 2 July, a week after Judy Garland had died in London after a night out with Brian Jones, when both were seen leaving Blaises night club so drunk and stoned that they had to hold each other up.

At the first gig in Central Park, Beck played the 'Star Spangled Banner' some six weeks before Jimi Hendrix was to immortalize his version at Woodstock. Then there was the obligatory appearance at Fillmore East, and it was while Beck was in New York that the group finally began to break up. Tony Newman was becoming increasingly annoyed about his salary – he'd have been even more upset if he'd known how much Ronnie was making – and was beginning to talk insurrection.

But the real killer came with a phone call from former Yardbirds roadie Bruce Wayne, now working with Vanilla Fudge. The American band's guitarist, Vinnie Martell, was ill, and they were due to record an advertising jingle. Would Jeff Beck like to step in? He would and did, and the subsequent version of 'Things Go Better With Coke' was played on all US radio stations throughout the rest of the year. But the most significant fact was that Jeff Beck once again met up with Vanilla Fudge's rhythm section, Tim Bogert and Carmine Appice. Once again the three men began talking about forming a new group together. The first time Beck met Bogert and Appice had been at the London Astoria on 4 October 1968. His enthusiasm for Vanilla Fudge's rhythm section then had then led to Ronnie quitting – 'So I just thought, fuck it, I'm not hanging around to get sacked' – and now history was repeating itself.

However, things were never that simple with Beck, as Rod Stewart remembered: 'It was all being done under our noses, which was bad. The original idea was that Jeff and I were going to join the Vanilla Fudge, at least with drummer Carmine Appice and bass player Tim Bogert. We were having these meetings throughout the tour, and it made the atmosphere unbearable. But the idea folded. Christ, it could have been an immaculate group, a world-class group – but there were differences. They wanted to work seven nights a week, and Jeff didn't want to know. He said, "We've got to rehearse in England, I'm not coming over here." And they said, "We're here and we're not coming over there" and all that. And all this was happening in front of Ronnie. I knew he wasn't going to hang about for all this.'

On the other hand, Beck must have known about the rumours that Ronnie was joining the Small Faces. Given the money he was paying his bass guitarist, it might well have seemed a little ungrateful – especially as Ronnie never complained about it. But then Beck never asked. Perhaps the deeper truth was that, in his mind, the Group had always been temporary. Their main function was to highlight Beck's own undoubted talent.

While Beck was off fudging, the rest of the group flew back to the UK for a week, for management hate putting musicians up in hotels unless unavoidable. Ronnie arrived home to find that Fleet Street was still feeding frenziedly on the rotting corpse of Brian Jones' reputation. Jones had been found dead in his swimming pool in July, having been sacked from the Stones the previous month. Everyone, from chauffeur to school friend, was crawling out of the woodwork, offering exclusive stories about his debauched life. Ronnie was intrigued that one man could still so dominate the headlines, little realizing that his own time to be dissected by the media was not that far distant. But he also felt a great sadness for Jones, and not just because the Stones were his favourite band.

'It's all fantasy situations, all hindsight,' Ronnie says, 'but I always used to think that if only I'd known Brian then maybe I could have helped him. Mind you, I used to think the same thing about Elvis too – that all I'd have had to do was get him away from all those bodyguards and doctors, that all he really needed was a mate! But I suppose that's what you do with heroes, isn't it? Of course, on today's scene I don't think there's anyone worth saving! Except mates left over from the old days, musicians who've paid their fucking dues.'

Ronnie arrived home in time to be approached by the Rolling Stones, who were looking for a replacement for Jones. In fact, it was the second time they had tried to contact him. Before he had gone to the USA, Mick Jagger and Keith Richards had drawn up a short list of possible replacements which, thanks to the rumours of a split with Beck, included Ronnie Wood. 'I was round at my mum's one afternoon and there was this phone call, apparently from Mick, asking what I was doing. I thought it was a wind-up, an impostor, so I said I was busy. And the impostor just said, "Oh well then, we'll see you around." I mean, I had no idea Mick ran the Stones, anyway. But it was him, of course, fuck it!'

Now, this second time, they had tried to reach him while he was rehearsing with the three remaining Small Faces. Once again, he never found out about it until a long time later.

'We were down at the Stones' practice studio in Bermondsey Street,' Ronnie winces, 'when the call came. I would have said: "Is sixty seconds too late to show up?" But apparently they got Ronnie Lane on the phone, who was fully aware of that fact, so he answered: 'No thanks, he's quite happy where he is!' I never found out about it until years later when Brian's replacement, Mick Taylor, was about to leave! The funny thing is that I coincidentally bumped into Jagger and Charlie on the way to the memorial gig for Brian, before I rejoined Beck in the States. I was walking around the edge of Hyde Park and they were coming out of their hotel. I shouted out, "Have a good gig", totally ignorant of the fact that it could've been me up there with them.'

Ronnie was going to join the Small Faces whether he wanted to or not. Yet even though Lane was an extremely determined and very shrewd character, he'd have been unlikely to have said no on Ronnie's behalf unless Ronnie had, for once, made some sort commitment; or at least Lane and the other two thought he had.

The Almost-Stone and the rest of the band returned to America to perform with Beck at the Baltimore Jazz Festival with Led Zeppelin, which must have hurt Beck's feelings, and at the Flushing Meadow Singer Bowl, where the headliners would be Vanilla Fudge. The tour was planned to end with Woodstock. No one knew very much about Woodstock, but the suspicion was it was going to be huge. The main reason for these gigs was to promote *Cosa Nostra Beck-Ola*, which actually reached a very respectable number fifteen in the US charts.

Things came to a head when the band reached the West Coast. Posters and advance publicity already listed the Jeff Beck Group as appearing at Woodstock, along with Crosby, Still & Nash, Ten Years After, Keef Hartley, and headliner Jimi Hendrix.

'It was a few days before Woodstock and we were all sitting round the hotel pool,' Ronnie explains. 'We had Woodstock on the cards and

Tony Newman started the uprising. Jeff didn't really have a lot to do with it, it was Tony against the management, he was calling them all cunts. He was like the union, getting us all together and saying, "We're not getting treated fair, we should get together and fuck that lot off . . . tell them that we're not going to work unless they give us more money, the cunts." Well, they weren't going to give us any more money. I was already on two grand a gig, I didn't know how much Rod was on – that was all part of the trouble, we were just looking after ourselves – so Tony led the uprising, he was like a slave-driver, saying, "Let's make a stand." No one realized how big Woodstock would be, but he was holding it to ransom, saying, "I'm not fucking doing it – how about you Rod, how about you, Ron?" I was really looking forward to it, knew a lot of the bands that were going to be playing and we were going to be amongst them. And I had the feeling it was going to be a big event. Tony had already said none of us were doing it unless we got more money – and so nothing happened. I would have loved to have kept the band together to play it, but with all the bad vibes – and they were so bad by then – the band couldn't have lasted a couple of more hours, let alone days. So we came home.'

The attitude of Beck and manager Peter Grant appears to make no sense at all. Until you remember that Beck was heavily courting Vanilla Fudge's rhythm section, and Grant could see far greater potential with Led Zeppelin.

'It was weird, we never actually broke up,' says Rod Stewart today. 'We came back from the American tour. I knew Woody had as good as left, but I didn't know what I was going to do and I never knew what Jeff was going to do because we never spoke to each other. He'd never asked if I was going to leave, or go with Woody. I never asked him what he was going to do and we just drifted apart. Next thing I heard was that Vanilla Fudge had come to England.'

But in 1970 Stewart had a slightly different slant on things. 'Woody and me had all the ideas behind the two albums. We wrote most of the songs, Hopkins as well and Tony Newman. Beck just used to come in and put the guitar track on afterwards. He used to call it playing "evergreens", meaning it was the same pattern every time. I'm sure it's why he hasn't got anything together now, because he hasn't got anyone to turn to. Beck's the sort of person who can't take anything on his own shoulders. I owe to him exactly what he owed to the Yardbirds. I think he's a great guitarist, better than Jimmy Page or Eric Clapton. You know, he was huge in America, really immense. We'd play on bills with the Moody Blues and Ten Years After and the whole audience would only want Beck. But they wouldn't recognize that success in Britain. I think that's why he's so bitter. I suppose having a huge chip on his shoulder didn't endear him to anyone, but not only did he never get recognition in his own country, but even when he was this incredible force abroad nobody even mentioned it.'

It's possible that Stewart worried too much about Ronnie's feelings of insecurity. After all, ever since he was a child Ronnie had believed that everything would always turn out right for him. Nor was he particularly wedded to the idea of the Jeff Beck Group becoming his musical home. As producer Shel Talmy said in May 1998: 'I don't think Ronnie ever really thought about any band as a long-term affair, not even the Stones, because even there he wasn't a full member for years. I remember he lived very much for the moment – that's how he manages to give his all in every situation, because it's for the now, not yesterday, not tomorrow, but now. And of course in those days [of the Jeff Beck Group] he would have been really happy to be back playing lead guitar, with Kim Gardner on bass, with the Creation.'

Beck eventually did get together with Bogert and Appice, but not until years later and not before he'd tried their patience to breaking point with his endless deliberations – forcing them to form their own new group, Cactus. In fact, Beck carried on going about his business in the usual haphazard way for months after his return from America. He tried out several ill-conceived rehearsal groups with the very same disregard and lack of foresight he'd shown when trying to form the very first incarnation of the Jeff Beck Group. Line-ups included Ace Kefford, brought in as a lead singer, when he was only known as a not very good ex-bass player with the Move. Beck continued to agree to gigs, only to cancel them at the last minute. He even travelled to Detroit to record an album, bizarrely conceived by Mickie Most, of Motown covers with drummer Cozy Powell, who was hardly noted for his subtlety.

'You want the Motown sound?' asked bass player James Jamieson, when he saw Beck's roadies replacing Kenny Benjamin's modest drum kit with Coy Power's gigantic set-up. 'Too bad, man. You just took it out.'

Ultimately, the album was considered so wretched by all parties concerned that it was deemed unfit for public consumption. But at least Mickie Most got something out of it – the singer Suzi Quatro, whom he discovered singing in a Detroit bar.

By the autumn of 1970 Beck was seriously considering a Yardbirds reunion, only to be told by their former singer, Keith Relf, that he wasn't in the slightest bit interested.

All this confusion had left the way clear for Led Zeppelin and Jimmy

Page to clean up in America. That last tour was the end of Beck's career as a concert headliner. One of Britain's most original musical talents appeared to have been consumed by mismanagement and his own ego. Or as Elton John (then comparatively unknown) said after also trying out with Beck in the summer of 1970: 'We had rehearsals that went just fine . . . but I would have ended up as Jeff Beck's pianist.'

Beck returned to England set on promoting the September UK release of *Cosa Nostra Beck-Ola* with a series of interviews which, as usual, he used for teasers to outline his future plans. He also let it be known that Ronnie Wood no longer featured in the scheme of things, but was hoping to keep Rod, and announced that two big names had been chosen as replacements for Ronnie and Tony Newman: 'It'll be big news when it comes together, but both replacements are under contract at the moment, so they've got to be careful. Ronnie says he's leaving because he wants to play lead instead of bass, and I wish him the best of luck. There's no bad vibes or anything, like there is with most groups.'

Assuming that the two big names were Bogert and Appice, about the only thing Beck got right was Ronnie wanting to play lead guitar. But then Ronnie had been leaving for some time, and the Small Faces were waiting. As he said recently: 'With Beck, even the roadies were telling us what to do.'

Actually, a little more than that, as Waller – 'I was a mouthy little so-and-so in those days' – remembers. 'There was one time when I mouthed back at one of them, Pete Saunders his name was, and he punched me so severely that I was in hospital with a ruptured spleen. Rod and Ronnie came to visit me, which was thoughtful. But all the same, what sort of band is it when the roadies can go around beating up the bloody musicians?'

10
'We needed a referee'

Throughout September 1969 Ronnie continued to rehearse every day with the Small Faces in their Bermondsey bunker, thrashing out a handful of hastily compiled new songs and various old soul covers. But the band lacked what Ronnie describes as 'a proper vocalist'. Songs would trail off into an improvised jam session, until the rehearsals became almost strictly instrumental run-throughs.

'We were all too scared to sing,' Ronnie remembers. 'Marriott had one of the best soul voices ever and he was a hard act to follow. All groups need an identity, and that identity usually stems from the lead singer. I'm not a lead singer, and a group needs a sound that is instantly recognizable. Mick Jagger isn't a great singer, but you know from his voice you're listening to a Stones record. Dylan isn't a great singer, but you know who you're listening to. I eventually called Rod [Stewart] and said, "Come down and see who I'm playing with now!"'

As Rod Stewart recalls it, Ronnie was always hinting that he should come and have a go. 'Oh the lads are pretty good,' Ronnie would say, 'but there's no one to sing' – which was invariably greeted by Rod with 'Oh, yeah, shame, innit?' For Rod had already started work on his first album, *An Old Raincoat Won't Let You Down*, with American producer Lou Reizener, who'd signed him for a mere £1500 – which just happened to be the exact price of a little yellow sports car Stewart had been after for months.

'He would have signed for however much the car was,' Kenney Jones later commented. 'That's how his mind worked then. If the car had been six hundred quid, that's what he would have asked for.'

Eventually, Rod agreed to visit Ronnie and his three new chums at the practice studio. He arrived giving the impression that he was just passing by, maybe even waiting for the pubs to open, but certainly not interested in rehearsing with a band he already partly knew from their Quiet Melon days together: Ronnie Lane could never be bothered to play live with

Quiet Melon, which was why Kim Gardner had been roped in. Of course, and as for the Small Faces themselves, Stewart might also have been a little wary of involvement with the three remaining parts of a spent force. And he must have remembered how the Small Faces had sabotaged the Jeff Beck Group's début gig on 3 March at the Finsbury Park Astoria.

A few 'hellos' were exchanged, after which Rod promptly departed for a half-hidden vantage point at the top of the stairs. From the safety of his hidey-hole, he could hear that the group lacked direction. It also lacked a forceful lead singer. He listened for a few numbers and left, but returned the following day and repeated the same process – brief 'hellos' followed by his disappearing act. This continued every day for well over a week, as Rod found that he liked the group's easygoing approach, and enjoyed their seemingly united spirit and humour. Their music appealed to him too, and it wasn't long before he was incessantly humming certain tunes that had wafted their way up the stairs and lodged permanently in his subconscious. 'I don't know if I could ever lead a band,' Rod was quoted in *Record Mirror* at the time. 'But I need the security of a band before I could get back in front of an audience.'

But Rod didn't want to appear obtrusive. 'I was too embarrassed to ask Woody if I could join.' He wasn't sure if the group would even want him as their lead singer, while Ronnie, who'd got Rod there in the first place, was being as vague as possible on the subject. It was left to Kenney Jones to stick his neck out, as he did at the Spaniards pub in Highgate.

'We'd tried out everyone as lead singer – Woody first and then Ronnie Lane,' Kenney explained, 'but it still wasn't right. Although their singing was nice, it wasn't strong enough for a front man. But we carried on every day and it got more and more painful, until I couldn't stand it any longer. Rod used to go to this pub near where he lived after he'd been to our rehearsals, so I asked if I could meet him there and went along without the others knowing. Then I asked him outright to join the band. I knew that he wanted to, but he wasn't sure the others were into it, except for Woody, who'd invited him in the first place. He said, "Do you think the others will let me?" So I said "Yeah, I didn't see why not," and I went back and told them. They hit the fuckin' roof! Ronnie Lane didn't want another lead singer. He was saying, "Oh fuck, no! We don't want another prima donna." '

From Ronnie Lane's point of view he was right to be worried. After all, he'd been one half of one of English pop's most successful songwriting teams, along with Steve. Maybe Ronnie Lane saw himself as the leader after Steve left. But he wasn't the only one worried, because Mac was saying: 'Yeah, we don't want another fucking Steve Marriott!' As Kenney recalls, 'We all went round to where Woody was living at Alvin Lee's house and sat up all night talking about it until they gave in and I got my own way.'

But without Ronnie, who'd left them to it, claiming he was tired and wanted to go to bed. Krissie vividly remembers his dismay, particularly at Lane's reaction. 'He couldn't understand why they thought Rod could be a problem. Jeff [Beck] was an ego, not Rod. He was saying, "Fuck! Rod's brilliant, he's not the sort to get carried away. When we were with Jeff, he used to stand behind the fucking amps to sing. That's how much of an ego Rod has!" All Ronnie knew was that he worked best when Rod was around. He used to say they were true soul mates, that they shared this special chemistry. That Rod had this cross-over swagger that appealed to both men and women. For me, the charisma really shone when they got together both on and off stage. Theirs was a truly great partnership.'

Maybe that partnership reminded Lane what he'd lost when Marriott walked out. Maybe he felt threatened by it. He'd achieved far greater success than either Ronnie or Rod Stewart put together, and for far longer, but thanks to Arden, Oldham and even the Small Faces themselves, had nothing to show for it. He was riding a bicycle, and Rod Stewart had the sports car. Even Ronnie had successfully passed his driving test, and was whisking Krissie around town in a (second-hand) Mercedes. Despite his diminutive stature, Ronnie Lane was a formidable character. He could cut anyone down to size with his savage wit alone. He and Rod Stewart were never at ease with each other, there was a natural standoffishness between the two men that at times would make the atmosphere every bit as unbearable as the Jeff Beck Group had been.

'The Faces were seen as poor man's Who,' Rod recalls. 'Somewhere between a teeny-bopper band and a progressive outfit. They were always one of England's finest bands, though. I've always dug the album *Ogden's* [*Ogden's Nut Gone Flake*], that was a masterpiece, but it was ahead of its time and *Tommy* got in there later, where *Ogden's* should have scored. There was always a link between the Small Faces and the Who, but actually there was a closer one with Free. The Small Faces played that tight sort of sound, but Free did it a lot better.'

Nonetheless, once Ronnie Lane had resigned himself to the inevitable, he began to see that the combination of Rod Stewart and Ronnie Wood did offer certain possibilities. 'I could tell the sound would make a nice band. We all played together easily, because we all listened to the same records: Booker T, Gladys Knight, mostly Black American stuff. Our taste was stuck back in 1964 – a good year, that. On the other hand, 1969 was a fucking gloomy year!'

Later Ian McLagan remembered the birth of the new band a little differently. 'With Ronnie we were a group again. Then along came Rod, which was even better. The Small Faces had gone stale, mainly because Steve was in total control. He never used to ask me to do anything, always used to tell me exactly how to play. But when Ronnie and Rod arrived, we began really supporting and encouraging each other. That would never have happened with Steve.'

McLagan's enthusiasm for Stewart was not to last – but for the time being, Rod was OK. Well, apart from one tiny nagging doubt that Jones, Mac and Lane harboured about their singer: was Rod Stewart gay?

'There would have been no problem,' Mac's former wife, Sandy Sargent, says positively today. 'But it was just like a question mark hanging in the air. They were all getting to know each other. Rod's great mate was Long John Baldry, and he was gay, and he was always saying things to Rod in front of the others like, "That was a lumpy bed we slept in last night, wasn't it, Rod?" They were both camping it up, and the others' little faces would be a picture, thinking, is he or isn't he? Except for Woody, who'd been on tour with Rod. They all found out in the end that Rod just liked something with blonde hair and long legs, and it didn't matter whether the collar and cuffs matched or not, as long as it was female, definitely female.'

Ronnie and his old pal had signed on with a group who were financially destitute, contractually beleaguered and facing a future that was nothing short of dubious. Moreover, Ronnie was the only group member without a contract. The three original members were still locked into a worthless deal with Immediate Records, and Stewart was now contracted to Mercury. Jones, McLagan and Lane were all bankrupt, Rod was living with his parents, while Ronnie was eking out what little money he hadn't blown since leaving Beck. But mostly he was relying on Krissie's wages.

Record companies still believed that the Faces were no more than the remnants of what had once been two very successful groups. The real stars had been Marriott and Beck, and they were the ones the industry wanted. The group obviously needed a manager to get them back on track, and Kenney Jones was appointed to find one. He approached the composer and arranger Jimmy Horowitz, whom he'd met early on in his Small Faces career, and explained the dilemma.

Now, it is generally believed that any good manager needs two basic skills. ('Good' here implies making the band rich, happy and content, as opposed to ripping them off, which is often the hallmark of a successful manager.) The first requirement is a brilliant business mind, and the second the patience of a saint. But the Small Faces also needed someone blessed with enough imagination and foresight to counter the industry's negativity and indifference. Also, someone strong enough to take on five very disillusioned and by nature, very uncooperative and volatile individuals. Or as Kenney pointed out: 'We needed a fuckin' referee.'

Horowitz knew just the man: Billy Gaff.

Twenty-two-year-old Gaff had studied economics at Woolwich Polytechnic, and gone to work as an agent for RSO (Robert Stigwood Organisation). His first assignment had been Cream. 'I told Robert I wouldn't know where to start,' he recalls, 'and he replied, "Have you ever looked after children?" So I said yes, my sister's got three. Stigwood said, "Good, just think of it like that and you'll be fine!" And I did. And it was.'

Horowitz arranged a meeting between Kenney and Gaff at the Speakeasy in London.

'Gaff had this little leather hat on,' Kenney recalls. 'I told him we basically couldn't get out of our deal with Immediate and we couldn't work as the Small Faces because of it. He listened attentively to all this and says that he thinks he can sort everything out. But our old solicitor had frozen everything up for the last two years, so I didn't hold out much hope.'

Under the heading 'Hang Ups Over Contracts', Gaff's intervention managed to get a mention in the 31 May edition of *Disc & Music Echo*, where he let it be known he was looking for a way to release the Small Faces from their Immediate deal. But he made no mention of Ronnie or Rod Stewart.

Gaff arranged a meeting with the group's solicitor for the following day, and immediately secured the release of Messrs Jones, McLagan and Lane from all previous contractual arrangements, much to the surprise of Milton Mark, the Small Faces' accountant, who recalls: 'I'd once gone to Immediate myself to try and get money for the Small Faces. I went to see Andrew Oldham and Tony Calder at the office they had in Gloucester Avenue. It was a listed Georgian building, a beautiful place, but they had these builders in smashing the walls down and building these huge alcoves. I said to Andrew, "That's a bit unusual. Are you sure you're allowed to do this?" and he replied, "Yes, that's where we are putting the thrones!" They were putting these huge great thrones on blocks set back in the alcoves for him and Tony Calder to sit on. I never got any money; it was too chaotic to deal with.'

Gaff phoned Kenny with the news, plus an offer to find a new recording contract, plus another offer of £500 to tide over the more impoverished members of the group.

'That's when we asked Billy to manage us,' says Kenney, 'and he said that he'd always had that in the back of his mind anyway!'

The Small Faces' next step was to play live. But with no gigs booked, and with no agent to arrange any, they quickly discovered that club owners were as unwilling to give the group a chance as the labels were to sign them.

Meanwhile Gaff was receiving more or less the same response from the record companies. Polydor had practically thrown him out of their Oxford Street offices, after informing him the band was nothing without Marriott. Track and Apple Records had simply asked if he was joking.

The problem was eventually solved by Gaff, when, on Saturday 1 November 1969, he managed to talk Warner Brothers into giving the Small Faces a £30,000 advance and a five-album deal. It was a victory snatched from the jaws of defeat, as the British arm of the label, headed by Ian Ralfini, hadn't wanted to sign the group. But the visiting American chief, Joe Smith, was eager to sign new British talent for the US Warner Reprise label. Smith immediately saw the hit-making potential of Ronnie and Rod, for both were well known to American fans courtesy of their time with Jeff Beck. The group breathed a collective sigh of relief and, as Kenny remembers, took great delight in letting the disbelievers know that a new group really had risen from the ashes.

'We still had this horrible accountant, another relic from the early days and he'd said, "Oh, you've started a new band then. How are you gonna pay for it?" I told him we'll get an advance, go on the road and make records. He said, "Oh yeah, on what kind of money?" really sarcastically. So I came out with the first figure I thought of, which was £30,000! And he went, "Ha! Telephone numbers!" So when Billy asked me how much we thought we needed, I said it again. He wasn't sure he could get it but he did. It was great telling that guy afterwards. Then we fired him.'

Although the Faces weren't exactly well off, Krissie was determined that Ronnie would make good on his promise. He had the Revox; now she wanted a secure home. Ronnie would probably have rather had a recording studio, or at least a new guitar, for in his heart he already had a secure home: 8 Whitethorn Avenue, Yiewsley, where the boxroom was always ready. Nonetheless, he turned to Perry Press's Little Pink Pig estate agency for help. Press arranged for them to rent the Old Forge in Henley-on-Thames while he applied a little creative accountancy to the Wood finances. This eventually helped Ronnie secure a mortgage on a spacious flat at the aptly named Ravenswood Court on Kingston Hill,

Surrey – not far from where he now lives when back in the UK. Not quite the stockbroker belt, which had been discovered by the Beatles a few years previously, but still a marked improvement on Shepherd's Bush – and, of course, Ronnie knew all the best pubs in the area. Old family friend Jim Willis, who'd first taught the infant Ron how to play the guitar, moved in with his wife Irene to help pay the mortgage.

'Actually, I've no idea how Ronnie and Perry worked it,' Krissie admits. 'Ronnie never used to involve me in money matters. He just came home one day and said he'd managed to sort out a mortgage, which was unheard of at the time for a musician unless they were the Beatles or someone. He came home with a second-hand Bentley as well. That was such a lovely car.'

As for a new agent, the group finally found one in the familiar shape of Robert Stigwood, possibly because he owed Ronnie a favour after standing by as the Birds had plummeted to earth. Gaff still worked for him, while Rod Stewart was tipped as a hot property. In fact, rather than a favour, this was a sensible business decision for Stigwood.

The first engagements that the new Small Faces undertook occurred later in November, when they played a week of low-key dates in Effretikon, near Zurich, Switzerland. Then, in December, they entered the Olympic Studios in Barnes, London, to begin recording their first album as the Faces. The shortened name 'was simply a way to separate the old configuration from the new,' was Ronnie's reasoning, 'plus Rod and me were a few inches taller than the others!'

Warner Brothers, however, wanted the group to capitalize on their only US success, 1967's 'Itchycoo Park', and retain the name the Small Faces. 'We told them to fuck off!' Mac explained. 'There was no way we were going to cover anything we'd done with Steve. I was heartbroken when he left, and there was still a lot of bad feeling around towards him, especially from Lane.'

Another comment from that time has Ronnie strangely talking as if he'd been in the original Small Faces: 'Now we're the Faces, I don't think we're heavy. That's a label, rather like being labelled a teeny-bopper. There's a lot of influences from the old Small Faces in the group, of course, but labels don't mean a thing. Now we're the Faces, everyone goes on calling us the New Faces. We're called the Faces, not New Faces, that's a label, too.'

Again, in 1972 he was to say: 'Steve Marriott had left us to get Humble Pie together, and we had to think seriously about what we were going to do. We had essentially, up until that time, been a group which was in the public eye all the time. Once people have decided what it is they want you to be, when you're in the charts then you're expected to keep fulfilling that image – which at times can be extremely demanding.'

If nothing else, this shows how at home Ronnie was to become with the Faces. It was as if he'd always been there. The Birds had never existed, any more than had the Creation. It was as if his entire musical past had been wiped out – except for the Jeff Beck Group, which he always mentioned.

A compromise was finally reached which saw the group agreeing to be the Small Faces in America, but the Faces in the UK. All the old band's repertoire would be replaced by new group compositions.

So it was that when the Faces entered Olympic Studios to begin recording, they weren't even sure if they still had an audience. First they assembled a grab-bag of a dozen half-finished ideas and completed compositions. Next Ronnie played the demo tapes to Glyn Johns, with whom he'd worked in his Creation days, hoping to persuade him to produce the album. Johns agreed, asking for a two per cent royalty per album. Given that Johns was one of the best producers in the country, and the band was yet to play live at any serious venue, two per cent was a good deal. Naturally, the band didn't agree, which resulted in a press statement saying: 'The Faces don't need a producer, they are a dying breed.' Many people wondered why the band would refer to themselves in such an unflattering way.

This meant the production seat and control room were deserted, save for lone engineer Martin Birch, and the group were without an encouraging or critical ear to guide them. The eventual production credit went to the Faces themselves. In truth, they had desperately needed a producer, if only to make them sound fresh and exciting.

Ronnie and the brilliant, lyrically astute Lane commandeered the lion's share of the songwriting credits, either penning or arranging seven of the ten finished tracks. Stewart lent a hand with three, leaving Mac to appear twice and Jones just once. It was a decent enough mix that combined the group's five individual styles and influences, from Lane's whimsical folky ode to reincarnation, 'Stone' and the soulful mournful ballads 'Devotion' and 'Nobody Knows,' to Mac and Stewart's solid working-class-rock-based 'Three Button Hand Me Down', a stellar tale of barstool advice concerning sartorial standards and cultural baggage. The public, however, thought it was about Grandad's old suit. The first inkling of any future songwriting partnership between Ronnie and Rod came with a reworking of the Beck period standard 'Plynth (Water Down The Drain)'. Originally credited to Beck-Stewart-Wood, it re-emerged as 'Around The Plynth' with Beck's arrangement omitted, along with his name, and the credit firmly assigned to Stewart and Wood alone. They'd got over being mad, and now they were getting even.

The album, released in March 1970, kicked off with Dylan's 'Wicked Messenger', it also had two instrumentals: Ronnie's salute to Booker T, 'The Pineapple & The Monkey', and 'Looking Out The Window,' essentially a rhythm work-out featuring Kenny and Mac. All very diverse, and neatly summed up by the album's title, *First Step*.

The cover shot showed the band sitting timidly in a row, with only Ron and Rod looking uneasily at the camera. Kenny, Mac and Ian are engrossed by three different Mickey Mouse caricatures. Ronnie is holding a guitar manual as a comment on the public perception that he was really only a bass guitarist. The overall idea was to pre-empt any critical bitchiness by admitting they were indeed just starting out. They could only hope that they hadn't actually shot themselves in the foot.

Rod Stewart's solo album, *An Old Raincoat Won't Let You Down*, had been out a month in America, under the title *The Rod Stewart Album*, and although it was selling a reasonable amount, there were still no plans for a UK release. At first, Rod didn't seem bothered about the situation, preferring instead to get behind the Faces and promote *First Step* and a single taken from the album: 'Flying', backed by 'Three Button Hand Me Down'. The group made their BBC TV début performing the song on *Top Of The Pops*, which was by now attracting a staggering 17 million viewers. Unfortunately, none of them appeared to like the song. Ronnie Lane tried to rationalize its poor showing in the charts when he said: 'We didn't really want to put out a single but our record company said that if we were good boys, there'd be some money in the bin for us. "Flying" is more a trailer for the album than anything else. We didn't really care if it was a hit, but it would have been nice if it was.'

It would have been nice if the album had been a hit, let alone the single, but it was not to be. Seventeen million potential record buyers had heard, seen and apparently disliked the Faces. For a while the group wondered whether *First Step* would turn out to be their own last hurrah.

Thankfully, live dates begun trickling in. The band had already played London's Lyceum Ballroom on New Year's Eve 1969, predictably billed as 'The Faces' First London Performance', where they'd showcased some tracks from the album. Now they began playing at various low-profile locations, ranging from a US Air Force base in Cambridgeshire to the University of Sheffield, and a Birmingham nightclub called Mothers. Have busted career, will travel. On 14 March they were again booked by the BBC, this time to appear on BBC2's late-night live-music programme *Disco 2*. Things, it seemed, were beginning to look up.

Wrong. By now reviews for *First Step* had begun to appear in the music press. *NME* reported: 'The Faces come up with some weirdo sounds on the ten tracks. They are striving for a heavier sound and getting it, but whether the former fans of the Small Faces will like it, remains to be seen.' 'The Faces have retained much of their original appeal, with a much heavier feel,' sniffed *Melody Maker*, 'but the album is rather patchy.' Only *Billboard* gave any genuine encouragement: 'The most together of any first album I've heard in a long time! A thundering great album.'

If Ronnie was in any way worried about the album's lukewarm reception, he certainly never showed it. If anything he was more upbeat than he'd been in a long while, and eager to get started on the group's first major tour, a twenty-eight-date trek across America: 'Rod and me had already made a bit of a name for ourselves in the States thanks to the Jeff Beck band, so I wasn't worried about getting a good reception, but it was all new for the others. Ron, Mac and Kenny had never played there . . . in fact, I don't think that they had ever set foot there!' (This wasn't totally accurate, for following their deportation from Australia, the Small Faces, with Steve Marriott, had actually spent one night in America in February 1968. Having missed their connecting flight at LA, they were put up at a Holiday Inn.)

Rod had helped smooth the group's imminent arrival Stateside some months earlier with a week-long promotional tour organized by Mercury Records to plug his first solo album. He also used the opportunity to enthuse about how happy he was to be working with Woody again and thanked the record company for allowing him to play with the Small Faces. He explained how he hoped that by promoting his solo work abroad it would, in turn, raise the band's profile. A reasonable assumption but one that was wasted on some newspapers and DJs, who turned up in some cities to ask: 'Was Rod Stewart the guitar player in the Jeff Beck Group?'

Still the band was geared up and ready to go, leading Rod to say: 'Half the battle is already won. The Faces will go down fantastically well because everyone in the band has improved musically so much. It's Ronnie, Mac and Kenny's first trip to America and they're all going to get very homesick. God, they went to Australia for a week and got homesick! This is going to be a great two months. I really think that Marriott was holding their playing back. Since he left, they really seem to have come into their own.'

Ronnie Lane hadn't wanted a leader for the new group. Now there were two.

'The whole set-up in the band was a bit stacked against us right from the very start,' Kenney stated. 'Rod and Ron were all cocky about going to America because they had been there before. They had their following, knew their way around, and became all flash by saying things like: "Oh, we know this great place in New York that does boiled eggs" and all that. We were seen as Rod's and, to a lesser extent, Ronnie's band, which I could see was going to be a problem, but it was a case of waiting and seeing.'

Nineteen-seventy was a good year for English groups in America. *Rolling Stone* was predicting a decade of 'Renaissance Rock' in the wake of the frantic chopping and changing that been prevalent among several top bands at the end of the sixties. Then it had been dubbed the era of the 'supergroup', with Cream at the forefront, followed by groups like Humble Pie and Jon Hiseman's Colosseum. The new Faces were awarded a curious, but sizeable, ready-made audience.

The tour started on 25 March at the Varsity Arena in Toronto, with the band playing third on the bill to home-grown crowd-pleasers such as Canned Heat and Detroit's demi-gods the MC5.

Unfortunately, the group was advertised in a way that was bound to cause trouble. 'They gave me hell!' Gaff remembers. 'I knew perfectly well that behind the scenes they were advertising "Rod Stewart & The Small Faces". Promoters would try and change the signs on the front of the theatres at the last minute, but not always in time. Anyway, they sent Ronnie to tell me that the American promoters were never, ever, to give Rod star billing. I didn't know him [Ronnie] that well, but he'd always seemed like a pussy-cat. I figured that it was mainly Lane and McLagan. Thing was, it was all pointless, anyway. Rod Stewart was going to be a star, one of the biggest the rock world ever saw, and there was nothing the band could do about it.'

Krissie Wood also believes that Ronnie was merely used as a front man: 'He loved Rod. I don't think he would foresee any conflicts. He went along with what the others wanted because he knew Rod better than anyone, so he was always the one to have to talk about Rod to Billy.'

From the first note that the Faces played during their opening American concerts, they had the crowd awestruck. Their magic was instant and it seemed the most natural thing in the world for them to create an atmosphere of snug-bar intimacy in auditoriums as big as aircraft hangars. Fuelled by enough booze to knock out an elephant, the band duly invited everyone along to their party.

Rod mastered a unique acrobatic baton-twirling routine with the metal mike stand. Ronnie Lane stomped around him in ever-widening circles, like a little drunken gnome, chugging out locomotive bass lines that accentuated Kenney's thunderous drumming and Mac's howling Hammond organ. Meanwhile Ronnie Wood, constantly puffing on a cigarette, swooped around the stage like a cartoon rooster, his guitar screeching in torment from a bottleneck pummelling that would reach such a climax that the group ended the show collapsed in a drunken and exhausted heap on the stage – and not always at the end of a number.

They soon gained the reputation as an impossible act to follow. Midway through the tour they were regularly blowing away the bill-toppers and anyone else who dared flex a musical muscle in the same city. Revered groups such as Savoy Brown and a Joe Cocker-free Grease Band learned the hard way.

'We thought no one else would take us seriously,' was how Ronnie described these early dates, 'so we would get plastered beforehand. Dutch courage – we were basically lacking in confidence, especially Ron, Mac and Kenney.'

News filtered back to England that the group was taking America by storm, but an indifferent English press were not impressed and column inches remained Faces-free. Who cared how big anyone was across the pond? If they couldn't cause a mini-riot on *Top Of The Pops* . . . if they weren't making the gossip columns or hanging out at the Speakeasy . . . if their management wasn't schmoozing journalists by the gross – well, they just didn't exist. And then there was the question of their heavy drinking.

Rod recalls: 'We didn't set out to be different or get a reputation going with the press with a gimmick, it wasn't a conscious thing. We just all enjoyed a drink. All the boys enjoyed a drink, we wanted to be drunks. There was a general smile whenever anyone played a dodgy note.'

'Booze – terrible stuff. The ruin of me mother. It's nice, really, quite OK. Why – have we a reputation of being a bunch of juice-heads?' Lane innocently inquired at a press conference.

Which was a problem because while drugs were hip and cool, booze was strictly down-market, even thuggish. Rock music had begun to be heavily influenced by class, and former working-class music journalists – never very many – were desperate to establish their middle-class credentials and the power of their intellect. As indeed they are today.

When the group returned to the UK in June, the first concert they played was at Dudley Zoo in Epping, on the north-eastern edge of London. According to Ronnie: 'We came back after a successful two months to nothing. We expected a flood of gigs but nothing happened, nobody had fixed up anything. We had quite a job to do at home, it just hadn't taken off. I remember saying I'd rather go back to the States than bash people's heads against a brick wall. Over there, they had nothing to go by except a couple of chart entries by the old Small Faces. They hadn't seen the band, only Rod and me, so there wasn't the problem we had in England, linking the old with the new. In the States we started fresh and new. They didn't have anything to match us to, so we didn't have to live anything down or prove anything to anyone. Someone did call out for "Itchycoo Park" though, which pissed Rod off. I wanted the band to make it in England, but by the back door, not by hype! People were very critical of the Faces at the start, or else they just ignored us. We weren't given a chance in England. Music journalists in England think bands simply play to please them – "Come on, entertain me" – and they have a preconceived idea of what they expect and if you don't pander to them they slag the band off and everybody gets on the bandwagon.'

As happened at the Dudley Zoo gig, where the band supported T Rex and were introduced by jazz snob Edgar Broughton as 'a bunch of drunken East End yobbos'. Maybe the Faces' real sin was that they were unashamedly working-class.

In fact, Ronnie had experienced something similar with the Creation: huge in Germany and Holland, minuscule in the country of his birth, just as Jeff Beck was always more popular overseas than in the UK. Today highly regarded groups and musicians like John Mayall and Ten Years After still command a large and respectful following abroad, but not in Britain and certainly not in the mainstream music press. Not because the foreign media and music industries are less knowledgeable or hip, but because they are less age-obsessed, more appreciative and far more broad-minded.

The UK slavishly copies marketing techniques developed in America, where a minority audience can be the size of the population of Holland. At the same time, the industry also suffers from the belief that if you're not big in Britain, you can't be big anywhere. People laugh and sneer at British bands that are successful in Germany, France or Spain. To draw attention to this nonsense – which still goes on – in the eighties a band even called themselves Big in Japan. You might have thought it preferable to be big anywhere, rather than small in Britain, but you'd be wrong.

Ronnie had realized all this when he'd toured with the Creation. All he wanted to do was to make a living as a musician, and where he did it wasn't important. Sure, it would be nice to make it in your own country, but if America and Europe were more open-minded, then that's where the Faces' future lay.

'We had strict ideas about the States,' Ronnie says. 'We had a direct approach. We knew how to go in and we pretty much organized it so that the places we played were the most important. The gigs we had previously done had got us the enthusiasm to slog it out. We could have gone back and done the Fillmore East but if we'd played a dud there, that would have had a bad effect on us, smashing what little confidence we'd built, so we didn't do it. We never played it until we were ready. Bill Graham wasn't the first businessman I'd ever met. I think we were the first band to turn him down. A lot of bands turned him down after that. He expected groups to kiss his boots. He was a slave-driver! He was one of the people you could do without. He got people at the lowest possible prices. At first you needed to play the Fillmore but as America opened up, you didn't. You could get by without it.

'We were learning the business side of things because we had all these raw deals and big debts we'd inherited from the old Small Faces days. We started off the new group full of new hope and old problems. It was enough to make us give up, but we got our heads down and ploughed through it all and America helped that. American audiences can discover a band, they can help break a group whereas in England they're used to having it on a plate, reading about it, letting the stories get back to them, so if they read about a band that has conquered the States, they're ready for them. But in England they figured the Faces were trying to make a second life for themselves, using a name that had been there and gone. Naturally, we stood little chance with that attitude!'

But then the Faces' own attitude wasn't exactly shy and retiring. As Ian McLagan's wife, Sandy Sarjeant, remembers: 'They all came back from that first trip to the States with the clap – Ronnie, Rod and Mac. Probably Kenney got away with it . . . it was a sign of things to come, I could tell that was how our lives were going to be. They all came back really excited, raving about something called Thousand Island dressing which they'd never seen before, as if having the clap didn't matter. So the trouble started straight away with all the wives and girlfriends – that was the biggest trouble they had, all the girls. They spent more time trying to sort out domestic situations when they should have been trying to be a band. Eventually it caused so much trouble that the record companies would fly the girls over to be with them: Ronnie Lane's wife, Sue; Kenney's wife, Jan; Krissie Wood and myself.'

The Faces' second US trip, which included four sold-out dates at the Atlantic City Music Hall in New Jersey on 7, 8, 9 and 10 August 1970, broke Joe Cocker's in-house record and netted them a handsome $30,000 profit. The band then flew directly on to Scandinavia for a further three days of concerts before flying home in order for Ronnie to join Rod at the Morgan Studios in Willesden to cut the latter's second solo album.

'Gasoline Alley', the album's title and lead track, was the first definitive evidence of Ron and Rod's maturing songwriting and musical partnership. The song, an entirely acoustic composition, deals with the stark realization that the grass is not, by any means, greener in pastures new. The lyrics originated with a girl whom Ronnie and Rod had met at an after-show party thrown for the Faces following their sold-out Fillmore East concert. That was the gig that saw the band take to the stage after Bill Graham's introduction: 'Ladies and gentlemen, the Mateus Wine Company presents . . . the Faces!'

The girl had casually mentioned to Rod that she should be getting home before her mother could accuse her of being 'down Gasoline Alley' again. The phrase struck a chord with both Ronnie and Rod, who were feeling a little homesick and lonely after so many nights on the road. The result was a beautiful lament that had the listener yearning for the old homestead. Or pub.

When Ronnie and Rod were asked about the song's 'no place like home' inspiration and where, in particular, they felt at home, Rod replied: 'Highgate, where I was born and bred.' However, Ronnie seemingly misunderstood the song's well-crafted message and simply replied: 'It's just about some prostitute we met at a party!'

The players on the album naturally included all the Faces, with the exception of a 'holidaying' McLagan, who blamed a 'bus strike' for his absences. Ronnie Lane and Kenney Jones might have taken Rod to their collective bosom, but McLagan was remaining aggressively neutral. Other musicians included Martin Quittenton, Mickey Waller and bassist Pete Sears from the pub-rock band Stoned Ground.

The Faces played as a unit on two tracks, 'I Don't Want To Discuss It' and a reworking of the old Small Faces classic 'My Way Of Giving'. The latter was a tribute to the group's fondness for Chris Farlowe's rendition as opposed to, according to Stewart, 'the monstrous version' cut by the original Small Faces in 1967 on their first Immediate album.

Ronnie's suggestion to cover the Bobby and Shirley Womack chestnut 'It's All Over Now' owed more to his admiration for the Stones' interpretation than the earlier, and superior, original. As it was, the Faces manage to inject their own particular brand of football-terrace singalong, complete with Billy Gaff's final whistle towards its crashing climax. It became an instant live Faces favourite, but strangely only a Rod Stewart solo single when it was released that September.

Ronnie doubled on bass and guitar on most of the remaining numbers, including 'Cut Across Shorty', where his fluffing of a chord change caused Stewart to miss out a line completely.

'That was Woody's fault! He forgot it when we were laying the track down, but I think it's great. It doesn't sound wrong, it's a lovely sort of mistake really,' was Stewart's unusual response to a recording error that he wouldn't have tolerated from any musician other than Ronnie. 'He's brilliant. I can't think of any anybody else I could use to play bass and guitar, and there are loads of good players about. I could have used musicians like Paul Kossoff, but as far as bass players go, you know I wouldn't look anywhere other than Woody. He'll be the only one out of the Faces that I'll use on a new album. I used to tell him he would never make as good a guitarist as he was a bassist. But he proved me wrong!' We can only imagine how well that comment went down with the rest of the Faces.

Rod also explained the loose working liaison that the pair were building: 'Woody comes up with a chord sequence or a tune and records it on a tape cassette, then I take it home and work out words for it. For instance, Ron's got this one called "Had Me A Real Good Time" which seems to suggest a party, so that's what I wrote about.'

Ronnie famously summed up his own contributions to *Gasoline Alley* in the album's liner notes, which read: 'Well, it's like this. Now I am definitely not one to complain, no way can I be accused of that. I turned up promptly at each session with my guitars, a shoe lace and a small wireless. I couldn't be fairer than that. Everyone had a good time. Nobody came without being invited and no one arrived who didn't come. All in all a finer gathering of vocalists and musicians I've yet to see. I mean, we all share a good deal of satisfaction and respect for Rod and the lads on this album and also . . .'

Which actually makes more sense than the self-serving and pretentious sleeve-notes to which the industry has become addicted.

The album, released on 11 September, climbed no higher in the UK charts than number sixty-two. Once again the sheer disparity between Stewart's standing here and his success on either side of the Atlantic was emphasized when *Gasoline Alley* peaked on the *Billboard* chart at number twenty-seven.

The Faces prepared for yet another North American marathon to follow the album's release, starting in Vermont at Goddard College in Plainfield on 1 October. The band intended to use the tour to work up new numbers for inclusion on a second Faces album. This was not altogether an unfamiliar practice, but one the Faces decided to take a step further, and they began excluding the songs that the crowd knew – and expected – in favour of new material worked up on stage. Like many British bands, the Faces had quickly become convinced that they were better – and more musically important – than they really were. Or, as was once said of them: 'Just a bunch of cocky little bastards, really, with an over-inflated opinion of their importance.'

However, never let it be said that the Faces weren't quick learners. The first time they informed Billy Gaff of their intentions to play a gig consisting of entirely new material, he was suitably aghast. 'I told them it was too early to even think about it, that to leave out what little numbers the crowd knew would be disastrous. Of course, they ignored me because they'd forgotten their job was to entertain. The show was a complete fiasco, the worst kind of flop and the audience let them know it. You should always try to at least meet the audience halfway. Anyway, they learned their lesson and the next night sang all the crowd-pleasers.'

Gaff's appraisal of the Faces' individual characters at the time is interesting: 'Ronnie Wood is a lovely bloke, one of the nicest people in the business. Kenney Jones is very straightforward and genuine. Ian McLagan and Ronnie Lane have their dark sides, can be quite vicious at times – and both are really jealous of Rod Stewart, who's one of the most professional people you could ever hope to work with.'

Although Gaff was obviously less than enamoured of two of the Faces, his view would change over the next few years. For each of them he later produced individual *This Is Your Life*-type books, listing those qualities that he thought made them special, complete with photographs and even a poem.

On 5 October, four days into the tour, the Faces breezed into Boston for a show at the Tea Party, only to find that the local promoter and publicity hounds had been up to their old tricks again. 'Rod Stewart and The Small Faces,' read the posters, and Ronnie Lane began sharpening his wit. Ian McLagan looked for something to kick, but Gaff wisely kept out of the way.

Rod Stewart managed to defuse the situation by spending most of the evening's performance hiding from the audience, except when he was singing. They sought him here, they sought him there, all to no avail as he was either behind Kenney Jones's drum riser, or McLagan's Hammond and Vox Continental combination. It worked – to some extent – and on occasion the Faces' familiar humour even managed to break through. As when, for example, Stewart bodily lifted up the vertically challenged Ronnie Lane for the first verse intro to 'Maybe I'm Amazed', instead of lowering the mike stand. There was the usual booze-aided pub chorus to close 'Gasoline Alley', and the obligatory collapsing-in-a-heap finale, but the show was quickly over and the band strolled off stage separately.

A point to remember is that the original Faces were East Enders, whereas Rod Stewart came from North London and Ronnie Wood from West London. There was no way on God's earth that the band would ever bond together as Marriott, Lane, McLagan and Jones had once done, for East Enders are nothing if not tribal. Besides, Ronnie and Rod might call themselves working-class, but they weren't really, not in the way that the others were. One of them had actually been to art school, and the other had once been a beatnik busking across France. Not exactly your traditional working-class, right? Not the kind of people you could count on in a ruck.

The following night the band were booked for two shows at The Club in Rochester, New York State. But at least the gig reunited the group: two shows at the same venue in Rochester, of all places, was a mistake, since in the early seventies the town wasn't best known for its live music or rock fans. The Faces said they'd be lucky to fill half a house at each performance. They were right. Most of the tickets had gone for the second gig, so the first became nothing more than an impromptu rehearsal for the main event – which turned out to be a marathon drinking session at the Holiday Inn.

It took all of Billy Gaff's emerging management skills to shepherd the band into the waiting cars and back to the venue. He began by fretting, which they ignored. Then he tried bribery, but they laughed at him. It was only when he tried pleading that they relented.

All the group were slightly the worse for wear, one or two had difficulty focusing, but their collective mood was up and everyone wanted to deliver a good performance. However, their happy dispositions were dampened by the news that the show was running an hour late, thanks to Savoy Brown's late arrival, and that the Grease Band were refusing to vacate the stage. According to the programme, the Faces would have just over three minutes to play their set. Gaff managed to negotiate an extra half-hour – still a ludicrously brief amount of time and in any case quite irrelevant.

It was now 12.30 a.m. and the Grease Band were still ploughing defiantly on with their own brand of pub rock. Well, they'd backed Joe Cocker, hadn't they? So they deserved respect. More to the point, their roadies were bigger and stronger than the Faces' roadies, and formed a protective ring around their employers. The Grease Band hit their final, cracked note at 1 a.m., allowing the Faces to clamber on stage and in double-quick time surge into an ironic rendering of 'It's All Over Now'. The set was quickly over, the audience cried out for more. The Faces were only too ready to oblige. Unfortunately, the heavily unionized stewards and stage-hands thought otherwise, and had bought along a dozen or so rent-a-cops with nightsticks to make the point. Faces and Grease Band roadies united against the invading Colonials, but to no avail, as the power was turned off.

All the audience could hear was Kenney Jones's drumming as the rest of the Faces crashed to a halt. Stewart slung his mike stand hard into the backcloth and all five Faces stormed off stage to join the fracas. Meanwhile the crowd began a fist-saluting chant, which lasted well over a quarter of an hour until the house lights were brought up in a vain attempt to empty the auditorium. That was met by a shower of small change hurled at the stage and the group's equipment, ricocheting tunefully off Kenney's cymbals.

Enter the real cops, with the message that unless everyone went home peacefully, that guy with the funny hairdo who slung the mike would be charged with incitement to riot.

Meanwhile the guy with the funny hairdo was swapping jackets with Gaff in a ridiculous attempt to disguise himself, while the rest of the Faces grabbed as many bottles of booze as they could carry. The band then made a dash for the exit and the safety of the waiting limos. Gaff stayed behind to try and sort out the mess. A manager's lot is not always a happy one.

Ronnie emerged first, to be met by a torrent of thrown bottles, beer cans and rubbish aimed at the venue's windows by an angry mob of fans who had congregated outside, screaming, 'Kill the pigs!' The entire band piled into the first car and sped off, whooping and laughing, towards the Holiday Inn, leaving the crew to, hopefully, clear the stage and maybe pick up some small change for their trouble.

The tour progressed down the East Coast to New York and then across country to Detroit, giving the band the opportunity to break in several new, live numbers like 'Had Me A Real Good Time', 'I Feel So Good' and Paul McCartney's recent composition, 'Maybe I'm Amazed'. In this way they managed to work up new material that would subsequently be included on their second album. Detroit had obviously adopted the Faces as its own since they had demolished the Motor City's very own MC5 a mere six months earlier. A giant banner proclaiming 'Detroit Welcomes The Faces' greeted the bewildered fivesome at the East Town Theatre, which had to post 'house full' notices for the next two nights.

On 18 October, when the group were playing at The Scene in Milwaukee, news broke that the remaining sixteen dates of the tour were sold out. Naturally, they celebrated by invading Billy Gaff's hotel room in the middle of the night in order to overturn his bed, steal his trousers, flood his bathroom and exit with the light-bulbs, leaving behind the bewildered and dazed Gaff naked under an upturned mattress in an inch of water, while his assailants whooped and screamed down the corridor.

This was the beginning of regular hotel rampages and wrecking sprees that came to be recognized throughout the seventies as a particularly English trait among rock bands visiting the USA. As Ronnie admits: 'Keith Moon, of the Who, turned it into an art form. But the Faces pioneered the craft of hotel demolition, [but] we didn't always get the blame for some of the worst examples of destruction, because a lot of the times we would book ourselves in as Fleetwood Mac, which caused them no end of problems, but got them a lot of press and I'm sure, a few lawsuits! A particular favourite on that tour was having parties in our room and seeing how many people we could cram in it. We'd round up everyone we could, all these strangers and people walking by and cram them into one room and get completely pissed, waiting for the first person to fall over, which would start the domino effect.'

Why did they trash so many hotel rooms? Aside from the obvious reasons of drugs, booze and aggression – defenestrating innocent television sets goes beyond youthful high spirits – the simple truth is that they could get away with it, so why the hell not? Think of little kids breaking windows in an empty house. Evelyn Waugh got it wrong: it wasn't only the English aristocracy who bayed for the sound of breaking glass. The Faces and their ilk were Britain's first working-class generation who hadn't had to learn discipline – and good manners – in the Armed Forces or on the factory floor. People indulged them, and they indulged themselves.

It also made great publicity.

The tour continued to snake its way around North America, crossing to San Francisco and Fillmore West on 28 October, Santa Monica on the 30th, then up to Canada before arcing back into the USA to begin the second leg in Wisconsin on 3 November. A further date in Detroit saw the Faces upgraded from the East Town Theatre to an open-air appearance at the Olympic Stadium on the 7th, which caused Gaff an almighty headache when it was noticed that the front-of-house billing announced: 'The Small Faces Featuring Rod Stewart'.

The group and Gaff sat in the limo, looking at the sign. After a few seconds, McLagan hit Gaff over the head with a bottle and told the driver to move on.

The blame was quickly shifted to the tour publicist Peter Burton, who said: 'I thought the game was up that early, the band so deeply resented those marquee signs advertising Rod separately to the Faces. They refused to be relegated to the backing band. Ronnie Wood was a charismatic performer in his own right, an awfully nice man, so he had his own space, somewhere to go. But Ronnie Lane felt marginalized as a writer as much as anything else. There was a lot of power play, whispering and jealousy adding to the tension and then the girlfriends started adding to it when they began flying in for certain dates.'

All things considered, it's a wonder that the Faces lasted as long as they did. Although Rod Stewart did feel uneasy enough about the duo billing to begin arriving at venues early, in order to check that promoters had removed his name from the hoardings. It was either that, or get a mouthful of abuse from the rest of the band except for Ronnie, especially from McLagan, who could be particularly ferocious.

The Faces played their final date of the tour at the Commodore Ballroom in Lowell, Massachusetts on 15 November and flew back to England to play the Marquee. Meanwhile they had released the single 'Had Me A Real Good Time' on 13 November to coincide with their return. It also served as a preview to the forthcoming follow-up to *First Step*, entitled *Long Player*.

Once again, the group produced the album themselves, continuing their determination to keep a tight grip on the artistic control and an even tighter grip on their finances. In England this was seen as an even greater example of their arrogance, prompting the *Record Mirror*'s headline 'Faces Ditch Producers' and an admission from Lane that: 'Some of the band's past efforts had proved to be disappointing.'

Nevertheless, the Faces were publicly adamant that they still viewed a producer as an unnecessary element; although Ronnie was not so convinced: 'I think it's a valid point that a producer can act as a referee if there's indecision, but a producer is only of value if he works the buttons himself. Back then, Glyn Johns was one of the few who did.'

But as Ian McLagan added: 'Producing is a musical thing and most producers didn't know or wouldn't know one note from another. We didn't really know the notes but we could play them.'

The problem of production made Ronnie think about the possibility of building his own studio, but as he had no permanent address big enough to house one in 1971, this had to remain a project for the future.

'One thing that bothered me was that in most studios the sound that came through the cans was never the same as the sound you got when you were playing. That's when I began looking for somewhere in Richmond – big house, and I fancied walking over the bridge in the morning to get the milk in!'

The Faces had been given an initial six months in which to produce *Long Player*. It was a reasonable time for a group as well rehearsed as they were, but left to their own devices they were revealed as sadly lacking in any form of self-discipline, as Kenney Jones admitted: 'Rod and I were very frustrated when it came to recording with the Faces. We had a bit of a drink and that's all. The others were already getting a bit out of hand on other things. Everybody else in the band took a lot of other things, we were night owls, we used to live through the fucking night! Rod and I would have preferred to have gone in the studio at eleven or twelve in the morning, worked through the day, finished at eight and then gone out and partied. That's sensible and that's how you do things. But in those days, the earliest we could persuade the others to come in was about seven at night! Rod and I would get there at six just to loosen up and play a while and we would inevitably be waiting there till ten o'clock and in most cases midnight. In the end we would think, fuck this! We couldn't handle it. It was the Faces' in-house behaviour that would let them down when it came to recording.'

To say that the Faces approached the recording of *Long Player* with a less than professional approach is an understatement. They may have insisted that their attitude towards the record-making process was, in fact, saving rock 'n' roll from taking itself too seriously, but the album proved this was just an excuse.

Only two weeks out of the allotted six months were ultimately used for recording the album's eventual nine tracks, of which the last was a two-minute, solo slide-guitar rendition by Ronnie of the hymn *Jerusalem*, for which, incredibly, he claimed the publishing rights!

The album also included two live recorded versions – 'I Feel So Good' and 'Maybe I'm Amazed' – together with the two Ronnies' 'On The Beach', recorded acoustically on a porta studio Revox at Lane's new flat in Richmond. This left only four fully recorded studio numbers and one of those, 'Bad 'n' Ruin', was recorded in the Rolling Stones' mobile studio, parked at Jagger's stately home in Hampshire.

It wasn't something that passed the critics by, either, as American *Creem* magazine's Ed Ward pointed out in his review: 'Well, the Faces took their first step and like any other first step it was greeted with reserve. After all, the baby might fall flat on its face with the second step. Here then is the Faces' second step and I think we'll have to wait a while before we can categorically state that the baby's learned to walk yet. After playing it numerous times, I find that I can still look at the label and not recognize some of the titles; nor I find, can I remember what most of the songs sound like, but why deal with the album's shortcomings and why bother with these babies at all?'

11
'If you ever do to me what he did to her . . .'

Long *Player* was seen by the critics as a step backwards for the Faces. Was this really fair? Even the first album had eventually, thanks to the group's high-profile touring persistence, managed to limp into respectable sales figures in the USA. Even the American *Rolling Stone* had decided to reappraise it and was currently hailing the band as its third favourite group of the seventies, winning over the normally unshakeable and heavy critic Jon Mendelssohn in the process. American hearts had warmed to the Faces' particular brand of humour and charisma, and applauded their readiness to flaunt their unmistakable Englishness in the wake of such Americanized Brit rockers as Free, Mott The Hoople and probably the most guilty, Humble Pie.

Yes, one has to admit, it was fair: the band hadn't bothered and the music sounded half-hearted. And the blame was placed squarely on the shoulders of Ronnie Wood.

Ronnie's guitar dominated the album and although it was some of his most innovative playing to date, it sounded laboured and hesitant, which *Rolling Stone* was quick to point out: 'The Faces seem to lack any clearly defined sense of direction. They are obliged (or disposed) to look aside from infrequent contributions in the grand old style by bass-ist Ronnie Lane, to late additions Ron Wood for direction. Wood most frequently fancying pleasant if dispensable bottleneck laden variations on De Booze is not the Face to provide that direction.' Meaning they didn't like him.

To be fair, Rod Stewart didn't escape unscathed either: '. . . and Wood's friend with the haystack haircut doesn't seem nearly so intent on so providing as deferring to the other chaps' tastes for purposes of saving the group from becoming Rod Stewart (with The Faces). But so intimi-dating is Stewart's presence apparently in what should, of course, but hasn't thus far been a mutually beneficial way, that the other chaps are all too eager to defer to Stewart's tastes. The present result being that instead of getting both Faces albums and Stewart albums, "Long Player" being nothing more than a grab bag of tit-bits good enough to tide us over until Stewart's third solo album.'

A little unfair, perhaps, that such writers can skewer a band, but that's rock journalism for you – and the Faces had asked for it.

Other reviews were equally damming and all singled out Ronnie as their target. 'Ron Wood is probably one of the best guitarists for a beginner to copy,' sneered *Disc & Music Echo*.

'First off you need to have played bass to have a good excuse for not playing fiddly!' was Ronnie's reply, referring to all the intricate guitar work that was then in vogue, courtesy of Beck and Page. 'When I started out I was copying riffs. I used to listen to early Motown records and try to find out what the hell the chords were, but that was hopeless and my playing was grinding to a halt. I came off a two-year stint playing bass and leaped into slide guitar, which I'd not tried before. I heard Duane Allman and it was "wow!" I felt a natural pull towards that. It was a whole new style of bottleneck because we started playing slide guitar using regular tuning and I tried to copy that. I never realized it was the most difficult way to start. I was aware of Steve Cropper, Buddy Guy, Kenny Burrell and Wes Montgomery, but Duane's playing on Aretha Franklin's version of "The Weight" was my main inspiration. That was what I was trying to do.'

Ronnie's intentions may have been understandable, and it was obvious he knew just what he wanted to achieve in his head, but *Long Player* ended up sounding half thought out. He was accused of gross self-indulgence by experimenting in public and using the Faces as a vehicle with which to pursue his own personal agenda, despite the obvious shortcomings and over-compensating clumsiness. This popular train of thought wasn't helped when Ronnie Lane, whose own compositions had been only slightly less rubbished than Ronnie Wood's – 'Horrendous production' and 'Insufficiently developed arrangement' – did little to help Ronnie's reputation on both record and in live performance: 'Ronnie's got this thing about jamming, but it usually means fuck all! Jamming is all right for a bit of fun on your own, but in front of paying audiences . . . I ask you, is that fair?'

Ronnie defended his performances on *Long Player* and blamed the impossible demands of constant touring, and the lack of any serious time with which to work up any new material or ideas. But he was honest enough to acknowledge that his attitude had become sloppy and accepted that maybe the drinking was, in fact, getting just a little out of control: 'I don't rehearse enough and I didn't practise. The only time I'd practise was when I put new strings on before a show, and then we'd usually be pissed anyway!'

His playing throughout the album may have received a trouncing, but his lyrical contributions to 'Had Me A Real Good Time', 'Sweet Lady Mary' and even 'On The Beach' [Wood/Lane] were met with grudging approval. In fact the second of these was regarded by most critics as the stand-out track. This story of separation, incompatibility and the doomed love of a travelling man may have owed its origins to 'Gasoline Alley', but Ronnie's harder-edged realism had perhaps pointed the Faces, for the first time, in the direction of a hit-making potential:

> Her Spanish habits are so hard to forget,
> The lady lied with every breath I accept,
> It was a matter of time before my face did not fit.

Even so, Ronnie was susceptible to any criticism just before the Faces were due to play to British crowds. They had a handful of UK shows lined up across the country and he grabbed the opportunity of an interview with *Melody Maker* before the first show at the Orchid Ballroom in Purley, Surrey, on 11 April 1971, to explain how he saw the band progressing in the UK. He also defended *Long Player* and the intended follow-up single, 'Maybe I'm Amazed'. The latter was eventually produced as a limited edition pressing of 500 copies given away free to the fans entering the Roundhouse, in London's Chalk Farm, on 29 April.

'The first album was simply to show the direction the band was taking and this one was us levelling out,' Ronnie told the journalist. 'But the next one, wow! that's how it should be. I don't think the band realize that we've got something to live up to. The next album will supersede *Long Player*, we've got to keep up a high standard of work and even the Stones have re-recorded "Honky Tonk Women", that's why we've re-recorded numbers today that would have been considered great about six months ago. I really think we get a very high standard of performance on stage. If there's more than a minute between numbers now, Rod goes potty and the rest of us get very edgy. I mean, I've watched the Grateful Dead constantly tuning up and it makes my nerves bad. Now when we go out on stage, there's no time to be messing about tuning up, so if the things are not in tune when you go out there . . . beware!"

The Faces had also come up with a novel and highly unconventional way of ensuring a convivial response from their audience. They had decided to dispose with the usual approach of using a support band at most of the shows in favour of distributing free crates of booze and wine from the stage.

'We'd get the roadies to dish out fuckin' great crates of the stuff,' Ronnie laughs. 'Crates of wine and then wait for about an hour and a half while the audience were soaking it all up and come on when they were completely pissed!'

The group had already performed shows in the US with the aid of a fully stocked bar on the stage, from which waiters dressed in white shirts, bow-ties and waistcoats would serve the band with drinks throughout their set. This set-up would later expand to two bars: the original bar, staffed by cocktail waitresses, and a little mobile one pushed from player to player by a dwarf in white tie and tails. Meanwhile the roadies cut and left neat lines of cocaine on the top of flight cases and amplifiers positioned just to the side of the stage out of view of the audience.

It was a devil-may-care approach to performing, born from sheer insanity. Not surprising that Ronnie remembers little of these shows: 'None of the Faces remember much, but that was just the beginning. Things got much worse on the later tours.'

Their attitude to playing in the UK was still very much that it was a chore, and the idea of getting the crowd as drunk as themselves was probably as calculated and self-indulgent as the Faces could get. But hey, it worked!

The images of Rod and Ron singing head to head around the one mike may have been reminiscent of Lennon and McCartney, but their cartoon-like features forged an identity very much their own, and it's an image that has stayed indelibly fixed in the memories of the Faces' fans ever since. The whole band had almost subconsciously honed their stage presence while on those long hauls across the States. They still retained their trade mark of slipshod, good-natured, men-of-the-people, but now they added a dash of panache which gave them that true pop star quality.

'I wouldn't say American audiences made us into a great band overnight. But they certainly made us into a big one,' Rod Stewart reflects today.

And Ronnie was a major reason. There was little doubt that he'd learned to project the very charisma and self-assurance needed to elevate himself from the shadows of Rod Stewart in very much the same way as Pete Townshend had done in relation to Roger Daltrey, or Jimmy Page with Robert Plant.

He was dressing the part, too, and had developed his own very individual style just as he had with the Birds, courtesy of his art school background. 'Ronnie had found this sweatshop in the King's Road,' Sandy Sarjeant says, 'run by a Greek guy called Andreas, and both

Ronnie and Krissie were having their clothes made down there, they were both so clothes-conscious! They were always finding these fabulous lengths of fabric. Ronnie had more of an eye for it than Krissie. He'd get jackets made in these fantastic colours, and he and Krissie fought over them like fighting dogs.'

Ronnie was also a lot less menacing, and a sight more entertaining than Jeff Beck had ever been in the same situation. And the magic didn't only work with Rod Stewart, for when he got it together with Lane the picture was perfect: the duo's plumes of thick cigarette smoke wreathing the air as one by one Rod and the two Ronnies chugged over to the bar in order to take more booze on board, like steam trains going to the water tank. McLagan and Jones competed the scene – Mac resplendent in one of his seemingly inexhaustible supply of satin waistcoats and forever craning his neck over his shoulder in the direction of the band's centre-forward and his pair of knock-about team-mates. All the while, Kenney would thunder relentlessly behind them, tight-lipped and staring madly heavenward. At times both seemed a little resentful of the obvious constraints their chosen instruments imposed on them. Especially when Rod and Ronnie would drag on a net full of footballs and, together with Lane, boot them into the crowd.

British audiences were finally waking up to something that America had known for more than a year: here was a band whose natural vitality, humour and undeniable hospitality set them worlds apart from anything else currently on offer, either side of the Atlantic. Britain was finally ready to take them to its own, often inebriated, heart. It's fair to say that at this point, had the Faces rapport fallen flat with a larger, home-grown audience, then Rod Stewart would certainly have taken to the road with his studio band. And it's true that they could have sustained a small part of the magic, but could never have brought together so perfectly this country's three major passions of music, football and booze. The Faces embodied a very real working-class dream. Two hours spent watching them strut around the stage bolstered the belief that if this bunch of befuddled piss-heads could take on the world and succeed, then there was a very real chance that the audience could too.

The success of these live shows even had a rejuvenating effect on the sales of *Long Player*, pushing it as far as number thirty-one in the UK charts, only two places lower than the US showing. Billy Gaff added extra dates, hoping to keep up the British momentum, and extended the live itinerary through April, May and into July, at which point another American excursion would kick in – their fourth in under two years. The band also managed a TV appearance on 22 April, when they were the stars of BBC2's *Disco Two*, where they performed three numbers from the album: Ronnie's 'Sweet Lady Mary', Lane's 'Tell Everyone' and Bad 'n' Ruin'. Ronnie and Rod added to their workload, whenever possible, by meeting between dates at Morgan Studios to record tracks for Stewart's third solo album, which Mercury had scheduled for release on 9 July – the date of the group's next live date in the USA.

The stupidity of such a gruelling schedule meant Stewart had to stick pretty much to the same established formula and components that had worked so well on *Raincoat* and *Gasoline Alley*. He kept the nucleus of Ronnie, Mickey Waller and Martin Quittenton as his studio band, recorded another Dylan song, some soul covers, a Tim Hardin number and two Stewart originals. There was also a new song from Rod and Ronnie: the title track and album-opener 'Every Picture Tells A Story'.

Stewart's ability to pick covers that suited his vocal style so well, while slotting perfectly alongside original numbers, is a skill that has made him one of the most enduring of all the rock legends.

Every Picture Tells A Story turned out to be as close to a conceptual, autobiographical album as it's possible to get without meaning to. The title track sums up the overall theme, which harked back to Stewart's days as a busker in Europe, albeit with large portions of poetic licence. It's familiar enough, with its trouble-struck wanderers and their meandering memories of unfulfilling relationships and lustful encounters in far-off lands. Which slightly begged the question of why Stewart gave it all up to become a gravedigger.

Even so, the title song was special and encapsulated the entire album in under six minutes, while displaying the definite coming of age of Ron and Rod's musical partnership. The album as a whole might well have stood as Rod Stewart's finest moment but for a certain track called 'Maggie May', yet another fabled slice of the Stewart sexual legend that referred to losing his virginity to an older woman, with a tent, at a rock concert, and his later joining the Faces: 'Find myself a rock'n'roll band that needs a helping hand.'

Ironically, both Stewart and Mercury Records had been slow to recognize 'Maggie May's' massive hit potential and relegated it to the B side of 'Reason To Believe'. However, for once DJs on both sides of the Atlantic knew a hit when they heard one, and took it upon themselves to flip the disc over in favour of 'Maggie'. It was played non-stop until it bounced simultaneously to the top of both the UK and US charts.

Some idea of how this affected the Faces' popularity in the UK is conveyed by their reception at the Weeley Festival in Essex, where they were booked to appear on 29 August 1971 as a support band for T Rex. 'WEELEY – A ONE GROUP FESTIVAL!' screamed the front page of *New Musical Express* afterwards, and told the story of how T Rex – at that time Britain's premier attraction – had been totally humiliated by a crowd shouting and banging beer cans together as they demanded more of the Faces, for a full fifteen minutes into the headliners' set. The report also said that 'Maggie May' brought the best response of the entire festival, with the hundred-thousand-plus crowd standing and chanting out the words. The reviewer's sympathies were with T Rex, with the caveat that the Glam Rock group couldn't hope to match the sheer brilliance of the Faces.

Three months earlier the Faces had played the Nag's Head in Northampton and the Greyhound in Croydon, with a maximum of two hundred and fifty drunken punters at each pub gig, invariably shouting out for that old Small Faces hit 'All Or Nothing'. Now they had knocked the sequins off Marc Bolan and T Rex.

But there was a downside. The score was now Rod Stewart 1, the Faces (plus Rod Stewart) 0. Even worse, the phenomenal success of 'Maggie May' propelled the album to number one, so that Rod now held the top spots on both the American and UK album and single charts – for the first time in recording history. He also had album and single number ones in Canada, New Zealand and Australia. Rod Stewart 7, the Faces (plus Rod Stewart) still 0.

The Faces' fate as Stewart's backing band was now cast in stone. For a while they would cling to the hope that his solo success might somehow rub off on his team-mates. This hope would prove to be a forlorn one.

But for the time being the Faces shamelessly plugged 'Maggie May' with the intent of making it look like a group effort – ignoring the fact that only Ronnie was a member of Stewart's studio band of regulars.

Mickey Waller, for one, was understandably shocked to see Kenney Jones uncomfortably miming to his drum fills when he tuned in to see the Faces appear on *Top Of The Pops*. 'To this day people don't believe it's me playing on "Maggie May", because they wanted people to think it was Kenney, to make the Faces look better than they were. It was all Rod's doing, he had the cheek to ask me one night before *Top Of The Pops* if I wanted to play mandolin on the show! This was in front of Ronnie, who was really embarrassed, and my girlfriend Nicole said don't do it. So they got John Peel to do it instead. But anyone who saw the Faces live knew they weren't capable of recording anything remotely as good as "Maggie May". The Faces couldn't make a fucking half-decent record, they were useless.'

Waller has a point. It's one thing to mime to your own record, quite another to mime to someone else's work. To their credit, the band did play with a football on that infamous broadcast – 'To show it wasn't really us playing,' as Kenney Jones later said – but this is a little disingenuous. In reality, the band wanted to have their cake and eat it. For those fans in the know, the clowning around demonstrated that the Faces weren't trying to take credit for 'Maggie May'. But the band were also banking on the fact that the vast majority of the record-buying public wouldn't have a clue.

Along with Mickey Waller, certain British rock journalists were also sceptical about the band's real abilities, since at the Weeley Festival they'd only triumphed over a field that included the best of British B-List bands.

The Grease Band had been given yet another hiding; as had Mungo Jerry, the Groundhogs, Heads Hands and Feet, Juicy Lucy and the newly bedenimed Status Quo. But although respected bands, these were little more than pub rockers. The Faces, it was felt, still had a lot to prove. Rod Stewart, however, was another matter. Rod-mania was about to break and everyone knew it.

The Faces' next show was at the more sedate, but prestigious, Queen Elizabeth Hall on London's South Bank, where it was announced that Rod Stewart had been voted Best Male Vocalist by the readers of *Melody Maker*. Maggie Bell, his chosen backing singer for the album, was voted Best Female Vocalist, and the single 'Maggie May' made third place in the International Singles section. Lane, McLagan and Jones all fared reasonably well in their instrument categories. There was no mention of Ronnie anywhere.

For their following show the Faces were second on the bill at the Oval cricket ground, South London, where they gave the mighty Who a run for their money in front of thirty-five thousand fans.

'For a live show,' wrote Chris Charlesworth in *Melody Maker*, 'it has long been my opinion that the Who couldn't be topped – but watch out, Who, the Faces are breathing down your necks.'

The Faces seemed to be silencing their critics – after all, the Who could hardly be accused of being a pub band. But all Rod Stewart could do was give them a brief pat on the head: 'I had a few doubts about the Faces to begin with, me and Woody used to think, Christ, we better ring Jeff [Beck], this isn't going to work. Me and Ron had come from the so-called underground, the Faces were more pop, and it was hard to match the two at first. But it's working out fairly well.'

Fairly well? Certainly for Ronnie and Rod, both obviously benefiting from the latter's solo career. The royalties were mounting up from their joint compositions, and it was time to go mansion-hunting.

Stewart bought his first obligatory rock-star mansion, Cranbourne Court, from Lord Bethell. It was a thirty-two-room monster near Windsor, surrounded by fourteen acres, with a lodge, stable block and swimming pool, for which he paid £89,000 cash – over £1.5 million today. Rod and his girlfriend Sarah Troops broke up during the move, and Dee Harrington became the lady of the house.

Ronnie, too, was looking to move up in the property world, encouraged by Krissie's conviction that they needed something a little more distinctive than the Old Forge in Henley. After all, every newly-wed couple dreams of owning their own house – Krissie and Ronnie were married on 27 September 1971.

'We'd been together about eight years,' Ronnie recalls, 'and her father started dropping hints, saying isn't it about time I done the decent thing, go on, make an honest woman of her, so I asked Kris to marry me. Her parents were living in Northampton, which is just about the dullest place in England. We all went up there together – Mum, Dad, Art and Doreen's son, little Simon, Ted and Gill. I wore a bright red suit, Kris was in this Hungarian-embroidered blouse and skirt with red shoes. Rod was me best man. He wore white and looked more like the bride than anyone, and we brightened the town up for a day. Rod said he'd never get married, this was as close as he'd ever want to get. He and my Dad just spent the whole day getting drunk as skunks.'

Ronnie and Krissie exchanged turquoise wedding rings – a turquoise and silver ring for Krissie and a turquoise American Indian mountain ring for Ronnie.

Lizzie was proud to finally see her youngest son get married and remembers: 'We all went up in this big, white limousine and Rod had little Simon with him in his white Rolls-Royce, and when we pulled up it said on the radio that "Maggie May" had just gone to number one and Simon and Rod were singing it at the top of their voices.'

Perry Press was set to work to find the couple something appropriate in the Richmond area. It's difficult to hide wealth from close colleagues. The rest of the Faces duly saw and noted that the two newcomers were doing vastly better than they were. Ronnie was now driving a new Bentley and Stewart had a Lamborghini. The rest of the Faces were doing OK, but nowhere near as well. It seemed to them that Rod and Ronnie were beginning to move into different musical and social orbits – leaving the boys behind. Whether the feelings of distance and resentment were warranted is beside the point. They were inevitable.

'We never saw the Rod thing being quite so big,' Ronnie said at the time, while trying to paper over the cracks. 'We were extraordinarily close and we'd all reached a stage when we co-operated with each other. With the Rod thing it was all of a sudden, Bang! and he was huge. He was getting lots of offers, people dangling carrots under his nose, but

Rod was incredibly good about the whole thing, and despite all the temptations of going solo he swore the Faces were still his cup of tea. But I don't think the others saw it like that, and they looked for someone to blame.'

Twenty-two years later, Ronnie sees the situation a little differently. 'The wives started the break-up. They were always setting their husbands up against each other, arguing and rowing with each other, just making life unbearable. It made you want to get away from it, because they acted as if they were the band, not us. That's one reason why we toured so much – but then they started to go tour with us, and that was the beginning of the end.'

The three original Faces had all married in their very early twenties, and would eventually divorce young, too. McLagan to and from *Ready Steady Go!* dancer Sandy Sarjeant; Lane, the singer Genevieve (in fact, a girl named Sue); and Jones, Jan Osborn, daughter of the band leader Tony Osborn.

None of the marriages survived the Faces; none of the wives remarried; and only Sandy, a particularly feisty character, reverted to her maiden name. Years later Krissie Wood summed up the First Rock Wife dilemma when she was asked why she'd never married the long-term boyfriend she'd had after her divorce from Ronnie: 'Well, in a way I'd wanted to . . . but that would have meant changing my name. I wouldn't have been a Wood any more.'

But then the wives did have to put up with a great deal from their husbands. In the following year, at a party in their own Richmond home, Ronnie Lane went missing – as did Sue's best friend and neighbour, Kate McInnerney, married to Mike, who designed the *Tommy* album cover. They were discovered having sex by an extremely put-out Sue – for although the Lanes had an open marriage, often swapping partners with other rock-world couples, this didn't extend to best friends. Besides, they were in her bed. She was even more put out when Lane announced that, all things considered, he actually preferred Kate.

Two marriages broke up that night.

This sent shock waves through the other wives and girlfriends, as they realized how easily they could be replaced. None of them was living a life that could be called conventional, and God only knew how much temptation their men faced every day. The worry and fear gnawed at Krissie in particular, although Ronnie was far too private a person to ever consider an open marriage.

'The business with Lane and Sue had obviously played on her mind,' Sandy Sarjeant remembers. 'We were in the States and the boys were on stage. Krissie was all done up in her usual manner – feather boa, big hat, silk dress. She was also pissed and one of her tits had popped out of her dress. She had really great tits, I would loved to have had tits like that. Anyway, she walked straight out on stage with a of glass of champagne in one hand, her tit still hanging out, in front of thousands of people and walked up behind Ronnie [Wood], who was in the middle of solo . . .'

Cut to Kenney Jones, the only one of the band who'd noticed Krissie's arrival: 'I saw her come on stage and thought, where the fuck's she going? None of the others could see her because they had their backs turned.'

Cut to Sandy: 'So Krissie tapped Ronnie on the back, he turned round, saw her and just couldn't believe it, and she started wagging her finger at him and shouting out: "If you do to me [points finger at an equally shocked Lane], what he did to Sue, I'm leaving you!"'

Except Sue wasn't on the tour. Her place had been taken by Kate McInnerney, also watching aghast from the wings. Kenney Jones takes up the tale: 'It was Rod who broke it up. He was so pissed off that he gobbed on her back, then hustled her off the stage. It was unbelievable.'

The next night, Kenney Jones showed up on stage wearing a T-shirt that read: 'If you do to me what he did to her . . .'

Sandy admits: 'I've never been able to work Krissie out even to this day. She was absolutely beautiful, everything that I had always wanted to be: blonde, blue-eyed, hair down her back, but it was like she was on another planet. She'd either be as thick as shit or she'd have flashes of brilliance, and I never knew whether she was playing the dumb blonde or whether it was real, and sometimes I still don't know.'

In October 1971 the band had left for America, for a two-gig tour including a sell-out concert at Madison Square Garden, where they had previewed what would become the Faces' first solo hit, 'Stay With Me'.

'That record, and in particular the intro,' Ronnie says today, 'was the turning point in my career. It was done at the time when everyone was kissing the arses of Led Zeppelin. That song and the album was when the Faces finally got it together.'

Not just the intro, but Ronnie's playing throughout the album – *A Nod's As Good As A Wink To A Blind Horse* – finally established him as a class lead guitarist. But it also led to one of the most musically embarrassing moments of his career.

'We were playing Madison Square Garden and we had this idea of walking through the crowd to get on stage, and [I] must have knocked my guitar out of tune. There was a big introduction when we got on stage: "Ladies and Gentlemen – the Faces!" and we were supposed to break into "Stay With Me", my cue to start the show with that big opening chord. Except I played the worst note I'd ever heard in my life! Then there was this dead silence, with the whole band standing their looking at me, except for Rod. who'd begun pacing nervously around the stage, and I had to go to the mike and tell twenty thousand people to talk amongst themselves I stood there and tuned my guitar. It put me off the rest of the gig – the Faces' biggest moment, and my worst nightmare!

'But I was still well pleased with all the attention I started to receive as a guitarist. I was getting worried that I'd always be in the background. It was nice when the little things you'd try to do got picked out, and you realize you've got your point over . . . at one time I was feeling like, well, that being stuck away was going to be my position for the rest of my life. I'd started out experimenting with slide [guitar] on *Gasoline Alley*. And then I went on to using twelve- and six-strings and overdubbing the slide. And I found I could get the same sound live by using open tuning [not tuned to any particular chord] and fiddling about. I found I could easily mould the guitar around the organ and bass. I think that guitarists had gone out of style for a while – it was the dawn of piano players like Leon Russell and Elton John, which came in when the Hendrix, Clapton and Beck thing started fading. It's like everything, it was a style whim the public has.'

There was one other contributing factor to the album's success: they'd hired Glyn Johns as producer, and it showed. Although Johns himself was afterwards less than ecstatic abut the experience. 'It was obvious to me when I first got involved that it was too much "Rod Stewart and his backing band". That wasn't necessarily anyone's fault. Rod was a success and the band weren't. I doubt if I'd work with the Faces again. Too much hoo-hah went down in the end and I made myself unpopular. I'd like to work with them, though. Rod's vocal abilities are wider than he gives himself credit for. Again, he was one person I never produced. You don't produce Rod Stewart. He has a particular way of recording and it works for him.'

A Nod's As Good As A Wink . . . reached number two in Britain and six in the US, while the single 'Stay With Me' reached number six in Britain and seventeen in the USA. The album would arguably have reached the top slot if it hadn't been for a last-minute recall by Warner Brothers, following outraged complaints by American record dealers. They were offended by the contents of the poster given free with the album that featured groupies in various states of undress.

Nevertheless, 1971 had ended on a high note for the Faces. But with the new year it was business as normal: a list compiled by the British

Market Research Bureau named Rod Stewart as the top-selling album artist, and number three as a singles artist. As Glyn Johns had said: Rod Stewart and his backing band. Or, as was becoming increasingly apparent, Rod Stewart and the Faces, also featuring Ronnie Wood.

12
'My whole family's good at emptying bottles'

The Wick in Richmond – now owned by Pete Townshend – is one of the loveliest houses in the London area. It's a classic Georgian, twenty-roomed house standing just below the brow of Richmond Hill, overlooking that lovely curve of the Thames which gave its name to a similar view in Richmond, Virginia. The garden slopes down to the tow-path, and includes a three-bedroom cottage – very important, the Wick Cottage, because without it Ronnie could never have afforded the asking price of £100,000.

He was doing well, but not that well. Not yet.

The problem was solved by Ronnie Lane, now homeless and separated following his continuing affair with Kate McInnerney. Ronnie bought The Wick and Lane bought the cottage, partly because he could also park his mobile recording studio, an Air-Stream caravan, in the garden. On the face of it, a good deal for everyone, and at first Lane was delighted with the deal. But not for long, for every time he walked out of his own home he'd be confronted by the evidence of how much more successful his band-mate had become – Ronnie owned the mansion, while he had the servants' quarters. Lane had always seen himself, along with Marriott, as the moving force behind the Small Faces. Now he'd been sidelined by two outsiders. The Faces weren't relying on his songwriting talents as much as before – it was all Ronnie and Rod, and there was that bloody great house to prove it.

Under the influence of Kate McInnerney – a great one for the myth of the raggle-taggle gypsy, o! – Lane himself began to adopt a gypsy-like approach to life. Possessions no longer meant anything, he would preach: 'I know big houses and big cars won't make me particularly happy. It's work, friends, the company I keep, and the old lady.' Subsequently, Lane began wearing earrings and allowed his hair to become romantically straggly.

The only exceptions to the no-possession rule for Lane were guitars and caravans:

'I had so much trouble adapting that fucking Air-Stream caravan for British electrics,' Lane joked in 1990. 'Nothing fitted, the plugs were all wrong – and when I'd finally finished it I realized the only reason I'd bought it was because I liked the look of it. Funny thing was, years later, after I'd split up with Kate, it got vandalized when I left it parked on a council estate in Hackney – and I discovered that only the wiring was insured.'

The irony was, of course, that here was a man trying to become a gypsy, while a real, full-blooded Romany lived in the big house on the hill. Meanwhile the caravan collection continued to grow, and came to include a traditional, brightly painted, horse-drawn example that remained slowly mouldering in the garden long after Lane had gone. His stage appearance began changing, too. The more glamorous the other Faces became, the more Lane would turn up wearing long costermonger scarves, high lace-up boots and a four-day stubble. In the Small Faces, Lane's persona – a down-to-earth East Ender from Plaistow – had seemed so right when surrounded by his three little mates from Mile End and Stepney; all cheeky, cheerful barrow-boys with an eye for mischief and a wicked sense of fun. Even in the early days of the new Faces, his dapper, Teddy-boy drape suits hadn't looked out of place. But from 1972 onwards his look of ragged introspection was totally at odds with the others' naturally flamboyant style.

Even so, Lane might have had a point about possessions. After he left the Faces, he finally got over his hatred of large houses and bought a working farm in Wales. Tragically diagnosed as suffering from multiple sclerosis, he later discovered that his condition had been worsened by the chemicals used in sheep-dip.

Ronnie had bought The Wick from Sir John Mills and his wife, the writer Mary Hayley Bell, who'd decided to move out of London – although they regretted their decision almost as soon as the papers had been signed, and asked Ronnie to sell it back. But in his mind he'd already spent £25,000 to equip the recording studio he planned for the basement. Besides: 'I fell in love with The Wick as soon as I saw it. I'd always wanted a nice, big house and Krissie and me had been living in chaos, always moving. Even when I'd lived at home with my mum and dad, it was chaos because there'd be parties every week – my family has always been good at emptying bottles. When we moved in to The Wick, I got Art's then wife, Doreen, to come in every day as my secretary and Mum used to come and cook breakfast every morning and do anything she could to help out. Art and Ted were always there, offering to fix things, which they were no good at, but it was lovely, just like being at home – there was always people coming and going, but mum was used to it, she'd known chaos ever since she'd had children. And my dad was so proud, too!'

Krissie, too, had fallen instantly in love with the place: 'Ronnie just said one day that he'd found this house for us,' she remembers. 'I didn't know he'd even been looking. When I saw The Wick, I couldn't believe how beautiful it was, and I kept on saying to Ronnie, "Is it really going to be ours?" And he just said, "Yep!" Sir John Mills had left a note on the mirror, saying, "Hope you will be as happy as we were at The Wick." He was such a lovely man – the fact that he and his wife had lived there for so long, and brought up their children Hayley, Juliet and Jonathan there, made The Wick even more special.'

Even so, not everything in the garden was lovely. While there had been no serious affair to disturb Ronnie and Krissie's relationship, nevertheless their idyll had begun to tarnish a little. They'd been together for nearly eight years. Ronnie had grown in stature as a musician, and Krissie had grown in stature as a musician's old lady. It was no longer the two of them against the world, no longer Krissie needing to work to help support them. As the band became more and more successful, they began back-to-back tours of Britain, Europe and the States – where they were regularly spotted around Hollywood fraternizing with the likes of Dustin Hoffman, Steve McQueen, Warren Beatty, Crosby, Stills, Nash & Young, the Allman Brothers, the occasional wayward Beatle and the Stones. All this while the wives seethed and bickered at home about only being allowed to join their men for key dates and for the occasional long weekend.

As it was, Ronnie's hectic 1972 schedule – Germany in March; UK and the USA in April; Germany and the UK in May; another major US tour in June; UK festival dates in July; yet another major US tour in August, their seventh; all interspersed with recordings for the next album, while the two Ronnies began work on the film score for *Mahoney's Last Stand*; and sessions for Rod Stewart's fourth solo album – had kept him apart from Krissie and delayed by months the moment that The Wick would become their new home.

So it was hardly surprising that Krissie began to suspect he was seeing someone else.

Ronnie had known George Harrison and Patti Boyd for several years, and introduced Krissie to George in Los Angeles in 1972 during the

Faces' fifth US tour. But by then the Harrisons' marriage was famously heading for the rocks. George had long since discovered meditation, sitting for hours in a darkened room in his Henley mansion, before disappearing London-wards for slightly more earthly pursuits. This gave Patti the impression that George was either thinking about sex or looking for it elsewhere.

Krissie believes that Ronnie began an affair with Patti around this time. But this has been hotly denied by both Ronnie and Patti even to this day.

But it's equally possible that Patti simply needed a shoulder to cry on and Ronnie is well-known for his sympathetic ear; or seemingly so, according to Krissie: 'Brian Robertson [Thin Lizzy guitarist] once said to me that Ronnie can make you feel you're the most important person in the room for that moment he's with you, but it's a mistake to hold on to that moment. I thought, wow! that's it, that's what was wrong, he can do that . . . and once you've moved on, it'll be someone else, and you're a fool to think otherwise – he never calls you back, he's got that wonderful thing that allows him to live in the now, he doesn't live for tomorrow or yesterday. People take it for innocence, but it's not. It's actually very intelligent. I was speaking to Pete Townshend just the other day and he agrees. There's also a cutting side to Ronnie: he can really cut you down very quickly with a smile on his face. I think it was something he developed from being on the road all the time. He didn't live life like an ordinary person who sometimes woke up with a hangover and went to the pub to get over it. He woke up like that all the time, but he'd have to perform for people both on and off stage. So he learned to develop this way of dealing with people who are naturally drawn to him.'

In other words, people gravitate to Ronnie and receive what they think is his total support and interest – and so it is, at the time. He's also incredibly discrete and jealously guards his private life – one of the reasons why his friendship with Harrison, the Quiet Beatle, has endured for so long. This privacy also makes him the ideal confidant – for him, a secret shared is one never to be repeated.

But whatever the truth of Ronnie's close friendship with Patti Boyd, Krissie was convinced of the worst. She felt more and more that the growing distance between them wasn't only a matter of miles, due to Ronnie's touring, but also because they were moving emotionally apart: such is the downside of being a rock wife, made much worse when the suspected rival was married to a Beatle. In rock wifedom's natural pecking order, there's no one more important than a Beatle's wife.

It wouldn't even have been necessary for Ronnie to have slept with

Patti Boyd for what came next to have happened. Simply being close to her was more than enough.

Krissie vividly remembers her first meeting with George Harrison, in Los Angeles at a party for the Faces. 'George started chatting me up. He had no idea I was with Ronnie. He was so calm, but still really charismatic with that great crooked grin. He seemed to be a million miles removed from all the rock-star madness going on around us. He just sort of glided in and suddenly there he was, talking to me. I never dreamed anything would ever happen between us. But I was just so flattered.'

The next time they met was at in October 1972 at a party at The Wick. Ronnie and Krissie had only recently moved in, which meant a succession of house-warming parties that would last for the next few years. George stayed over that night and the next morning, Krissie breezed into his room to offer him a cup of tea. She was never to forget her third meeting with the Beatle, and still giggles at the memory. 'The first thing I saw was George's naked bottom, bouncing up and down in this big brass bed. But I didn't recognize the girl he'd met at the party. I thought the tea could wait.'

George had obviously made a lasting impression on Krissie – one that would ultimately lead to her first serious affair.

Mansions, luxury cars, a seemingly inexhaustible supply of money – ditto drugs, especially on tour in America – famous friends, the adulation and jealousy of their fans, and an entourage of twenty-four-hour ego masseurs. The average age of a rock star was twenty-five, and they felt like gods. There was nothing they couldn't do, and they were almost expected to behave with wild disregard for society's values.

This was the world that Krissie and Ronnie now lived in – and someone had to keep it in check, and the worst parts out of the newspapers. Enter Shirley Arnold, who, as former secretary to the Rolling Stones, understood all about drugs, chaos and scandal, and how to control them. She'd started with the Stones as a naïve sixteen-year-old. Nine years later, she'd seen it all.

'I was working in the Stones' New Oxford Street offices, when Ronnie Wood and Ronnie Lane came up to see Stu [Ian Stewart, Stones roadie and session pianist] about the film soundtrack they were working on, and Ronnie Lane's car got towed away from outside, and they were so vague: "Oh, blimey, me car's been towed away!" They didn't know what to do. But the Stones' organization was very professional, we could sort anything out. So I got the car back – and it was if I'd pulled off the most amazing thing, they were so impressed. And I thought, God! they need someone to look after them. I'd been thinking about a change for a little while, but wasn't sure I wanted to go from one band to another. They were like two little kids, saying, "Oh, we need a secretary. Shirl, you wouldn't fancy doing some stuff for us?" I said, "I might, Ron, I might give it a try." There was a lot of nonsense starting with Billy Gaff: some of the band didn't think they were being well managed, and I think they thought I was more high-powered than I was. They thought I could take them away from Billy, they all did – except for Woody, who didn't seem to care either way. So I went to work for them and after about two weeks I realized what a mistake I'd made. There was no way you could do anything with them, they were so unreliable. And there was so much bitching going on amongst themselves and amongst the wives. Ronnie Lane was always bitching about Billy, Kenney was always bitching about Woody and Mac being late for rehearsals, Mac and Kenney bitched about money, and they all bitched about Rod, and the "Rod Stewart and the Faces" banner they'd seen in the States. God, they were not the happy band everyone thought they were! They were all so incredibly moody over the pettiest things. This was when Kenny started insisting his name be spelt with an extra "e" – "Kenney" – and it got so bad at times I'd be relieved when they finally got on stage and the bickering would stop. I started going outside the theatre when they were on, to have a quiet cigarette and wonder what I'd done. And all the time I was trying to keep the rumours about Woody and Patti out of the papers.'

The Stones threw a leaving party for Shirley. 'Mick organized this big cake, he hadn't wanted me to leave. And it was hilarious because all the Faces were downstairs, frightened to come in because they were frightened they'd upset the Stones. But Woody was already helping himself and the other Faces slowly drifted in one at a time.'

Shirley joined the Gaff organization as a secretary, not manager, but none of the Faces except for Stewart seemed to realize it. They wanted to be looked after, which was what managers were supposed to do, and Shirley did just that and extremely well. Ergo, she had to be a manager. Simple as that. It was the looking-after that was important: 'Krissie wasn't very good at the domestic side of things. So I offered to cook for them one day, and he [Ronnie] asked if I could do a shepherd's pie, and I remember doing it in their kitchen and everyone coming back for seconds. I once saw Kris trying to cook toast. It was just as well Ronnie never ate very much. I eventually realized that he wanted something normal in his life, he was surrounded by so much that wasn't normal.'

The media rumblings about Ronnie and Patti Boyd finally died down.

Shirley needn't have worried, however. Krissie would soon give the papers something and someone really worth writing about.

Shortly before the Faces started the Christmas, 1972 UK tour, Ronnie and Krissie were invited to stay at the Guinness family's castle in Ireland by Mick and Bianca Jagger. The invitation hadn't come out of the blue, for Ronnie and Mick had become good friends over the past few years. While Keith Richards would eventually become Ronnie's true soul mate, it was Mick who'd initially taken Ronnie under his wing.

'He's a shrewd boy, Mick,' Ronnie says. 'He'd always kept one eye on what I was doing, right back from when he'd rung my mum that time. And I'd started hanging out with Mick a lot, way before I joined the Stones. When we went to Ireland he wrote and played me, "Daddy You're A Fool To Cry", which is an amazing song.'

Krissie, however, spent most of the time in Ireland alone. Mick and Ronnie had immersed themselves in their music. She found it difficult to connect with Bianca and the Guinness family. Finally, the feeling of being out of place became too much – fuelled, as she now admits, by perhaps a little too much hash. She flew back to England, metaphorically as well as physically, and went directly to Friar Park – and its owner, George Harrison. She was looking for reassurance and a little ego-boosting. Or maybe she wanted to prove something to Ronnie.

'What people don't appreciate,' Krissie says today, 'is how young we all were. And I mean really young, because none of us grew up normally and we were still very childish in lots of ways. And suddenly we had all this money and there was no one to tell us how to behave. Lots of people giving advice, but only because they wanted something.'

The affair with George Harrison lasted only a few months, yet even though Ronnie and Krissie would stay together for a few more years, in effect it signalled the end of their relationship. She'd proved that one of the most eligible men in the world found her desirable, and Ronnie was no longer the centre of her world. How could he be, when he was so rarely home?

They'd met as kids, and in many ways their relationship had never grown up. Krissie had never had a career, or any thoughts of one. She did harbour the idea of becoming a model, and definitely had the looks – but then, didn't most rock wives nurture similar dreams? Anyway, being Ronnie's old lady and part of sixties London's pop scene had been career enough in itself. Now she began to feel the first real glimmerings of discontent – and the vague suspicion that just possibly she was living in a fool's paradise.

Krissie and George's relationship never did make the media splash that Patti Boyd and Eric Clapton's affair did. In part this was a testament to Shirley Arnold's professionalism, but mainly it was because Harrison has always managed to control the prying into his private life, and of all the pop stars of the era appears to be the one who genuinely dislikes personal publicity.

Rod Stewart's fourth solo album, *Never A Dull Moment*, had come out in July 1972 and notched up another number one. When the Faces' UK Christmas tour started, the fans asked for numbers like 'You Wear It Well', another number one single, which Stewart had promoted on *Top Of The Pops* in August, and would again on Christmas Day. Once more Kenney Jones found himself in the awkward position of miming to Mickey Waller's drumming: 'I sometimes wonder what I did to upset them,' Waller says. 'But I've never been able to forgive Rod and Billy Gaff – I don't think they cared who they upset. The saddest thing was, my father had recently died and I remember my mum getting into an argument with a neighbour, after Mum had told her I was Rod Stewart's drummer. The neighbour had seen *Top Of The Pops* with Kenney pretending to drum, and called Mum a liar, which made her cry. I've never forgotten that.'

The band were never comfortable playing Stewart's solo hits, except for his cover version – and second single hit from the album – of the Jimi Hendrix classic 'Angel' (from which Waller was excluded again).

Things were becoming very confused – Ronnie Lane had sent a cardboard cut-out of himself to the *TOTP* edition promoting 'Angel', indicating he was no longer prepared to take part in the farce. For Ronnie Wood, there was no such problem: he'd played lead on the album, and had every right to mime to his own music, especially as he'd co-written most of the songs.

One might think that the rest of the band would have been as critical about Ronnie as they were about Stewart. One would be wrong. Even though he was an integral part of Stewart's solo career, his charm and disarming air of not being totally involved very much with anything – and certainly never to be blamed – deflected any anger. 'Woody was so incredibly easygoing,' says Shirley Arnold. 'Everything went completely over his head. He wouldn't have anything to do with all the jealousy, either.'

A good deal of that jealousy was directed at Ronnie himself, but it was a nice sort of jealousy, a 'I wish I was more like you' jealousy, especially when it came to his hair. As Sandy Sarjeant says: 'Ronnie had this mop of black hair that you could take a pair of garden shears to and it would still end up looking fantastic. Mac tried to copy it, but his was finer, he was always at the hair-spray, setting lotion and gel. And they all loved Ronnie's clothes – oh, God! it was a disgusting era, just look at those old films and press cuttings!'

Or as Ronnie's dad used to say to him: 'If you want to go out looking like that, son, it's up to you.'

As 1973 began, any impression that the Faces had regained some ground on their lead vocalist's meteoric rise to super stardom was purely illusory. Stewart and Ronnie had written most of the songs on *A Nod's As Good As A Wink To A Blind Horse*. Even a song Rod had recorded as a session singer for Python Lee Jackson had reached number three when re-released in 1972. He could have made it into the top ten by reciting the phone directory.

By now two distinct but interlocking musical styles had successfully emerged, based on two very different aspects of Ronnie and Rod's collaboration. There were the folky, introspective, story-telling ballads reserved for Stewart's solo outings. And then there were the boozy, bar-room rockers they shared with the Faces.

Sure, *A Nod's As Good As A Wink . . .* had fared just as well as any Stewart album, and the Faces even had a current number two with the single 'Cindy Incidentally', but it was still Rod's solo efforts that caught the world's imagination – leaving the rest of the band still ordering at the bar.

In truth, Stewart had a shit-load of what none of the others – except for Ronnie – had: star presence. They may all have shared a similar sense of humour, Ronnie and the three others more so, but none of them was charismatic enough to grace the front cover of a publication like *Rolling Stone* or even *Melody Maker*. It was all too easy to ignore the writing contribution made by Ronnie Lane – and it was ignored. His material was always of a more gentle nature; wistful warblings that were actually closer to the more nostalgic material Stewart reserved for his own solo albums.

Not just the clothes, but everything about Lane was now at odds with Stewart. His voice was frail, but blessed with sincere emotion. Stewart's voice, soaked with booze and cigarettes, had a powerful rawness that belied his very real skill. Lane's humour as expressed in his songs was of a resigned nature, while Stewart's was cocksure. The songs that Lane had first contributed to the Faces had served to diversify their ramshackle repertoire, but now seemed far too parochial, still deeply rooted in old-time music hall of the war years. They now sat uneasily in the Faces' stadium-rock, crowd-pleasing set list.

Ronnie's genius was the ability to flit easily between the two different styles – and why not, since he had a hand in both of them? Yet he'd made no secret of his unhappiness at the band's seeming inability to find that all-important cohesion: 'Some tracks on the Faces' albums didn't even sound like us.'

Rod Stewart was a little harsher: 'People must hear something I can't hear. The Faces sound so out of tune to me and so out of time! We never had the musicianship. Individually we were good, but we did not come together as a band. Don't get me wrong – it was a great band to be in.'

Lane believed that Stewart had a coldly calculated agenda that included cherry-picking his own best work and holding it for his personal career. Not only did Lane believe this, he said so loudly on the increasingly few occasions the band ever got together, gigs excepted, in the same place at the same time.

'Ronnie Lane was such a lovely man,' says Shirley Arnold, 'but he was extremely unhappy with the Faces' situation. He saw Rod's solo success as being promoted by Billy Gaff at the expense of the Faces, and it really hurt him.'

Lane started travelling separately from the band, commuting between gigs whenever possible in a hired Range Rover. When he, Mac and Kenney weren't complaining about Rod, they were doing so about Gaff.

'Billy was a nice guy,' Shirley remembers. 'He was a good manager, but they treated him badly. I remember one day Billy had a car crash and they were all ringing the hospital because they didn't believe he'd really had a crash – can you believe how gutted Billy felt? He was in pain and in traction and they were saying, "When are you going to go back to work? When are you going to be back in the office? When are you going to get us some publicity?" Then Kenney threw a moody one time, before going to the States. He rung up and said he wasn't going. I don't know what was going on in his mind, because I'd never had this with the Stones, because the Stones lived to tour. Kenney was adamant he wasn't going, and me and Billy were so exhausted by it all, I rung Rod and said, "You know what I'm going to do? I'm going to ring Woody because he's a great mediator and tell him that you've asked me to get in touch with Mickey Waller." So I did just that, and two minutes after I put the phone down to Woody, Kenney rang me and said, "Oh, hello, Shirl, I'll go on the tour now."'

Sandy Sarjeant sees it a little differently: 'Around this time all the girls had gone to New York and we were in a hotel. It was when I first got the feeling this was the beginning of the split. We'd all been out the night before, after the gig. Everyone was all hyper, we'd gone clubbing – boy, what a night! The drinking and drugs were absolutely ridiculous! I remember trying to find a chemist for Mac because he was in a real mess. All the girls were due to leave as the boys went on to LA. When I got back to the hotel Ronnie [Lane], Mac and Kenney were all sitting around feeling like shit, they were really deflated because they'd just been told by Reception that Woody and Rod had already flown to LA without them.'

It was only a matter of time before the Faces finally broke up. And even when they did, everyone blamed everyone else.

13
'Far too many brushes with Rod'

Amazingly enough, amid all the anger and bitterness, the Faces somehow managed to produce a fourth album. It had taken them the best part of a year to get it together. Media speculation was rife that at last they were going to give up that one, crucial album: their own *Sergeant Pepper* or *Pet Sounds*. With each consecutive release they had shown a gradual improvement, silencing their critics on both sides of the Atlantic. It had been a hard, uphill slog to *A Nod's As Good As A Wink* . . . and surely the next album – with so much collective experience behind them – would be the one to establish the Faces firmly at the top of the rock tree at last. Yes, *Ooh La La* would be the album to do it. Only it wasn't.

'It's a bloody disgrace,' Rod said to *Melody Maker*'s Roy Hollingworth in a controversial interview a few days after the album's release in April 1973. 'It was a bloody mess. But I shouldn't say that, should I? The public aren't gonna like me saying it's a bloody mess. Maybe I'm too critical. One of the best tracks is one I don't sing on, and that's "Ooh La La". All that fucking about to do an album like this doesn't prove anything. But I'm not going to say anything more about it. That's it.'

When Hollingworth asked if Stewart was thinking of leaving the Faces, he replied: 'Er . . . no. We're together for life. I don't think there's really anything else I could do. I just want to make good albums.'

As fence-mending, it was a case of too little, too late. Nor was *Ooh La La* as bad as Stewart painted it. It reached number one in the UK, and number twenty-one in the States. But it wasn't the seminal album the band wanted and the critics expected. Nor was it up to the standard of Stewart's solo work.

Also, there'd been far more input from the rest of the band. So while *Ooh La La* wasn't rubbish, it did emphasize one awkward truth: the Faces were essentially a live band.

Ronnie diplomatically defended the album without direct reference to

Rod's earlier comments: 'I think the work's been spread more evenly throughout the band this time. Five of us getting involved equally does help. It takes a lot off Rod's back for a start. It's certainly the closest we've ever got to our stagework. Every track stands up. I feel that with this album, more than any of the others, there are no throw-aways. But I also think some of the tracks aren't very identifiable as us.'

Ronnie obviously didn't like it very much, either – even if the track 'Ooh La La' had marked his singing début. But today he's scornful about Stewart's oft-quoted comment that it was the Faces' lack of studio discipline that lead to substandard material, and that only he and Kenney Jones took the Faces' recording sessions seriously. Stewart always complained that the two of them would be waiting to begin work while the others were still pissing it up in the pub, giving the impression that they were the only two professionals among a crowd of irresponsible drunkards. This begs the question of why he worked so much with Ronnie in the first instance, and even used one or two of the Faces as backing musicians on his solo albums.

'Rod's always telling that story,' Ronnie says wearily, 'and it's a fucking useless story. All Rod and Kenney used to do was jangle their car keys at a Faces' studio recording. They couldn't wait to get out of there. They never put their hearts into it – or maybe for one song they might have done. I used to have to bribe them to stay there most of the time. Rod was in the pub as much as we were – "old short arms and long pockets", as Ronnie Lane used to call him. He'd always make an excuse and be off to the toilet when it was his turn to buy a round. We were a heavy-drinking band – used to turn up at pubs at opening time without having had any breakfast. We used to have the greatest time with that Liverpool supporter, John Peel. He was great to go round the pub with and get totally pissed, then back into the BBC studios and go out live on air. Never having any idea about the set list or who was doing what, giving each other piggy-back rides to the stage, with Ronnie Lane always on my or Rod's back. Shame no one ever filmed any of it. Rod can say what he likes now, but he was there and very much part of it all. Matter of fact, that's how Rod, Mac and me came to write "Cindy Incidentally" – it came out of a pub session when every sentence you spoke had to mention the word "incidentally". Like, "I'll have a pint of Guinness, incidentally."'

It's worth noting that at the time of writing, Rod Stewart's new single is a cover version of that old Faces classic, 'Ooh La La', as originally written by Ronnie Wood and Ronnie Lane, and sung by Ronnie Wood.

Perhaps an interview Stewart gave back in 1970 pinpointed his real problem with the Faces' recording sessions: 'If I have to be frank, I must admit that I tend to enjoy my own recording sessions best. It's just that I'm producing them and everything is arranged around my voice.' The inescapable truth appears to be that Stewart really did only ever see the Faces as a means of promoting his solo career, as did Gaff. Justified, perhaps, on the grounds that he was destined to become one of rock's greatest superstars – but that was small comfort to Lane, McLagan and Jones, who also dreamed of producing brilliant work. Whether or not they could ever have done so is beside the point: with Rod Stewart as lead vocalist, they never had a chance to be anything other than his backing band. And this despite the fact that the Small Faces' *Ogden's Nut Gone Flake* was and is recognized as being one of the all-time classic albums.

Ronnie, too, was beginning to carve out a celebrity solo career for himself. On 2 January 1973 he'd begun rehearsing at The Wick for two concerts at the Rainbow Theatre (as the Finsbury Park Astoria was renamed) that would mark Eric Clapton's return from heroin addiction. The concert line-up included Clapton himself, Pete Townshend, Stevie Winwood, Rick Grech, Jim Capaldi and Jimmy Karstein. But none of the three original Faces. The two concerts and the resultant live album were a triumphant success. However, Ronnie was given equal billing with Clapton and the rest of the élite, which further underlined the widening gulf between him and Stewart on the one hand, and the rest of the Faces on the other.

By the time *Ooh La La* came out, the entire band was distinctly unhappy with their own performances, either on stage or in the recording studio. Two months earlier, in February, they'd even walked out of a BBC recording for Radio 1's *In Concert* series. As a somewhat shocked BBC memo states: 'Halfway through the recording, the band walked off stage and returned to their dressing rooms. They were unhappy about repeating all their old material and, in fact, some members of the band had not wanted to accept the booking until their new material was ready for a stage performance, but they had been talked round by the other group members and the Agency [Gaff]. After about twenty minutes they were persuaded to finish the recording but the result was a bit of a shambles and no one was really happy with it. Unfortunately the producer, Jeff Griffin, was in the States so the final decision had to wait until his return. He has now listened to the tape and decided against broadcasting it as it "was not as good as we would all have wished".'

The memo went on to say that under the circumstances the BBC would not be paying a fee, but would pay £20 to cover the Faces' expenses. It stated also that Jeff Griffin wanted to re-book the group as soon as their new material was ready; but added that BBC management should be 'put in the picture' and the event should be duly noted in case anything similar ever occurred again.

Stewart's comments to the media had done nothing to soothe the dissatisfaction felt by the rest of the band over their artistic direction. Jones in particularly was far more forceful in his response than Ronnie.

'I didn't fucking understand Rod saying that,' Jones said recently. 'How could it have been a fucking bad album if it got to number one?'

Listening to Stewart's solo albums provides another clue to the problem. His work was always far more polished and, as he himself admitted, centred around the subtle use of his voice, which had as much in common with Sinatra's approach to singing as it had with basic rock 'n' roll. By contrast, the Faces cherished their raw, more funky and dangerous attitude to recording; one that echoed their stage act, when anything could happen, and often did.

In fact, two tracks on *Ooh La La*, 'Flags And Banners' and 'Glad And Sorry', had to be sung by Lane, and then Lane plus Ronnie, because, although they had originally been written for him, Stewart had simply refused to sing them. 'The album began with a bang, then lapsed into monthly obscurity,' Lane complained. 'We'd do a song, then a month later Rod would hate it and refuse to sing it. That's why me and Woody end up singing so much on *Ooh La La*. Thing was, those songs were in the wrong key because they'd been written for Rod.'

One of the tracks that never made it on to the album – courtesy of the lead vocalist – was 'It's Only Rock And Roll (But I Like It)', conceived by Ronnie and based on one of his own favourite sayings. In the event he recorded this track at his own studio with Jones and McLagan plus Mick Jagger (lead vocals), Willie Weeks (bass), and David Bowie (backing vocals and handclaps). Jagger wanted to release the song under the Rolling Stones banner, and offered Ronnie a Jagger/Richards composition called 'Black Limousine' – a somewhat bizarre exchange that Ronnie immediately accepted. And that is why one of the world's greatest rock anthems is credited to the wrong people.

'The song pretty much stayed the same as we'd done at The Wick,' Ronnie explains. 'They kept Kenney's drums because Charlie said he wouldn't have done it any different. Mick released it as the next Stones single and it was the title of their next album. So I was on a Stones album before I was even a Stone.'

Unfortunately, Billy Gaff had remained neutral throughout the falling-out, not even bothering to call a meeting to try to resolve the group's personal differences. Somewhat strange behaviour from a manager whose band had just been rubbished by their lead singer. Considering how much damage Stewart's remarks could have done to record sales, Gaff's failure to even mildly reprimand him gave the impression that he was firmly on his side. And that if there was anything wrong with the album, Stewart was definitely not to blame.

Did Gaff see Stewart's involvement with the Faces as an irritable intrusion in a far bigger game plan? Had Gaff believed for some time, in fact, that the band was merely a necessary, but always only temporary phase in the career of Rod Stewart, superstar? 'To me, Rod Stewart will always be a great performer,' he told *NME*. 'I'm one hundred per cent sure he'll be singing in twenty years' time, simply because he can manage any sort of material.'

Ronnie for one could see the writing on the wall. All of the bands he'd ever been involved with had broken up, and he knew the signs better than anyone. He still clung to his teenage dream of one day becoming a Rolling Stone – but Mick Taylor still had that job, and even though Jagger had become a close friend, it was still just a dream. In the past Ronnie had always been able to find a musical home, but he was astute enough to realize that now it would prove far more difficult. To begin with there were only a limited number of bands he could join, those whose musical roots echoed his own. More importantly, he was now so high-profile that most bands would have seen him as a threat. (By 1973 the same fate had befallen Jeff Beck and Eric Clapton.) Naturally, his thoughts turned towards going it alone, but he wasn't about to rush into anything yet. The Faces still provided him with a musical base, and a pretty good income, so he simply announced that he 'had my own album to do' – a common enough practice and one not always taken too seriously by the industry.

Ronnie Lane was far less calculating. The situation had already gone too far and the crisis finally blew up on 3 May in Providence, Long Island, during the band's eighth American tour – their eighth in under three years.

They had just come off stage when Stewart, dressed in satin trousers, a feather boa and running mascara, looked at Lane, who was wearing a three-piece suit, like a rag-and-bone man in his Sunday best, and sneered: 'What are you, a fucking spiv or a Teddy boy?'

'I'd rather be a fucking Teddy boy,' Lane snapped back, 'than a prostitute who's going through the change of life.' And with that he took a swing at the band's star performer.

Shirley Arnold watched in horror. 'It was very sad. It developed into a full-scale punch-up in the dressing room, with lots of shouting going on. Pete Buckland, one of the roadies, had to pull Ronnie Lane off Rod. Woody was there too, but I can't remember what he was doing. (If past history was anything to go by, Woody had sensibly left them to it.) The next day we had to take a small plane to the gig and Ronnie Lane said he wasn't going, so we took off without him. I rang him later and he told me he was leaving, wanted me to go and work for him. But I couldn't leave the others, and managed to persuade him to rejoin the tour – which he did, hiring a car and driving himself to the next gig. Then he told Billy Gaff he'd finish the tour and the forthcoming London dates but that was it, he was definitely leaving.'

Sandy Sarjeant blames it on competing egos: 'Those were terrible times. There was no loyalty any more. They were all acting like superstars. With hindsight, you can understand how difficult it was for them and how egotistical it all got. They looked like the people we knew. Ian [McLagan] still looked like my husband, but he started acting like God. One morning at home he demanded to know why I hadn't cut his bread up into soldiers to dip into his boiled egg. That was the last straw. I packed my bags and went.'

Lane was as good as his word, making his final appearances at the Sundown in Edmonton, North London, where he was greeted by banners saying: 'Goodbye Ronnie, We Love You'. When the band had finished the last song, Stewart told the crowd: 'We're off down the pub.'

'Too late,' Lane quipped, 'they're shut.'

Which pretty well summed up their relationship.

It would be ten years before the two men could bring themselves to speak to each other again. Ironically, though, the episode helped Lane renew his friendship with Steve Marriott. 'I went over to see Steve,' Lane remembered in 1990, a few yeas before he died from multiple sclerosis. 'I'd always missed him, because we'd been so close once. I hadn't been able to give him any help when he'd left the Small Faces, because I'd never left a band before, but then I understand how he must have felt. I suppose I'd have been better off talking to Woody!'

'I knew that was the end of the Faces,' Ronnie said very recently, 'because you couldn't replace Ronnie Lane – he was the heart and the soul of the band. He'd had one too many brushes with Rod for me not to understand why he'd left. But it was very sad and sobering to us rowdy rock and rollers what eventually happened to him. By the way – how's Rod's version of *Ooh La La* doing? Because Rod and I want to give the money to Ronnie's family.'

*

The band needed a new bass player, and one that wouldn't mind joining a sinking ship. They found him playing for a band that had disintegrated even faster than the Faces.

Tetsuo Yamauchi was the first Japanese-born musician to make a mark on the English pop music scene. He'd joined Free as a replacement for Andy Fraser, endearing himself to fans less for his playing – willing, but musically questionable at best – than for his undoubted ability to drink most other people under the table: a true R&B rock 'n' roller in spirit if not ability. Joining the Faces was like a dream come true for Yamauchi – one of the greatest live bands in the world, and people who always got their round in.

Unfortunately, within a matter of weeks Yamauchi had to be tied to an amplifier to stop him falling over on stage. To this day, Ronnie can't remember why he was hired in the first place. Perhaps it was because they had a Far Eastern tour coming up in January 1974. 'The other thing: Tetsuo must have lied about his age. Years later, we were trying to get the band back together for some function or other, and Kenney looked him up and reckoned he resembled the master kung fu instructor out of the movies! He reckoned Tetsuo had to be at least a hundred. He wasn't even mine and Rod's original choice – we'd wanted Phil Chen, but he was too busy. It was only because the Union made such a fuss that we kept him.'

Yamauchi joined the Faces at the beginning of August. On the 18th he was banned by the Musicians' Union and the British government on the grounds that he was depriving a British musician of a job. However, his application to join the Union was accepted a month later.

The Faces left for their first Far Eastern tour in January 1974. Whatever musical reservations they may have had about Yamauchi were compensated for by the welcome waiting in his homeland – although Stewart didn't see it that way, as Shirley Arnold remembers only too well: 'Rod had the right hump when we flew into Tokyo, there was this huge crowd all screaming for Tetsuo. I think Rod really wanted the Faces to split up then, he just didn't want to be the one to do it. He felt he'd proved he was the big star – but here were all these fans mobbing Tetsuo and ignoring Rod. He was so pissed off that when we got back to the hotel Rod locked himself in his room and sent a message down saying he wasn't going to play the show. He made out he had laryngitis, but everyone knew it was because of Tetsuo. Cancelling the show caused a riot in the stadium, and then there was another phone call from Rod, saying he was feeling better and could he have a meal. Billy [Gaff] said, "No, stay in your room, they're tearing the stadium to pieces and it's getting us great publicity." Everyone was pissed off with Rod, except for Ronnie, who once again stayed out of it. That band had been breaking up for five years.'

In addition to the Japanese dates, the band also managed to fit in a first Australasian tour. By playing in Sydney, three of them were revisiting the scene of an earlier fracas, in 1968, which had led to the Small Faces being deported from the country. Incredibly, no one in the Immigration authority connected the two events.

To coincide with their Australian trip, a live album, *Coast To Coast Overture for Beginners*, recorded on their recent American tour, was released by Mercury Records. This was the subject of a strange deal orchestrated by Gaff and Stewart whereby Warner Brothers simultaneously issued the same album, but only on cassette. Naturally enough, this led Warner Brothers to issue an injunction against Mercury, prohibiting Stewart from delivering any new material to his own label. The lawyers had a lucrative few months, and the situation reverted to normal – or what passed for normal where the Faces were concerned.

With no new material available, the Faces put out an EP in June, featuring both 'Cindy Incidentally' and 'Stay With Me' again, plus 'Pool Hall Richard' (which had been released the previous December and reached number eight). The record-buying public saw this as one filler too far, and stayed away in droves. The EP failed to chart.

Back in May 1974, the *NME* had floated a rumour that Stewart had already decided to leave the Faces, and that Ronnie Wood was to form a new group to back him. The reality couldn't have been further from the truth. Yes, Rod was planning to leave – but he was going to take not Ronnie, but Kenney Jones with him. However, at the last moment Jones would renege out of loyalty to McLagan, who wouldn't have gone to the corner with Stewart, and hauled his drums off the plane when Stewart left for tax exile in America.

McLagan was plan-less, but didn't care as long as Stewart wasn't involved. At the same time he was having problems with his wife, the long-suffering Sandy, who would eventually walk out, leaving him free to become dangerously involved with Kim Moon, wife of Keith.

By now Ronnie was planning his own solo career, while dreaming of Rolling Stonehood. Domestically, too, it was soon to be all change for him, for Krissie was to discover a new love in her life who just happened to be one of Ronnie's oldest acquaintances.

14
'I drew the short straw on that one . . .'

Krissie Wood had first met Jimmy Page in his Yardbirds days. But that was way back in rock history and now she was married to the Faces' lead guitarist while Jimmy was playing lead for arguably the biggest-grossing hard rock band of the time. Ironically, Ronnie could have been playing bass with Led Zeppelin, but he'd turned down the offer in order to tour America one more time with Jeff Beck.

Krissie, Ronnie and Jimmy met up at a party in Los Angeles on 19 October 1973 during the Faces' ninth American tour. Observers noted an instant attraction between her and the latest rock demi-god – an attraction that Krissie later ascribed to the fact that Jimmy was one of the most interesting men she'd ever met. As luck would have it, both the Faces and Page were booked on the same flight home from New York.

'I can't remember whether he came and sat next to us, or we went up to him,' Krissie says now. 'But I do remember that Ronnie must have felt very threatened, because he sat between Jimmy and me all the time we were talking about stuff that didn't really interest him. I started getting embarrassed because Ronnie was making an issue out of nothing, because I didn't fancy Jimmy and I didn't think he fancied me, but Ronnie obviously picked up and felt very threatened by our energy and the fact that Jimmy and I communicated. And we did, we really could talk about things other than rock and roll.'

Ronnie wasn't the only one to be concerned.

'It was obvious he sensed something was up,' Kenney Jones said much later. 'So did we – especially the wives, they were either giggling or being really sarky. But they always thought Krissie was a bit stuck-up, anyway. I think they were jealous, too, because Jimmy had this reputation for being, well, a bit dangerous.'

It was Aleister Crowley's fault. Or more precisely, Page's openly admitted fascination with the man once known as 'The Great Beast'.

Crowley was at one time a member of the occult society known as the Golden Dawn that had included the poet W. B. Yeats among its flock, back at the turn of the century; founder of the Abbey of Thelema in Sicily – from where he was deported following an unexplained death and several cases of insanity among his followers, not to mention the orgies; a noted mountaineer and scholar; and writer of embarrassingly bad pornography. Crowley had been given the title 'The Wickedest Man In The World' by a *Daily Express* journalist back in the thirties, and had been used by Somerset Maugham as the model for the central character in his novel *The Magician*.

Whether or not Crowley was a Satanist is debatable. He certainly saw himself as a magician and heir to an esoteric tradition that pre-dated Christianity. Magic was rediscovered by the rock scene and hippies in the sixties. They particularly liked Crowley's well-known saying 'Do What Thou Wilt Shall Be The Whole Of The Law', but many tended to get bogged down in his 'magickal' writings; even to begin to understand these called for a knowledge of Latin, Greek, Hebrew and comparative religions.

Page's interest in the subject would lead to a collaboration with Kenneth Anger, ageing Hollywood bad boy and rumoured Satanist, on a film called *Lucifer Rising*. This ended badly when Anger pulled out, claiming that Page's music was far too sombre and depressing. The guitarist had also developed a reputation for being sexually adventurous, and there was much dark talk about whips and chains. What can be said about Page is that he was, and still is, highly intelligent and has a wide-range of interests. That old-fashioned expression 'a cultivated man' describes him very well. This was the superstar whom Krissie found so deeply fascinating on the flight from New York to London, much to Ronnie's obvious concern – especially as Page had recently split up with his long-time girlfriend, Charlotte.

The three of them had gone back to The Wick after the plane had landed at Heathrow, and there Krissie and Page continued communicating. But that was as far as it went and Krissie had gone to bed alone, leaving the two men to stay up for the rest of the night. The next day Page left, having invited Ronnie and Krissie to visit him any time.

Some months later, in the summer of 1974, Ronnie and Krissie took Page up on his invitation and decided to drop in on the guitarist at his country home at Plumpton Place, in Sussex.

'Actually, we were looking for coke,' Krissie now admits, 'and we knew Jimmy would have some. His home was beautiful – a moated castle surrounded by an orchard, and with a drawbridge. I walked over the drawbridge and I went to the left, and I was laughing all the time, saying,

"Come on, Ronnie, I know the way", and he was following me. I just knew, somehow, where the back door was, and stranger than that I knew how to open it. There was a set of wooden handles that you pulled, and I knew just how to do that. I pushed the door back and it opened and there was Basil, Jimmy's black cat, which would have normally clawed anyone but just stared at us as if it knew us. It freaked Ronnie out, who was saying, "Fucking hell, Kris, let's go." But I had to go on. It was dark inside, but I instinctively knew where the torch was and how to find the stairs. I even knew how to find Jimmy's bedroom, which was the last straw for Ronnie – he found the whole thing too spooky. I turned the light on and we saw Jimmy was in bed asleep with Charlotte, and I said, "Oh look, Ron, Jimmy's back with Charlotte", and I was really happy for them. Then we saw that Jimmy had a gun on his bedside table, and Ronnie said, "Fucking hell, Kris, he could have shot us!"'

To this day, Krissie professes wide-eyed amazement at how she was able to find her way around. Yet one assumes she was nowhere as amazed as Ronnie, who, despite being fairly superstitious – 'One of the reasons I liked The Wick so much was because no one had died there that I knew of' – had to have wondered initially whether Krissie had actually been to Page's bedroom before. Yet she swore that she hadn't. Maybe Page really was as accomplished a magician as he was a musician. Ronnie believed his wife.

If Page was annoyed to wake up to find a beaming Krissie and a puzzled-looking Ronnie at the foot of his bed, he didn't show it. Well, he certainly didn't shoot them. And pretty soon a mini-party was in progress downstairs, where they were joined by Jimmy's house guest, Gerry Beckley from the band America.

'You know how some parties are,' Krissie remembers. 'I fell asleep on the floor, and the next thing I knew it was morning and someone was covering me up with a fur coat. I thought it was Ronnie and turned round and kissed him, then opened my eyes and saw it was Jimmy. At that point Charlotte walked in and I think no one knew what to do. I'd thought it was Ronnie, but Jimmy obviously knew I wasn't Charlotte. Anyway, I stood up and looked out of the window, I mean I was only wearing dungarees, I wasn't dressed to kill or anything, and it was a really lovely day, so I suggested we all go out for a walk. And Charlotte said, "No, I don't want to go for a walk." She was pissed off, but Jimmy said he did. I can't remember where Ronnie was, he was off still partying with Gerry, I suppose, or in the loo. The castle was surrounded by three lakes and we walked for miles across the meadows and streams until we came to a water-mill and we just fell asleep there. When I woke up it was night-time, pouring with rain, and I was in Jimmy's arms. He was keeping me warm; I mean, nothing had happened. And I said, "Jimmy, listen, we're in trouble, we're on the missing list, this is serious." We could see the lights of the house in the distance and Jimmy said, "Don't worry, I'll get us back", and he led me across the lake because he had these stones just below the surface, which gave the impression he was walking on water. But it was raining so hard we had to stop at the keeper's cottage – I was soaked through. And I was sitting there trying to warm up with my feet in a bowl of hot water, and suddenly I heard a car coming and it was Ronnie, Charlotte and Gerry, really pissed off, and they drove off to London before I could explain what had happened, which was absolutely nothing. So I just stayed with Jimmy. I never left. All I had was the clothes I stood up in. I had nothing. Charlotte went back to The Wick with Ronnie.'

Outwardly everyone concerned tried to pretend they were happy with the new arrangement. However, the affair with Charlotte proved to be short-lived, and one Ronnie hadn't particularly needed, as he later confided to Zeppelin road manager, Richard Cole: 'I drew the short straw on that one. I got the worst end of the deal.'

Before Krissie went to stay with Jimmy Page, she had done one thing for Ronnie that would eventually help to change his life. 'It was when I'd begun recording my album in the basement,' Ronnie explains. 'Krissie had gone to the Speakeasy one night and she'd noticed Keith Richards was with a crowd of people he obviously didn't want to be with. So she interrupted them and asked Keith if he wanted to come back and hear what I was doing in the studio. Keith was grateful for the get-out, came to The Wick and fucking stayed for five months in the cottage that I'd just bought back off Ronnie Lane so he could buy that farm in Wales. And me and Keith have been best mates ever since, give or take the odd punch-up.'

The first time Art Wood saw his younger brother and Keith together, he thought they were like book-ends.

This is not a time in his personal life that Ronnie likes to talk about, other than saying it was 'fucking horrible'. Krissie's brief affair with George Harrison had been one thing. Going to visit Jimmy Page with Ronnie and then staying on, was quite another. The trouble was, rock stars were supposed to behave with a certain insouciance as regards conventional morality. Someone who's spent several years trashing hotel rooms; graduating from speed to cocaine; and taking advantage of groupies whenever the mood took him – 'a blow-job isn't like you're really being unfaithful' – could hardly complain when his wife took it into her mind to go off and do her own thing. Anyway, as Shirley Arnold pointed out, Ronnie Wood doesn't have a malicious bone in his body – nor even a slightly cross one – so that, unlike the average person in roughly similar circumstances, he couldn't even enjoy the relief of a good old bitch and moan, and certainly not in public.

He'd been very hurt by Stewart's scarcely hidden conviction that the Faces were no more than a backing band for his admittedly prodigious talent, a view which had led to many rows and great uncertainty among the members. For the Faces were family, and Ronnie had always needed the comfort of a family atmosphere to best flourish: it was how he'd grown up as a child. But he'd only shared those feelings with his immediate family and a few very close friends, and he wasn't about to go even semi-public with any anger or resentment or hurt that he felt over Krissie.

Besides, rock stars are often well shielded from the reality of their own emotions: groupies and hangers-on provide a twenty-four-hour ego massage; booze, acid and cocaine dull the pain; and when all else fails, you can go shopping. The net result is maybe twenty minutes of naked reality every forty-eight hours – which sobering angst Ronnie could always blot out with his music. Even so, there are those few seconds on waking when you realize that the body you've been used to cuddling is no longer there, and if there is a replacement, she doesn't react in quite the same way. Ronnie's solution was to start staying up for days on end, generously tutored by Keith, who still holds the all-time record – and was hardly likely to have been teaching Ronnie yoga.

'I can't do the nine-day-and-night stints any more,' Keith recently admitted. 'About three days is all I can manage.' Later he capped that idiosyncratic remark with the statement that the older you get, the older you want to get.

For her part, Krissie has no doubt why she spent a year with Jimmy Page. 'It was just something I needed to do,' she says today, and for a moment you're looking at the sixteen-year-old who first attracted Ronnie's attention. 'I'd been terribly lonely with all the touring Ronnie had done, and Jimmy could teach me about all sorts of things, especially to do with the countryside. But no, never anything to do with the occult – I mean, he owned Aleister Crowley's cloak and his stick, but I never saw anything like that going on. If it was, he kept it from me. I just needed some time to grow, and someone to help me do it, and Jimmy was perfect. Once I got away, I realized I couldn't live Ronnie's lifestyle any more. So I put my true feelings on hold for a while. Jimmy always said I was just infatuated with him [Page] and in hindsight he was probably right. George and Jimmy were both incredibly calming and sensitive men

Quiet Melon: Kenney, Art, Kim, Rod, Ian and Ron

The Jeff Beck Group: Rod, Aynsley Dunbar, Ron, Jeff Beck

Art, Ron, Shirley Arnold and Doreen Wood

Nervous Faces at Shirley's leaving do in 1972

Above: Ron and pregnant Krissie

Right: Ron and Chuch

Below: Waiting for the Man: Krissie, Ron and Keith wait for their connection

Jo Wood

The bookends

Rolling his own in 1994

Ron and Keith – shiatsu. 'You'll feel worse…'

An unusually cold Miami

Ron and Kim Gardner at Art Wood's 60th birthday party

Ted, Jo and Ron

Art and Ron

Ron's 'Wild West' 50th birthday party

Noel, Ron and Meg

Jess and Dad

Honest Ron

– they could both be crazy, but not like Ronnie. George had always known Ronnie was the only one – but he let people find their own way.'

Meanwhile Ronnie still had his own album to do, and threw himself heart and soul into his work. During the rest of 1974 Keith helped him pursue his solo career, appearing with him on 13 and 14 July at the Kilburn Empire, North London, in a line-up that included Willie Weeks (bass), Ian McLagan (keyboards) and Andy Newmark (drums). It was clear, even at that early stage, that Ronnie was not destined for solo stardom. His voice had the same qualities as Lane's or Harrison's – slightly fragile, expressive, quintessentially English – and these lend themselves more to folk than rock. More importantly, he is a man whose talent is most evident when someone else is fronting a band. He's far too easygoing to be a successful leader – all that Ronnie's ever really wanted is the security of a group in which his abilities can properly flourish.

And talking of groups, the Faces were still gamely carrying on, rather like a wounded animal desperately looking for someone to put it out of its misery – only to find itself surrounded by Animal Rights campaigners, none of whom can bring themselves to do the merciful thing. They'd topped the bill at the Buxton Festival on 6 July, when one of the supporting bands had been Steve Marriott's Humble Pie.

By now the Faces' record output had equalled Rod Stewart's: four albums apiece, not counting Stewart's greatest hits compilation, *Sing It Again, Rod*, another number one when released in August 1973, or the Faces' live outing, *Coast to Coast Overture And Beginners*. Stewart had already recorded most of the tracks for his fifth LP, using his usual studio band; but the legal problems between Warner Brothers and Mercury Records flared up again, with both claiming to hold the only binding contract with him. This fight over the singer's lissom body would delay the LP for a further five months.

Meanwhile the Faces had no real plans to follow up *Ooh La La*; nineteen seventy-four looked like being a barren year for new product from either Stewart or the Faces. Nevertheless, Stewart continued to record and Ronnie went on working on his own album. Naturally enough, the news that two solo projects were underway only served to fuel rumours that the Faces were about to split. But all of this passed Ronnie by, shut away as he was in his basement at The Wick with Keith and assorted musical cronies.

'Keith just sort of stayed and stayed [at the bottom of the garden], Willie Weeks and Andy Newmark were supposed to be in a hotel but ended up staying at The Wick as well. George Harrison came by and we did "Far East Man". At times, the house was like a fucking hotel,' Ronnie laughs. 'The album cost around £40,000 and that was just the booze. I was going to set up a bar and charge for drinks for all the people that just dropped in. Everyone had roadies and friends with them. Then the neighbours got a bit annoyed at the constant rehearsals. So I don't think you can say it was well organized. Fun, but definitely lacking on the organization front.'

Mickey Waller remembers one instance that seems to have been fairly typical: 'Ronnie and Keith wanted a drummer for one track they were doing, and they just came and got me from a studio I was working in. We went to a pub, where Ronnie tried to explain the song, and took several hours, then got back to The Wick around midnight to do it. Ronnie and Keith were so stoned that they played the same riff for the next six hours! I finally put down my sticks because I was so tired, and said, "This is bloody ridiculous! I'm going home!" And Keith looked up and said, "That's the trouble with you, Mickey, no stamina." I just got up and left, just as Ronnie was saying happily, "Yeah, Keith, this is a different class, isn't it?"'

Ronnie now thinks that his own album had far more effect on the rumours of a split than anything Stewart did, if only because Stewart already had an established solo career. But, a little disingenuously, he points out: 'Rod did sing on my album, and it was obvious to me that any one of us could have made a solo album at any time. Even Kenney did a single eventually, and he never used any of the Faces.'

The single was called 'Ready Or Not'. Unfortunately, Kenney wasn't. It sank without trace.

'I just couldn't resist trying to do my own album,' Ronnie continues. 'But I was worried that people would think, What's so special about him? Is he on an ego trip, a name-droppery ego trip?'

By 'people' one assumes Ronnie means the industry. As far as the record-buying public was concerned, the more names a musician could drop, the better.

As the year wore on, Ronnie toyed with the idea of playing more gigs with his studio band (including Keith), while denying any prospect of the Faces splitting: 'We're rather like the Who in so much as we don't see much of each other when we're not working. I think that's what keeps us together, it's the secret to staying successful.'

In fact, the secret to staying successful as a world-class band, in addition to being a great live act – which they were – is an agreed musical direction, a leader and at least one seminal record. One out of four wasn't enough, and Ronnie must have known it. Which is probably why his insistence on the Faces' solidarity sounded so weak.

I've Got My Own Album To Do was released in September 1974 by Warner Brothers, who organized the obligatory party at which Ronnie saw someone else he'd rather lost touch with over the past few months. Krissie showed up on Jimmy Page's arm, but they both left rather quietly and quickly. No fights, no fuss, no tantrums but as Krissie explains: 'Jimmy was so worried about what Ronnie thought. He didn't want to upset Ronnie, he really loved him.'

So why show up in the first place? Perhaps the answer lies in the rest of Krissie's explanation: 'But the situation had gone on for so long, I was going to marry Jimmy, and we had the divorce papers drawn up and everything.'

It was that kind of era, and those kind of people. Just as long as you were sincere and meant well, you could do and say almost anything, and if anyone criticized you they were a bad person. Worse, they were uncool. In time, that sincerity would become political correctness.

Despite Ronnie's stellar line-up, *I've Got My Own Album To Do* had sunk without trace by the time Stewart's new album, *Smiler*, saw the light of day in October 1974. Sure enough, *Smiler* shot to number one in the UK, totally overshadowing Ronnie and Jones's efforts, although in the US it made a less impressive number sixteen. There was clearly only one star in the Faces good enough to achieve solo success. Which was why Mac quite wisely decided that any solo effort by him would not be a good career move.

But then came a sold-out winter tour around the UK which put the Faces back on the map, so renewing the group's confidence enough for them to begin developing new material. This would include what is perhaps their finest single, co-written by Wood and Stewart: 'You Can Make Me Dance, Sing Or Anything'. 'It was a great single,' Ronnie remembers happily. 'It was a good step towards how we were feeling. It started off as about four different riffs and we sewed them all together with the lyrics we'd rehearsed at The Wick. But the guitar part didn't come together until the last minute – I pretended I was Barry White's guitar player.'

But once again, Stewart poured scorn on the single, saying: 'I don't think it's our best release, I don't think it's our best single. I think "Pool Hall Richard" was.' Interestingly, the song was credited to all of the Faces, in an attempt to promote a feeling of solidarity within the band.

Presumably, solidarity as in 'we're all equal' was the very last thing Rod Stewart wanted.

The British tour had been the largest-grossing one by any band in 1974, netting the Faces over £100,000 in only twenty-four days; taking into account inflation and money skimmed off the top, the equivalent of over £1.5 million today. This encouraged the band to forgo the pleasures of an English winter, so they headed off for another tour of Australia, New Zealand and Japan ... just as the rumours about Ronnie joining the Stones began to surface.

Mick Taylor – a genuinely gentle man – had been with the Stones for a little under four years. He was a gifted guitarist, but had never managed to connect personally with the rest of the group. Nor could he cope very well with the pressures of touring, while Stones fans were becoming divided into two main camps: Stones plus Brian Jones, or Stones plus Mick Taylor in terms of the band's best material. It was bad enough to be haunted by the memory of a dead psychotic – 'Brian was a lovely bunch of blokes,' as Keith used to say – but even worse to be seen as the vehicle for a lead guitarist who'd come late to the party – especially one who'd discovered heroin, and had never quite learned how to handle his habit, or had gone for a twice-yearly blood change to a discrete little clinic in Switzerland. Publicly, Taylor was making noises about wanting to return to playing more classical blues – an excuse similar to Jeff Beck's when he'd left the Yardbirds. Privately, he was cracking up and there was nothing anyone could do to help. It takes a very strong type of character to remain even relatively sane as a Rolling Stone. Taylor didn't have it. He wasn't even a real Rolling Stone either, inasmuch as he was still on a wage.

Ronnie was the obvious replacement for Taylor, if only because Keith was living at the bottom of his garden and, as Ronnie claimed at the time, the two men had become inseparable. Even so, he made a point of adding: 'Despite all the rumours I will not be joining the Rolling Stones – we've never even talked about it. I suppose in another time or era I would join the Stones. Aesthetically I'd join because my roots and influences are there. But it's like I said – another time, another era. It just couldn't happen while I'm with the Faces, the Stones know that and that's why they wouldn't ask me.'

Actually, they had already.

'Mick sort of sidled up to me at this party,' Ronnie now admits, 'and said, "What if Mick Taylor left, do you think you'd be interested in, you know, helping out?" But I said no, I couldn't do anything to upset the Faces, to make them break up. And Mick's going, "No, no, no, no, I wouldn't want to break up the Faces." And I'm thinking, "Fucking right I'd join!" '

In February 1975 the Faces were on tour once again in the States, where the debauchery would reach all-time records, even by the band's demanding standards. Strangely – or not, given Tom Wolfe's acid comments about radical chic – they still managed to attract America's most socially prominent, and the ladies-who-lunch. But only Stewart took the celebrity circus at all seriously. He discovered that George Harrison had received a First Family audience on his recent US tour, President Ford and all. So it seemed only natural to invite the Ford daughters to the Washington DC gig.

The best-laid schemes of mice and social climbers gang oft a-gley. Only Susan Ford showed up with a few friends – no President, no First Lady, and Harrison's tour hadn't even been all that successful, either. Still, Billy Gaff and the Faces press officer, Tony Toon, made the most of it and ensured that the press got their shots of Susan chatting to the band backstage. Immediately afterwards, a put-out Stewart flew off to New York for a party being thrown by Led Zeppelin. Ronnie and the rest stayed behind, Ronnie because he knew that Krissie was accompanying Jimmy Page. And oh! how they laughed when they discovered that Stewart had just been sent an invitation, at his Washington hotel, to join Gerald Ford and his family for dinner at the White House, as a thank you for being so kind to Susan. For by now Stewart was in New York, and the fog was rolling in. All civilian flights were grounded. No private jet or helicopter would attempt the journey. Somehow, no one seems to have thought of the train.

To make it even better, or worse, depending on who you were, a rumour planted by Tony Toon surfaced in the British press that Stewart was now dating Susan Ford, causing Stewart to send a bouquet of red roses to the White House by way of apology. Unfortunately, the gesture merely looked crass.

The band reunited in New York for a sold-out show at Madison Square Garden. Jones remembers that gig particularly well: 'Ronnie called me into his room backstage after the gig, and there was blood everywhere. His nose had fucking come away at the top with all the coke he'd been doing. And he made this looking-down-nose face, and said, "Fuck me, Kenney, I can see the sink from here!" Anyway, we cleaned him up and stuck his nose back on with gaffer tape, then put on this huge pair of dark glasses to hide the join. But he wasn't worried, only said, "I'll just get one of those things that Stephen Stills has got, he's had a couple." '

So Ronnie became the latest in a long line of rock stars to have a plastic septum inserted in his nose.

Stewart later admitted that this led to some members of the band using pessaries. They'd empty out what was already there, usually a cold cure, and replace it with cocaine since Ronnie's wasn't the only nose that needed treatment. Besides, they mistakenly believed it would do less physical damage that way. No one told them that the lower intestine was far more fragile than the inside of one's nose. Thankfully, plastic-nose surgery improved radically, allowing a return to the old, preferred method before any rock stars' guts fell out.

At the end of the tour the promoters, Pacific Productions, threw a lavish party for the Faces at a Hollywood eaterie called the Greenhouse, where the band rubbed shoulders with the music and film-world's élite, including Paul and Linda McCartney, Cher and Greg Allman, Joni Mitchell, Jon Lord, Ryan O'Neal, Tina Sinatra, Bob Dylan, the odd Beach Boy and even Kim Gardner, who had taken up US residency after the failure of Badger, his last musical venture. And Stewart unveiled his latest blonde babe, Britt Ekland.

Billy Gaff announced that the tour had gone so well that it would stretch on throughout the rest of the year, but would allow the band a break from June to July, before once again visiting Australia and Japan. That break would allow Stewart to record another album and the band to spend time at home. There would also be the possibility of a short UK tour, including five dates at Wembley's Empire Pool, and even a new Faces album. The old camaraderie seemed to be back in full force.

It all sounded too good to be true. It was.

No sooner had the band returned to the UK, plus Britt Ekland, than Stewart flew back to the West Coast – again, plus Ekland – for what he described as a working holiday, otherwise known as his next solo album, *Atlantic Crossing*. For the first time, Ronnie wasn't going to feature, either as co-songwriter or session musician. Not because he didn't want to, but because he simply hadn't been asked. Nor had any of the others – their places had been taken by Booker T and the MGs plus guitarist Jesse Ed Davis and the Memphis Horns. Aretha Franklin's producer, Tom Dowdg would replace Glyn Johns.

Not that Ronnie was worried, for he had his eye on a temporary job abroad and one that paid far better. On 15 April 1975 it was announced that Ronnie Wood would be joining the Rolling Stones in June as a replacement for Mick Taylor for the Stones' American tour. It had all happened very quickly.

'I was at a party for Eric Clapton at Robert Stigwood's house,' Ronnie explains, 'when Mick Taylor told Mick Jagger that he was definitely leaving, told him right in the middle of this do, and Mick was shocked, he wasn't happy, and came up to me and said, "Mick Taylor's just told me he's leaving and there's a whole tour lined up." But I still said, "Well, I don't want to break up the Faces, but give me a call if you get stuck, keep in touch." The Stones had everyone wanting to join, Steve Marriott, even Wayne Perkins. Clapton auditioned too, but he didn't work out although he still says, "I could have had your job", but I always say "No you couldn't, you need a personality." The Stones were holding auditions for the band in Germany and I got a call from Mick to come out. I went and they'd rented a load of rooms in the Munich Hilton. Jeff Beck was in a room next to me – just don't mention his big, pussy spots.'

The announcement that Ronnie was joining the Rolling Stones was read with great interest by the Metropolitan Police's Drugs Squad. The accompanying press articles also mentioned that Keith Richards was a frequent house guest at Ronnie's home, and the Drugs Squad had been wondering where Keith had vanished to for some time. In fact, since returning from a year's tax exile at his home in France, after the by now obligatory drug bust, he had moved back into Cheyne Walk, Chelsea, with Anita Pallenberg. The couple had been welcomed home by another bust in June 1973, and arrested for possession of cannabis, heroin and Mandrax. Bail had been set at £500 and a court date set for 31 July. They had sought sanctuary at Keith's Sussex retreat, Redlands, which then inconveniently caught fire, delaying the trial until December 1973, when Keith was found guilty and fined £200. All of this had made Keith understandably nervous about remaining in any one place for too great a length of time. The Wick Cottage offered a convenient bolt-hole. Besides, when he was working – as he had been on Ronnie's first solo album – he liked to shut himself away from the outside world.

The Drugs Squad, still smarting over what they'd considered the ludicrously light fine imposed on Richards, had been seeking him here and seeking him there. He'd been showing up infrequently at Cheyne Walk, but now they had another address for him. Moreover, it was the home of another probable drug user called Ronnie Wood. Why, he even looked like Richards and had just joined that well-known group of criminals, the Rolling Stones. A bust at The Wick was surely long overdue, especially as the local police confirmed that the neighbours had been complaining about the noise.

Enter Krissie. 'I'd gone to dinner with some friends in Earls Court,' she explains, 'and it was too late to get back to Jimmy's place. I just felt the need to go home, and The Wick was still my home, far more than

Plumpton Place. I knew Ronnie and Keith were away in Amsterdam, and I asked a girlfriend, Audrey Burgon, to come back with me because I didn't want to go home on my own.'

As far as the watching police were concerned, two women, one of them a tall blonde, turned up at The Wick. Anita Pallenberg was tall and blonde. And wherever Anita was, Keith was sure to be close by. Although, officially, the police were acting on 'information received'. When they broke in, they discovered Krissie in bed with her friend. Naturally, they jumped to the obvious conclusion.

'It was a huge bed, bigger than a double bed, and the only reason I'd asked Audrey to share was I was frightened of sleeping alone. I remember waking up at around six-thirty in the morning, and there were about twenty men in the room – I thought I was going to be kidnapped, I had no idea they were police. They'd even kicked in a two-hundred-year-old door. There were no policewomen there, and all Audrey had on was a pair of panties, and I had a nightie. So obviously we had to be lesbians!'

The raid netted a pestle and mortar containing the faintest residue of cocaine and an antique rifle; the latter had been left behind by Sir John Mills. While the police waited for a female officer to arrive, to search the girls, they played Ronnie's jukebox, banged his drums and strummed his guitars. Both girls denied the subsequent charges of possessing a controlled substance.

When the case finally came to trial, Krissie painted a harrowing picture of the pressures that came with being married to such a high-profile musician. She told of the hangers-on and parasites that surrounded their lives, any one of whom could have been responsible for the minute amounts of cocaine found in the mortar. The jury believed her and both women were acquitted. The trial received extensive coverage, but nowhere was it mentioned that Krissie had actually been living with another man at the time of her arrest.

The legal proceedings would last well over a year, and by the time they were over, Krissie would be back with Ronnie – pregnant and married to a Rolling Stone.

15
'Not a bad birthday present . . .'

Ronnie's long-time friend Rick Cunningham remembers that Nils Lofgren desperately wanted to join the Stones: 'He phoned up Woody and asked him if he would put in a good word for him. Ronnie was laughing because it was a foregone conclusion he would get the job, but was going, "Of course I will, mate, I'll talk to Keith about you", and then saying to me, "How out of touch is Nils Lofgren?"'

Ronnie's own press statement said that at first he couldn't accept the job because it would have meant leaving the Faces, that he was too close to the idea of the Faces to turn his back on them and that Mick Jagger understood this as well as anyone. But that finally they had arrived at a satisfactory compromise: 'I will become a part-time Rolling Stone but will remain a full-time member of the Faces and still be free to carry on with my solo projects.'

Who was kidding whom? Stewart was thousands of miles away doing his own thing, and even an abandoned-feeling Jones and Mac were talking of reforming the original Small Faces.

Ronnie had waited twelve years for the chance to join his boyhood idols. He wasn't about to blow it, even if, like Mick Taylor, he would only be on a salary – and would stay that way for a very long time.

'I was very worried for Woody,' Shirley Arnold says. 'I pulled Mick aside before they left, and I said now listen, Mick, you can't go and treat Ronnie in the same way you treated Mick Taylor and just give him a wage, you've got to give him a cut of everything. Of course they didn't, but Woody was happy. You could tell it was the happiest he'd been all his life.'

Ronnie was on a wage, but a bloody good one: reportedly £50,000 for one tour. Even so, he still managed to come home almost skint. According to Rick Cunningham: 'He'd basically spent all the money without realizing it. He had signed for everything. Imagine, there'd been eight of them in a club and the waiter comes up and says someone has to sign for whatever they'd had, and it needed someone in the band to do it. Ronnie would be, "Oh, I'll do it." What he didn't realize was that it was going on his fucking bill, he thought he was signing on behalf of the band, but he wasn't and he did it all the time. It was easier for a waiter or whoever needed something signed to come up to Ronnie than it was to approach Mick or Keith, who terrified most people. But Ronnie was the new boy, and he'd go, "Yeah, sure, how you doing, give it here and I'll sign it." And in the hotels he thought everything was free, courtesy of the hotel management. But everything was charged – you open a bottle of champagne and you pay for it. And it all came off his wages. He said to me that after all the deductions he'd signed for, he got a cheque for £2500 at the end of the tour.'

Ronnie's joining the Stones set the stage for the burning question of 1975: who hastened the eventual break-up of the Faces? Ronnie? Stewart? All of them? Or was it Her Majesty's Inspector of Taxes, who had been taking a keen interest in the band's careers and in particular their bank accounts?

The top rate of tax stood at eighty-three pence in the pound. And while many businessmen managed to avoid paying any tax at all, or paid very little – the Vestey family, for example, with their fortune from meat-packing and butcher's shops – entertainers always seemed to be caught out. Not for them the sensible luxury of trusts based in Lichtenstein, and a web of companies all apparently running at a loss. Instead, rock'n'rollers opted for a lifestyle conspicuous by its consumption, and an income that even the most junior tax officer could easily estimate. Also, the bands were often badly advised and even seemed to be the fall-guys for an industry never noted for its financial integrity.

Talk of tax was in the air, for Rod Stewart failed to return from Los Angeles, announcing on 9 May that he'd become a tax exile, was applying for American citizenship and had told Billy Gaff to sell up everything he owned in Britain. A month later he contradicted himself, saying the rumours of tax exile were false, that he was merely working abroad for the next few months, and that his mum would never forgive him if he quit home for good. On 23 July the British press reported that he'd refused to leave the International Lounge during a stop-over at Heathrow, to avoid being served with a writ for £750,000 in unpaid taxes. Stewart subsequently initiated legal proceedings against the news-papers and journalists who'd reported the story. However, at the time he had been on his way to Dublin for a press conference he'd called to begin promoting *Atlantic Crossing*.

Eventually safe in Ireland, Stewart continued to fan the flames of the Faces' break-up when he told the *NME*'s Steve Clark: 'I believe this album is the best one I've ever done. I definitely needed new blood around me. Suddenly I've seen the light of day. This is what I should have been doing two years ago.'

He then revealed his plans to tour with a full orchestra – a reference to his plans for a solo concert that was already booked for 1976 at London's Royal Festival Hall, where his backing band would be Booker T and the MGs. (The concert was cancelled in October 1975, when the MGs' drummer, Al Jackson, was shot dead by an intruder at his home in Memphis.)

The announcement of the Festival Hall concert started a rumour that Stewart planned to replace Ronnie Wood with the MGs' guitarist, Steve Cropper. When a reporter asked him about this, Stewart replied: 'I don't even know if our guitar player is still alive. I've spoken to him three times, twice he sounded really on top of the world and the last time he sounded really down.' His only passing reference to the Faces came when he added: 'We'll all be down in Miami in three weeks to start rehearsing and obviously there's going to be a lot of ego floating around. I wanted desperately to re-create what I've done on this album on stage. I'd do anything to do that, literally anything. We've already got a fifteen-piece orchestra [that is going to tour] with us, which Mac doesn't like. He's going to have to lump it.'

When journalists repeatedly asked about a break-up, Stewart wearily replied: 'If we don't break up soon we never will. We're now as close to breaking up as we've ever been.'

But note what Stewart was really saying: that the Faces tour was, as far as he was concerned, intended to help promote *Atlantic Crossing*, which had nothing whatsoever to do with the rest of the band – hence his concern about the need for extensive rehearsals before the Faces' tour began. This was the first time Stewart had promoted a solo album this way, and he couldn't have done any of it without Billy Gaff's encouragement and organization.

On a cold day in May, when Stewart was or wasn't becoming a tax exile, Ronnie was in New York riding down Fifth Avenue playing lead guitar with the Rolling Stones, on the back of a flat-bed truck that was slowly winding its way through the rush-hour traffic. The world's press had been packed into the dining room of the Plaza Hotel, expecting the band to turn up there, never realizing that they were about to witness their appearance in the street, accompanied by the deafening sound of 'Brown Sugar'. The Stones were arriving in their own inimitable style to announce that their 1975 tour of America would soon begin.

'These New York cops came up to the truck as we playing,' Ronnie recalls, 'and shouted out, "Hey, Ronnie, can you get us some tickets for the concerts? We couldn't get any for the Faces." '

New York's Finest never miss a trick.

Ronnie played his first real show with the Stones on his twenty-eighth birthday, on 1 June 1975, at Baton Rouge, Louisiana.

'I was thinking, "Not a bad birthday present for a kid who'd always dreamed of being a Rolling Stone." '

People who were there said he never stopped grinning.

Meanwhile there was consternation in the remaining Faces' camp.

'I feel pretty browned off,' Jones said in July, 'ever since Rod moved to the States everything's got disorganized. The Faces haven't worked in four months and I've lost £80,000 because we're not playing Wembley any longer.'

There was also the little matter of the new album, which Billy Gaff had announced a few weeks earlier. Jones, McLagan and Yamauchi desperately wanted to begin recording. But without either a lead guitarist or a singer, that too had been put on hold – as had the start of the Faces' next American tour, when Mick Jagger announced that the Stones' own tour would be extended.

Rod Stewart was not amused: 'We've had to cancel three concerts in Miami at a loss of $20,000 because there won't be enough time to rehearse new numbers with Ronnie. I'm particularly fed up because I feel the Stones should have let me know about their tour extension earlier.'

Ronnie eventually did rejoin the Faces in Miami and at last rehearsals began. It was the first time the band had seen their lead singer for five months, and their lead guitarist for two-and-a-half months. Even so, expectations were high.

'I'd been playing with a lot of different people, too,' Jones later said. 'Like Paul and Linda McCartney – she was actually a pretty good keyboard player – and what with Rod playing with Steve Cropper and "Duck" Dunn [Donald Dunn, the MGs' bassist] and Ronnie playing with the Stones, I thought the added experience would have made the Faces sound better. I knew Rod wanted the band to sound like his studio records, and we could have done it. But we never delivered it because we were still getting pissed as ever. And Ronnie had gone away as a Face and come back as a Rolling Stone.'

Stewart might have planned that Faces tour to reproduce *Atlantic Crossing* live, but once confronted by bloody-minded McLagan, a drunk Japanese bass player whom he'd never wanted in the first place, and a lead guitarist whose mind and loyalties were elsewhere, Stewart had to think again. Only Jones seemed to understand or even care about what he was trying to do.

'Going back to the Faces that time,' Ronnie admits, 'I realized how unprofessional we'd always been, and how much more organized the Stones were. In the Faces we'd all treated it too much as a laugh. The Stones had set lists and everything worked out beforehand, they knew exactly what they were going to do. They all worked together, they were the most professional band in the world. Spontaneity is all right, but for years in the Faces we never even used to work from a set list – you wouldn't know what number you were going to play next and we'd all be shouting at each other, "What number are we doing now?"'

Unable to stamp his authority on the band, and so re-create his new album live, Stewart changed tack. The orchestra was trimmed down to twelve players, and eventually individual string quartets – pick-up musicians – were hired in each city where the band played. Mac had been against the idea from the start – 'That's Liberace, that's Elton John, that's show business' – and suffered it for only a few dates before simply refusing to pay his share of the cost, leaving Ronnie, Stewart, Jones and Yamauchi to pick up the tab.

The set list also changed. Only two numbers from *Atlantic Crossing* were included – 'Three Times Loser' and 'I Don't Want To Talk About It' – while the rest was made up from tracks cherry-picked from almost all of Stewart's solo albums, leaving only two bona fide Faces tracks: 'Miss Judy's Farm' and, naturally, 'Stay With Me'. Effectively it was a Rod Stewart's Greatest Hits Tour, as played by a six-piece Faces band since Stewart had insisted that Jesse Ed Davis also join the tour.

Ironically, that Faces tour proved to be the most lucrative one ever. It stretched into November, giving Jones, Mac and Yamauchi the forlorn hope that the band would continue. But it couldn't have escaped their notice that only three-fifths of the Faces had returned home.

Ronnie had gone to Jamaica to join the other book-end for a holiday, before rehearsing in Switzerland for the Stones' next album.

Stewart had remained in Los Angeles, in Beverly Hills splendour. Billy Gaff had also moved to LA, now calling himself Stewart's personal manager and leaving Shirley Arnold in London to take care of what little Faces business remained.

Nonetheless, the three-fifths gave a series of press interviews in which they expressed their belief in a future for the Faces. The interviews began to sound increasingly desperate, and then out-and-out embarrassing as they refused to admit what the rest of the music world had long seen as patently obvious: the Faces were finished.

All it needed now was someone to administer the final *coup de grâce*.

The honour fell to Stewart's personal publicist, Tony Toon, who told the British press: 'Rod feels he can no longer work in a situation where the group's lead guitarist, Ron Wood, seems to be on permanent loan to the Rolling Stones.'

Gaff also added his tuppence worth: 'Rod thinks the world of Ron Wood. I have repeatedly tried to telephone Ron, who is touring Europe with the Rolling Stones. [In fact, he was recording.] I've left messages for him to call me, but I've heard nothing. The Faces' proposed tour of Britain and the Far East [always tentative at best] has now been called off.'

Incredibly, McLagan commented: 'I won't believe he [Stewart] is leaving the Faces until I hear it from his own lips.'

Whereas Jones said: 'If this means the end of the Faces, I'm not bothered. I expect I'll survive.'

No one asked Tetsuo Yamauchi what he thought about it. But the British press had never seen him as being a true Face anyway.

'Billy told me he wanted nothing more to do with Mac and Kenny,' Shirley explains. 'When they finally learned the truth, they smashed up the office and sent the roadies up to take the furniture because they felt they'd paid for it. Even the roadies were fighting each other. Pete Buckland went for Chuch [Ronnie's guitar roadie] and there was nearly another punch-up there. I called up Doreen [Art's first wife, Ronnie's first secretary] and we went for a drink and I never looked back. It was all over.'

Ronnie was doing his McCavity impression again, staying well away from all the arguments. As well he might, because on 19 December 1975 his face grinned out from front pages throughout the world when it was officially announced that he was to become a permanent member of the Rolling Stones.

And aside from that, he'd recently become reconciled with Krissie while he was on holiday in Jamaica. Between her and rehearsing with the Stones he pretty much had his hands full.

'I hadn't spoken to Ronnie in a year,' Krissie says. 'He wouldn't talk to me on the phone. Jimmy [Page] had asked my Dad if he could marry me and I'd sent Ronnie the divorce papers, but he still wouldn't talk to me, never even said if he'd received them. He just ignored the whole thing. He was in Jamaica with Keith and I said to Jimmy, "Ronnie won't talk to me on the phone, I'll have to go and see him," which upset Jimmy – it was so hard, but he understood that I had to go. Jimmy cared about how Ronnie was feeling . . . because none of this had been planned and he knew we had to get something sorted out . . . because there'd never been a big scene about it . . . nothing had been brought out into the open, there'd never been guns out, blazing.'

It must have been obvious to Page that the bonds between Krissie and Ronnie were still in place – especially as far as Krissie was concerned. She'd repeatedly said how uncomfortable she felt sharing Page's wealth and success. 'I wish I'd helped you achieve all this,' she used to say, while walking around Plumpton Place. 'I'd be comfortable with it all if I'd been there to help you get it. It was the same with George [Harrison]. I did it all with Ronnie, we were like soul mates.'

Page had once told her that she was only infatuated with him. He must have felt that the infatuation was wearing off.

'I went to Jamaica and met up with Ronnie,' Krissie continues, 'and he said no to the divorce. Just seeing him again made me realize I was still in love with him. And I never went back to Jimmy.'

16
'There's still a lot to do . . .'

B ack in 1997, when this book was a mere hopeful gleam in the author's bank manager's eye, Ronnie had decided that his years with the Stones needed their own appraisal, separate from his earlier career. For the Stones are a phenomenon, one of the few rock and cultural icons that the world will remember well into the next millennium. They've lasted longer than any other band. Their impact, not just on music but also on society itself, has been immense. For sure, Ronnie played with many other great musicians. But no matter how good or revolutionary the Birds, the Creation, the Jeff Beck Group or the Faces were, only one other band besides the Stones will be remembered as much for their effect on society as a whole as for their music. Arguably, the Beatles were far more musically innovative than the Stones, who have mostly remained true to their R&B roots. But Art Wood was absolutely right when he said: 'The Rolling Stones is a way of life.'

The move from Face to Stone might appear to have been relatively seamless, but in fact it took Ronnie many years to get used to the opportunities and the limitations of his new role. Over twenty years as a Rolling Stone deserves a book in itself, doesn't it? Not necessarily. For the truth is, Ronnie hasn't done a great deal in those twenty years – at least, not in terms of his solo output and writing, which was once the core of his existence. It's a popular view that, like mathematicians, rock musicians tend to do all their best work in their twenties. There are exceptions in both professions, like Ronnie's old pal Bob Dylan or the late genius physicist Richard Feynman, although generally the innovation and drive begins to lessen from the early thirties.

But the fact remains that Ronnie joined the Rolling Stones as potentially one of the ten best guitarists and songwriters, and certainly one of the best-loved, that Britain produced throughout the sixties. He was, and still is, an inordinately talented musician. Yet it was as if, once he'd joined the Stones, his ambition had semi-deflated, like a party balloon the morning after the night before. In terms of Ronnie's own personal musical development, the past twenty years appears to have been a time of coasting.

True, Ronnie has managed to survive a bad case of drug addiction. But so have many other musicians. Like record company executives and music journalists, they either use or they don't, and no one in the business seems to care either way.

True, he went from being relatively broke to amassing a fortune in excess of £50 million. This didn't happen overnight, however, for when he first joined the Stones he was a hired hand on a wage. It was quite a substantial wage, but it wasn't until Bill Wyman left that Ronnie became a shareholder, as it were. But he is not the only wealthy musician, and he's hardly a conspicuous spender. The recently purchased private jet has to be seen as a business expense. He does own racehorses, but so do many other people, not all of them multimillionaires. Aside from racing, Ronnie's favourite form of non-musical relaxation is snooker. Once you can afford the room for the table and the table itself, there's not exactly a huge overhead required. It would be nice to write about cues made from the rarest woods, inlaid with gold and platinum – or a chalk-holder fashioned from a single emerald. Sadly, there's nothing so extravagant to report.

And while Ronnie's family know they have only to ask if they need help, he hasn't moved the whole Wood family to his home in Ireland, as Keith Richards took his to New York.

Ronnie still cares about his art, too, and art in general. In fact, in his early days with the Stones, when he was still on a wage, his art had helped him survive financially. But while his studies of various musicians do carry an obvious interest and are professionally done, there is a sameness and a commercial slickness about them. This wouldn't matter much if it wasn't for the sketches he can also produce, more for himself and his family or close friends than for sale. These demonstrate a natural talent that is achingly good, and they tell you something about Ronnie himself. Perhaps this is significant, because the Rolling Stones live so much in the media spotlight that they become extremely reluctant to expose their private emotions. And maybe Ronnie is still too much in awe of the Glimmer Twins, Mick and Keith. His take on the relationship showed in his painting based on the photograph that appeared on the sleeve of *Beggar's Banquet*. There are the rest of the Stones in quasi-Last Supper mode, with Ronnie in the role of a humble waiter. Or perhaps as a man come late to the party and pretty damn grateful to be there.

True, Ronnie's marriage to Krissie didn't survive. But that was hardly unique. Often, people who've lived together for many years divorce soon after they marry. It's as if the marriage itself was a last-ditch attempt to paper over the cracks, a magical ceremony that will somehow make everything OK again.

The seeds of Ronnie and Krissie's divorce had been sown long before. They had met as adolescents and although they might have matured to some extent as individuals, the relationship had remained stuck in the 'everything's groovy, wow, man' atmosphere of the sixties. Both of them had developed outside interests from time to time, although Krissie's open affairs with Jimmy Page and George Harrison – it was to be a long time before Ronnie learned about her brief, return-fixture fling with Eric Clapton – had actually hurt Ronnie far more than he'd admitted at the time. Krissie always came back to him. Nor was the fault all hers: Ronnie often gave the impression of putting his music and career above everything else, and he was hardly a celibate saint on tour. Nonetheless, Krissie had given the impression that she'd left Ronnie for someone more famous. Her flight to Jamaica – ostensibly to ask for a divorce, and amid rumours she was pregnant by Page – when Ronnie joined the Stones, could almost be seen as her affirmation that yes, he'd finally made the big time. It might well have been emotionally satisfying for Ronnie to see that he was now ranked above Jimmy Page, but it was no way to restart the relationship. All of which totally passed over Krissie's head. For her, she was simply pursuing the first, great love of her life. But their closest and oldest friends privately wondered how long the latest new beginning would last. Most of them gave it no more than a year.

'Why did he sleep with her that time in Jamaica?' mused a close friend. 'Put it this way. Maybe he wanted to prove a point. A last-time shag.'

By the time Ronnie had finished proving it, Krissie was pregnant with Jesse James Wood.

But the truth was, Ronnie had something far more important to do than mend a broken relationship. As he saw it, he had to mend a broken band, and in the process, willingly sacrifice his own musical individuality for the good of the group. He'd spent the last two decades becoming a Rolling Stone, but always in the musical shadow of Mick and Keith – and even of the long-dead Brian Jones, whose ghostly presence still hovers malignantly above the stage.

Ronnie certainly divides his life into before and after becoming a Stone. Aside from anything else, there is the difference between being financially comfortable but always just a tad concerned about the next gig, and being a multimillionaire tax exile. To him, you write about an episode in your life only after it's over, like a love affair. 'I don't think the Stones are any way finished yet. There's still a lot to do. I'd rather wait and see the outcome.'

Meanwhile, his solo career hasn't been exactly illuminating, any more than has Mick Jagger's. Keith Richards has fared a little better, but only Charlie Watts' solo career has really earned the respect of other musicians. Maybe Art Wood got it wrong. The Rolling Stones isn't just a way of life. It's the only life for most of its members.

Even so, Ronnie's been a Stone semi-part-time, part-time and full-time for twice as long as Brian Jones and Mick Taylor put together. As Krissie says: 'I think Ronnie's been a very strong character and he's a very strong part of the Stones. He is a Rolling Stone now and he was meant to be there. I don't think he got sucked in – he made a choice at the time, even though it was difficult, and with twenty years down the line he's still doing it and doing it magnificently, so I think he's handled that whole aura, energy, really well – he's still alive.'

Why is it that so many people see joining the Stones as being tantamount to a death sentence?

Ronnie has also weathered the criticism of the Jones fanatics and the Taylor aficionados. ('Weathered' is the critical word here: at fifty-two, Ronnie's craggy features increasingly resemble an Easter Island statue struck by lightning, or a mountainside with soul.)

He survived his early years through a mixture of 'talent and bullshit', as Keith Richards said recently, adding: 'It's still there.' And as the band continues with its God-only-knows-what-number world tour, Ronnie is still there with the same spiky haircut ('my saving grace'), fag in his mouth and still playing the odd bum note.

But Keith also says: 'Ronnie has the same ability as Brian of being able to pick up on any instrument.' The kid who surprised his mother by learning to play the harmonica in a night will still play occasional bass, drums, saxophone or pedal-steel guitar on a Stones album. Given half a chance, he would probably play even more instruments. Ronnie has never suffered from a lack of musical self-confidence.

'That spell on bass with Jeff Beck gave me a different understanding of the guitar by the time I went to the Faces,' he says. 'I'd got in a rut and the bass gave me a new ground to build on. I learned to understand how important what you don't play is – as [important as] what you do. My son Jesse has only just reintroduced me to those old albums and I honestly can't believe it's me playing. With Beck I got that driving-along rhythm going and I still look at the guitar with the same driving idea. Hearing the guitarist on Aretha Franklin's "The Weight" got me into bottleneck and I never looked back. George [Harrison] is one of the great slide-guitar players, I love his playing, in the same way I rate the Burrito Brothers' Sneaky Pete's pedal-steel playing. I've got a double-necked, seven-pedal steel guitar which I just plonked in my lap one day and worked it out for myself. I once went through a sax phase which I really enjoyed and I think I could go a long way with it. Bobby Keys taught me a lot, though – I've even played in the Stones' horn section, standing next to Bob and all right, you can tell the difference! But I have to be careful and make sure I don't wander too far, because that's what happened to Brian Jones, that was a big part of his demise. He started playing everything – recorders, flutes, the sitar – and he lost his focus. Mick Taylor was also into experimenting with different instruments. But I'll always be a guitar-player at heart.'

But first and foremost, Ronnie has always been a Stone. Which was just as well, because he really did play a big part in getting the band back on track.

By 1975 the critics were writing off the world's greatest rock 'n' roll band, citing 1972's *Exile On Main Street* as the final parting shot. Two other albums – *Goat's Head Soup* (1973) and *Black And Blue* (1976) – had been at best a ramshackle collection of songs drawn from a period when the Stones could scarcely call themselves a band. And although *It's Only Rock 'n' Roll* (1974) had reached number one in America, it had been recorded at a time when Keith seemed determined to travel his own personal path to destruction. Mick – who'd written the title track with Ronnie, a number that featured more Faces than Stones – seemed to have forsaken most of his rock 'n' roll links in favour of becoming a Sunday-paper socialite. Bill Wyman was seriously considering working with Crosby, Stills and Nash, and Charlie Watts looked even more bored and uninterested than usual.

In retrospect, Ronnie's joining the band in 1975 wasn't the sure-fire career move it might have appeared to be. The Faces were definitely finished, but the Stones were following a similar downward spiral. They had recorded *Black And Blue* mainly as a four-piece group, with as many guest lead guitarists as possible filling in the solo spot. Along with Ronnie, the sessions featured a decent six-strings' worth from Rory Gallagher, Eric Clapton, Jeff Beck, Wayne Perkins, Steve Marriott and Harvey Mandel. In fact, Perkins was convinced he'd got the job permanently, especially when Ronnie was relegated to backing singer on the Perkins-heavy track 'Hand Of Fate'.

The ludicrous number of inner-sleeve credits demonstrated just how far the Stones had drifted from their original formula of a basic five-piece band plus the occasional guest percussionist or pianist, and brass when needed. Each track's personnel read like the rolling credits of a Hollywood sequel. It all looked and sounded forced, and the music press were happy to say so. 'There are two things to be said about the new Stones album, *Black And Blue*, before closing time,' bewailed *Creem* magazine. 'One is that they are still perfectly in tune with the times and the other is that the heat's off, because it's all over. They really don't matter any more or stand for anything. Which is certainly lucky for both them and us. I mean, it was a heavy weight to carry for all concerned. This is the first meaningless Stones album, and thank God.'

There was no getting away from it. Leaving aside Mick Taylor's departure and personal problems, the impression had been given that the tax-exiled Stones didn't give a damn any more. But, in saying as much, the critics had totally missed the point. The band was in crisis, yet it was a crisis of transition, not boredom. They'd been around too long to be rebels, but they weren't quite old enough to settle into that hard-driving middle age that would become their hallmark for the next two decades. There was also the slight problem of a power struggle between Mick and Keith.

Generally speaking, each rock band has a single leader. Very rarely have there been two – maybe Page and Plant in Led Zeppelin – but even John Lennon was seen as leader of the Beatles, as was Ray Davies of the Kinks, Pete Townshend of the Who and Steve Marriott of the Small Faces. The list is endless, and for good reason: without a single leader, anarchy breaks out. The problems arise when another member of the band thinks he should be leader, or at least co-leader. Normally, the leader will be the lead guitarist, who is also usually the chief songwriter.

But the Stones had changed the equation. The original leader, Brian Jones, had been quickly sidelined by their new manager, Andrew Loog Oldham. All other considerations aside – photogenic good looks, musical ability – Jones simply hadn't been dynamic enough on stage; nor could he write songs. This had allowed the Jagger/Richards partnership to flourish and given the band one front man but two leaders. Mick and Keith had been close since childhood, but times change and with Keith's descent into heroin addiction the old partnership was no longer working. Mick had the ability to stand back and take an overall view. Keith's life had become bounded by his relationship with Anita Pallenberg and the next fix.

Mick wanted total control over the band, primarily for business reasons, although he probably also had his own creative ideas about its future direction. Unfortunately, he wasn't a musician, except for playing the harmonica, and with all due respect to both Larry Adler and Ronnie's dad, harp-players aren't seen as being musicians, especially when it comes to writing song music. Later Mick would become an extremely accomplished musician, but at the time of *Black And Blue* the musical practicalities were in Keith's hands – as and when he showed up. Yet, spaced out or not, Keith was not about to surrender one iota of creative control. Like all addicts, he knew he could still function perfectly. It was just a question of managing to keep awake and remembering which country he was supposed to be in.

Mick Taylor had never been a kingmaker. Brilliant musician though he was, he lacked the drive and the will to support either Mick or Keith against the other, no matter how much they individually canvassed his support. It was a lousy situation to be in, and one that had helped him make up his mind to leave. Besides, he'd always been on a wage rather than being a full band member, and had never really looked as if he truly belonged. He was simply too nice. But once he was gone, the way was clear for Mick or Keith to bring in their own choice of lead guitarist.

Chris Spedding had known Mick Jagger for years. The guitarist's band the Battered Ornaments had supported the Stones at the Brian Jones memorial gig in Hyde Park in 1969. Even so, he was a little surprised to be called by Jagger one day and asked: 'What are your plans and are you free?'

Spedding knew that the Stones were looking for Taylor's replacement, although his departure was yet to be officially announced. And even though Spedding had plans of his own, he was intrigued enough to go and meet Mick and Keith.

'I soon realized the power struggle that was going on,' he recalls. 'I realized both of them were playing games against the other one. Both had their own agendas and lists, both had their own guitarists in mind – one that would side against the other. It wasn't a question of who was good enough to play with the Stones, but who could be easily controlled. It was all so obvious that I didn't even entertain the idea. I wasn't surprised when Ronnie got the job.'

Keith thought that Ronnie would take his side against Mick Jagger. But Mick had also known Ronnie for a long time, and had wanted him in the band before Mick Taylor had joined. Both were looking for a loyal lieutenant, but would settle for a harmless compromise.

Enter Ronnie Wood, also known as Mediator Man, believing that the job had been preordained, for wasn't Keith one of his best mates?

Yes he was. But above all Keith was and is a consummate musician with an abiding loyalty to his band. He wanted Ronnie, but other guitarists also had to be auditioned – including Rory Gallagher. In the event, Gallagher played just two-and-a-half numbers before Keith stopped the band, looked straight at him and said: 'That's enough, mate. You got the job.'

'Ah, thanks but no thanks,' Gallagher replied. 'See, I don't really like your songs.'

Ronnie was hired the next day. There would be no such insubordination from him.

Power struggles weren't the only things stacked against the Stones, for both London and New York had begun shuddering to a different musical wavelength: Punk had arrived. 'No Beatles, Elvis or the Rolling Stones in 1977,' screamed the Clash, and they seemed to mean it. Although, in truth, many seminal Punk bands secretly held the Faces and the Stones in awe.

Those passionate Punk slogans 'Never Trust A Hippy' and 'Rock Dinosaurs' looked and sounded good. Johnny Rotten had even slammed the door of Malcolm McLaren's King's Road shop, Sex, in Mick Jagger's face. And while that story was later dismissed by Jagger as pure fantasy, the fact that so many people took pleasure from it was enough to worry the Stones: a new gunslinger was in town. Of course, Jagger et al. weren't to know that the Sex Pistols – with the exception of Sid Vicious – had been in the audience at all of Ronnie's solo shows. Nor that Pistols Steve Jones and Paul Cook would happily break into The Wick to 'borrow' the occasional guitar from Ronnie and Keith, but always leave a note saying: 'Thanks mate, Steve was here.' For, as they later admitted, who better to 'borrow' from than your heroes?

Nowadays both Mick and Keith say – a trifle smugly – that Punk had never phased them. Really? Rewind to 1977 and Keith's comment about a certain track called 'Shattered': 'Why the fuck did Mick want a punk-sounding guitar? Why not have a Stones-sounding fucking guitar sound?' In fact, they ended up with a Ronnie Wood-sounding guitar, in one of the best solos he's ever played.

Looking back on his departure from the Stones, Mick Taylor would later say: 'I have the rare distinction of having left the Rolling Stones and lived.' Also: 'I left the Stones because they couldn't afford me.' Other rumours spoke of his drug addiction: if he'd stayed, he would have died. Whatever the truth, his leaving allowed Ronnie to help shape the band's recovery by bringing to it two key ingredients that had been missing for some years: reappraisal and youth. Never as good a player as Mick Taylor – who, according to Keith, ranks as one of rock's greatest lead guitarists – Ronnie nonetheless rejuvenated the band in a way that the self-effacing Taylor never could. 'When I joined the Stones,' he recalls, 'they weren't interested in playing "Satisfaction", "Paint It Black" or all the old classics. But that's what I knew the Stones to be, I knew all those songs and that's what I wanted to be up there playing. And I already knew all their back catalogue.'

Ronnie was twenty-eight when he joined the band – slightly strung out, a bit sycophantic but unmistakably rock 'n' fucking roll. He had actually travelled to Paris to audition for the Stones with Bobby Womack, so sure of landing the job that he asked the legendary soul man how much money he should demand for the upcoming tour. 'Half a million,' Womack replied, talking US dollars. Ronnie got two hundred and fifty thousand – pounds sterling. History doesn't record how much Rory Gallagher would have got.

The Stones hadn't tried to replace Brian Jones with another multi-talented psychotic; nor had they tried to replace Mick Taylor with a young guitar whiz-kid. Each change marked another stage in the band's development. In fact, the pairing of Ronnie and Keith allowed them to return to the dual lead and rhythm approach to live performances which had been absent since Brian had died, for Taylor's guitar had swamped the overall sound. Just as importantly, Keith had a new buddy to tour with; someone who thought like him, drank like him and took drugs like him. He'd found another little Keith.

But Ronnie also supplied an energy on stage that had been lacking for some time, as Mick Taylor had been the quintessentially laid-back guitarist. The band already had two members performing that ultra-cool role: Bill Wyman and Charlie Watts. Three had been one too many. It was hardly surprising that within twelve months the Stones decided to issue a double live album, *Love You Live*, recorded mainly in Paris.

Even though *Black And Blue* had been a musical hotchpotch, there had still been requests for over four million tickets for the British leg of the subsequent European tour. In fact, demand for the Stones' live work had increased dramatically following Ronnie's first tour with them, while he was still nominally a Face. He'd meshed perfectly into the Stones' live sound.

Also, he'd outshone them on stage. On that very first tour Ronnie had worn outfits from his Faces days that were as familiar to the fans as his custom-made guitar and haircut. In particular there were the tight, outrageous silk trousers overprinted with the Japanese artist Hokusai's *The Wave*, making his thighs look as if they were under permanent attack. The Faces had always been more of a show band than the Stones, and Ronnie used that heritage for all it was worth. He was positioned at the end of the stage, but his flamboyance even overshadowed Mick, whose lime-green ruffles and sun visor looked tame by comparison.

In addition, Ronnie brought a much-needed sense of danger to the act, if only because he played the occasional bum note. 'It's natural,' he was to say. 'I still don't practise anything. I don't want to remember the songs exactly. I love the risk, that's what keeps it interesting and different each night – although that approach can backfire. That's why I'm still getting better each time we go out on the road – that's my practice, that and five minutes in the dressing room beforehand!'

Art Wood pinpoints another quality that helped Ronnie give the Stones a new lease of life. 'He's got his own thing. I don't mean his solo albums – I mean Ronnie's thing is that he's a team player. Even when he did his New Barbarians [the band Ronnie formed to promote his second solo album, *Now Look*] he always wanted to share the spotlight. It was a big line-up, but with three mikes taped to the one stand, he doesn't want to be the leader, never had the genuine aspiration to be a solo star. Even if his albums had sold millions, I'm sure that he'd still be the same. Rod wasn't like that, and Mick wasn't for quite a while, but all Ronnie's ever wanted is to be part of a band.'

Or as Keith said in 1977: 'Woody and I can start playing together until we don't know who played the last lick. It's as close as that. He has the right feel and spirit for the Stones even though he's still the new boy, he's the one I communicate with the most.'

Love You Live was released in 1977 and, if nothing else, showed that the Stones had recovered all their old confidence. It reached number three in America and number five in the UK. Few bands really like live albums, since they never recapture the atmosphere but faithfully record every bum or missed note. The fact that the Stones released *Love You Live*, after albums that had been remembered more for their cover artwork than the music – witness *Sticky Fingers* and *Goat's Head Soup* – was testament to their new zest. Leaving aside compilations and reissues, the albums and singles that followed *Love You Live* – *Some Girls*, *Emotional Rescue*, 'Shattered', 'Miss You' and 'Beast Of Burden' – were respectable for any age, and showed the band was more productive than it had been in years.

A few months earlier, at the High Court in London, Krissie too had been making headlines when the case resulting from her gun and drugs bust at The Wick had finally reached its climax. Krissie and her co-defendant Audrey, also known as Lorraine to her friends and the wife of Richard Barnes, the man who renamed the High Numbers the Who, were found not guilty by a jury of the illegal possession of a firearm (the antique belonging to Sir John Mills) and possession of cocaine, which had nothing whatsoever to do with Sir John. Despite the jury's decision, the two women were still ordered to pay costs amounting to £12,000 by a sceptical judge, who commented: 'If I were to believe you were telling the truth, then in turn you must expect me to believe that fifteen police officers were lying.'

'Well, fuck, yes!' commented Ronnie.

The point was, Krissie's card had been marked 'possible addict'. It was not a good time to become too publicly linked with the Rolling Stones – still a thorn in the Drugs Squad's side.

The following month, May 1976, Keith crashed his beloved Bentley into the central reservation of the M1 near Newport Pagnell, Buckinghamshire, in the early hours of the morning. When the rescue service and police arrived, they were intrigued – some said delighted – to discover something in the car that looked suspiciously like cocaine. Keith was allowed to go free pending lab tests – which would eventually confirm the presence of both cocaine and LSD. Keith was at a loss to explain how they got there. He was ordered to appear in court at Newport Pagnell the following October, when he would arrive two hours late for the hearing, claiming that he'd been waiting for his trousers to come back from the dry-cleaner. This imaginative excuse – on which the judge's comment was: 'I would have thought that a man of your means would own more than one pair of trousers' – resulted in Keith's bail being increased from £100 to £5000. He would eventually be found guilty of possessing cocaine, but cleared of the lesser charge involving LSD and fined £750 with £250 costs.

The case was nothing compared with the trouble waiting for him in quiet, sedate Canada, but more than enough to worry Mick Jagger. A famous rock rumour circulated that Ronnie had been hired simply as a precaution, in case Keith was refused entry into the USA. Both Mick and Ron were later quick to deny it.

'There's no Rolling Stones without Keith,' Ronnie insisted. 'It's ridiculous to imagine that was ever a possibility.'

17
The Mounties get their man

On 25 February 1977 Keith mistook the people rifling through his and Anita Pallenberg's luggage at Toronto International Airport for Stones roadies – only to discover to his horror that they were Customs officers. Reportedly, they declared it an early Christmas when they discovered ten grams of hashish, a blackened spoon that revealed traces of heroin and a packet of Tic-Tacs that were taken away for analysis – along with the spoon – and never returned.

Three days later the Royal Canadian Mounted Police came looking for more drugs. A search party blitzed through the Harbour Castle Hotel and arrested Keith for possessing enough heroin to qualify for a trafficking offence. There were those who claimed the bust was Anita's fault; that she'd attracted the Mounties' attention by buying it locally herself. Whatever the facts, as usual Keith got the blame.

No one had ever beaten a heroin-trafficking rap in Canada – a fact that didn't escape Ronnie Wood, who quietly disappeared a few days later. Keith last saw him waving goodbye as the lift doors closed behind him.

'The hardest memory in all our years of friendship,' Ronnie says, and it's easy to imagine how difficult it had been to leave Keith on his own. To be fair, Ronnie did have his own problems at the time, mainly concerned with his nearly – if unwittingly – toppling the Canadian government.

God only knows what he had been thinking of when he slept with Canadian Prime Minister Pierre Trudeau's much younger wife, Margaret. Actually, it's pretty obvious what he was thinking of, but how on earth did he think he'd ever get away with it?

Ronnie and Maggie had first met on 4 March, when she'd gone backstage after a concert at Toronto's El Mocambo club. Maggie Trudeau was an early Diana, Princess of Wales-type of figure, married to a man who'd been a world leader when she was still at school. Two sons had quickly arrived, and soon Maggie was showing signs of boredom and wanting a life of her own. She, too, longed to glitter on the world stage, but in her own right. She was beautiful, vivacious, a little self-obsessed and ambitious beyond her talents. Ronnie had been mixing with women like Margaret Trudeau for most of his life.

On the evening of 6 March 1977 Ronnie was seen wining and dining Maggie in the Harbour Castle restaurant. After the meal they were seen walking around outside, alone. Much later Ronnie was to say that he'd hoped to persuade her to intercede with the Canadian authorities on Keith's behalf – that is, get her to persuade her husband to order the police to drop the charges. One thing led to another, as it so often does with Ronnie, and they ended up in his room – via a brief detour to meet his good mate Keith.

A few hours later Maggie was discovered in the corridor off which the Stones' entourage had their rooms and suites. She was clad only in a hotel bathrobe and alternating between euphoria and sheer bloody-mindedness. Pete Rudge, one of the people responsible for the Stones' security, asked her to get dressed and leave, but when she wouldn't, he called Mick Jagger, who repeated the request – although less politely. Meanwhile the hotel management desperately wondered what the hell they could do, eventually deciding to give Maggie her own suite and hope no one had noticed. She left the hotel early the next morning.

When the news first broke – for people had noticed – the media made the obvious assumption that she'd been visiting Mick Jagger. After all, she was the Prime Minister's wife, and Canadian honour demanded no less than the Stones' lead vocalist.

'You could hear them sharpening their skates,' Ronnie cracked.

When Mick proved it hadn't been him, suspicion fell on Keith, partly because he had been mistaken for Ronnie when Maggie had been seen in the restaurant, partly because she'd also been seen going into Keith's room – although not, apparently, later seen going into Ronnie's. Or, as Art Wood would later claim, tongue in cheek: 'Ron was innocent, he was never in that restaurant. He hasn't eaten since 1975.'

Art had a point. To this day, no one has ever seen Ronnie finish a meal. Some of his closest friends have never actually seen him eat at all.

Whether she knew it or not, Margaret Trudeau was under government surveillance – as much to make sure she didn't embarrass her husband as for her own security. Keith, too, was under surveillance, but of the police variety: it was later announced that a tiny electronic bug had been found in his room. By mid-morning the following day the Royal Canadian Mounted Police, who are responsible for state security, knew that Maggie had spent the night with Ronnie. They also knew that he'd previously introduced the Prime Minister's wife to a man accused of drug trafficking. Not exactly the smartest thing Ronnie had ever done. But he'd meant well.

Then the media arrived. Much of the local press tried to downplay the incident, as any responsible journalist would. Not so the Rottweilers from the USA and Britain.

Ronnie and the other Stones, apart from Keith, quietly faded away and regrouped in New York. Because his passport had been confiscated, Keith had to stay in Toronto with only Anita and the faithful Ian Stewart for company. February in that city can be a deeply depressing experience, even without the possibility of a jail term hanging over one's head. The sky often remains grey and overcast for weeks on end. And if the snow doesn't get you, the freezing rain will. While Keith was stranded in his hotel room he taped songs that mirrored his somewhat bleak outlook. 'Apartment Number Nine' was an apt Tammy Wynette number, and 'Worried Life Blues' was an old blues standard into which Keith inserted the poignant line: 'My friends have all left me.' And so they had, to party with David Bowie and Iggy Pop in New York and show up at the Eagles' sell-out gig at Madison Square Garden, where Ronnie couldn't help joining the band on stage.

One likes to think they thought of Keith every day. Certainly someone was doing some very fast thinking about who could replace him if the worst came to the worst.

Meanwhile the Canadian media were finally figuring out the truth about Margaret Trudeau, who was now on the missing list. Or rather, editors and proprietors were wondering if they dared print the truth as seasoned journalists looked at each other open-mouthed: 'What? Not Jagger, not Richards, but Ronnie Wood? Isn't he in the Faces?' But no one wanted to be the first to publish the story that put cuckold's horns on the country's Prime Minister. There was the matter of national pride and besides, Trudeau had a long memory and could be ruthless.

So it suited everyone, including the Stones, to pretend that it was all an innocent misunderstanding. Mick simply dismissed the entire episode when he said: 'Oh, Margaret, she just dropped by. Someone said she wanted to come to the gig, so we took her. I'd never met her before, but I guess she likes to go out to clubs and go rocking and rolling like anyone else.'

The *New York Daily News* eventually broke the story, announcing that Ronnie Wood was indeed the true object of Margaret Trudeau's affections and ending the piece with a quote from Mick: 'Ronnie Wood could probably tell you more about where Margaret Trudeau is staying than her husband.'

Not surprisingly, Ronnie was nowhere to be found and for a while the affair remained in limbo. The US media grew tired of constantly needing to explain where Canada was, while the world and UK media were more interested in Keith Richards. Only the Canadian media broached the subject, with more circumspection than rigour, while outrage there was none – except in the Midwest corn belt, but that hardly mattered.

Margaret Trudeau finally surfaced at home in Ottawa for the obligatory 'Sorry!' photo-call with her family. Husband Pierre looked even more sardonic than usual. He was a proud and highly intelligent man, one of the few world-class politicians who genuinely deserved the title. But he was not the first or last to make the mistake of marrying a much younger wife whose excitement with her new status in life gives rise to delusions of personal pop-stardom. It happens to rock star wives all the time.

Ronnie was fast becoming used to a Stones-style massive media intrusion into his life. But with it came an increasing police interest, and that was another matter. Earlier that year he'd publicly announced that he and Krissie had reunited and were thinking of moving to Los Angeles.

'I love Britain but I haven't lived there for nearly a year,' he said, adding, with an obvious reference to Krissie's arrest at The Wick: 'mainly because I don't feel safe in my own bed.'

He'd also received hate mail. 'Yeah, I got some. Well, one actually, and it wasn't just about me – it was about all the pop stars that were leaving the country for tax reasons, and it said: "I wish you'd fuck off with them!"'

Following Ronnie's announcement, he and Krissie had been stopped by Customs when returning to England from a holiday in France. A pregnant Krissie had been strip-searched for drugs, watched by her outraged husband. Both Customs and the police had been misinformed that Krissie always carried Ronnie's stash through Customs on the basis that no one would search a pregnant woman. 'Aren't you something to do with the Rolling Stones?' they'd asked her, displaying either a surprising naïveté or heavy-handed sarcasm. Either way, the result was intense humiliation for both Krissie and Ronnie, and a pay-off – or possibly a news story – for the original informant. But the lesson had been plain: Ronnie was now a target, like the rest of the Rolling Stones. He needed a place that understood celebrities, and thus America beckoned.

The move to Los Angeles had not been a success. As a close friend remembered: 'Krissie was always a flirt. I'm not saying she was easy, but she often gave that impression – probably because she can be so bloody dizzy at times, like she's not really aware of the signals she's sending. Or she is aware, but is a bit of a tease. And suddenly she's in LA, and the guys there are predators. Like, no one plays games – it's all bloody business, and the wife of a Rolling Stone would be one hell of a scalp. Especially this beautiful, blonde, typical English girl, because all the local girls were either bimbos or actresses, often both, and as hard as fucking nails.'

Meaning that both Ronnie and Krissie were flavour of the month, albeit for slightly different reasons. And that Krissie possibly mistook the compliments and adulation coming her way, believing that now she was shining in her own right. Dammit, she had a career and a life of her own, independent of her husband. Didn't she?

You can count on the fingers of one hand the number of rock wives who could truthfully answer yes to that question. The problem is that the traditional wife/mother/partner role has never translated very well into show business. It's not just the groupies – except in the sense that the most surprising people want to sleep with a rock star, people who one would normally think were beyond such juvenile nonsense. It's the sheer adulation and devotion given to the performer, which derive from the assumption that he or she also belongs to the fans. While many a performer is happy to belong in this way, it doesn't leave much space for a traditional family life.

But, quite apart from the Wood family's efforts to cope with Los Angeles, the Trudeau affair came as a shock to Krissie. Nevertheless, with commendable loyalty she still keeps a fairly open mind on the subject, explaining: 'I'd just had Jesse, so it was very hurtful for me. I don't know exactly what happened there but I know it was pretty serious . . . I'm reluctant to talk because I don't know the facts. The reporters turned up and it was horrible for me, you know. They were suggesting that my husband was sleeping with Margaret Trudeau and that was the first I knew. So slowly, slowly I started to get really disillusioned with it all. But I didn't see that as the end of our relationship. I just wanted to make some changes in our life.'

Fast forward to Keith, still languishing in a Toronto hotel room and a Canadian winter. Eventually, with his preliminary hearing set for June, he was given bail and allowed to leave the country. He joined the rest of the Stones in New York to re-sign with Atlantic Records in a $21-million deal that made them the highest-paid recording artists in the world. All except for Ronnie, that is, who was still on a wage and facing a mammoth tax bill left over from his years with the Faces. He had no alternative but to sell The Wick for £300,000. He kept the Wick Cottage as his London base and relocated to Los Angeles.

Keith failed to show up for his Toronto hearing in June 1977. His lawyer explained that he was unavoidably detained in a drug rehabilitation centre and asked for an adjournment. The hearing was rescheduled to July, the judge asking for medical evidence to be produced to show Keith's progress.

Come July, and Keith was apparently still in the clinic. In between making an album, that is: *Some Girls*, recorded mainly in Paris. The hearing was re-rescheduled to December and this time Keith did show up – with the tragic story that he had tried to give up drugs. Oh God! how he'd tried, but each time a tour came up he began again. The hearing was rescheduled yet again, this time to February 1978. People began betting on when the case would finally go to trial.

Meanwhile the Trudeaus were quietly separating. All very dignified, and although nothing explicit was said, it was widely understood to be a question of when, not if. The events at the Harbour Castle Hotel the previous March became to be seen by many Canadians as one more foolish – but basically harmless – indiscretion, similar to the time that Maggie had once posed in her underwear for a fairly respectable magazine. No one mentioned Ronnie Wood. Anyway, wasn't he still with the Faces?

Of course, if Keith's case had gone to trial earlier, then the two different elements – his drug bust and, a few days later, Margaret's scene in a hotel corridor – might well have combined as one major scandal. But luckily the seemingly endless adjournments helped defuse the situation. It was just as well, because the Harbour Castle Hotel episode was widely held responsible for causing a knee-jerk run on the Canadian dollar. True, it was only a very small run that didn't last very long, but how many other rock stars can claim to have blipped the economy of a major industrial nation? Rock on, Woody.

Funnily enough, many of those Canadians who had remained interested still assumed that Keith was to blame – even those who'd read the American or British newspapers, which anyway had quickly lost interest in the affair. Actually, the fact that those newspapers had named Ronnie was enough in itself to make Canada's glitterati look elsewhere. For the bulk of the citizens, Keith's supposed affair with Maggie had become a cocktail-bar confidence, exchanged between self-important people with a knowing smirk. But that too eventually became shrouded with disbelief, for, judging by the medical evidence given at the various adjournments,

Keith was obviously an ill man. 'Sex Tryst With PM's Wife'? He'd have been hard pushed to hold hands. Or so it seemed as time dragged on, and in the minds of many Canadians Keith became a tragic figure, heroically battling his addiction. Torontonians would openly applaud him in the street. Little were they to know that the man has the constitution of an ox – and the determination of a Churchill. Great lawyers, too.

If the media and public opinion had been manipulated, it had been done superbly. If not, the gods were smiling on Ronnie, Keith and Margaret Trudeau. Not to mention the Canadian Prime Minister, the Liberal Party, which he led, and – who knows? – even the Canadian dollar again. Whatever the case, the broom of time had swept the dust of Maggie T's frolics under the faded carpet of obscurity. Of course, there was always Keith's trial to look forward to – that is, when it finally happened.

On 24 October 1978, nearly two years after the original offence, Keith surprised everyone by not only returning to Toronto for his trial, but also by pleading guilty. He didn't even bother to claim that he was looking after the heroin for a sick friend. Watching journalists began composing their stories detailing his inevitable prison sentence and the end of the Stones, but then rapidly had to rewrite the intro when Judge Lloyd Graburn instead gave Keith a one-year suspended sentence and ordered him to play a concert for the blind in Toronto within the next six months. Keith was also ordered to see a Toronto probation officer within twenty-four hours, and then again on 7 May and 24 October 1979, to report on his treatment for drug addiction. He flew back to New York a considerably relieved man. Two days later tickets went on sale for his concert at the Canadian Institute of the Blind – it would have to be a small concert, for the auditorium seated only 225. By pleading guilty, Keith had ensured that the trial would be over before all the old gossip and innuendo could resurface.

And perhaps Ronnie's cunning plan to get his best mate off the charges had actually worked. But not, of course, in the way he'd intended. As it was, the match between the Rolling Stones and the Canadian government had ended in a draw, with only one player being stretchered off when the Trudeaus officially separated shortly before Keith's trial (as, in fact, did Krissie and Ronnie). Pierre was given custody of the children, and Margaret moved to New York with thoughts of hosting a TV chat show. But basically she was too nice to make up for her lack of talent, so her media career came to nothing. Nearly twenty years later, in early 1998, the mental instability that so many people had suspected finally surfaced and she was admitted to a psychiatric hospital in Canada.

Nagging doubts over Keith's liberty had unsurprisingly led to his keeping a low profile while awaiting trial and during the recording of *Some Girls*. The album was predominantly conceived and written by Mick, but the sessions also provided a songwriting opportunity for Ronnie. He ended up with his first Stones co-writing credits on two tracks – 'Black Limousine' (the track he'd traded for 'It's Only Rock And Roll') and 'Everything is Turning To Gold' – two songs which would later appear on the albums *Tattoo You* and *Sucking In The Seventies*, respectively. *Some Girls* stands as probably Ronnie's seminal Stones album, and his heightened presence is heavily felt on each track – never more so than on the cod-Country effort 'Far Away Eyes' and the vaguely Punk 'Shattered'. In addition to his lead guitar work on the album, Ronnie contributed bass, pedal-steel, rhythm and acoustic guitars, backing vocals and the occasional wallop on the bass drum.

Just as importantly, he encouraged Mick to play guitar on several tracks, and tutored him daily. Ronnie might have been Keith's best mate, but there was no way he was going to be seen taking sides. His job was to mediate between the Stones' two leaders and he did it as well as anyone could. But there was another reason for teaching Mick how to play guitar: if Keith's trial went the wrong way in Toronto, the band would be minus a rhythm guitarist. It made more sense for Mick to learn the job, for two newcomers would have diluted the Stones' sense of exclusivity.

Ronnie also brought in a grateful Ian McLagan, fresh from the re-formed Small Faces débâcle, who fleshed out Ian Stewart's keyboards. This in itself established that he was going to be his own man, and even if he wasn't on an equal financial footing, he was now an integral and vital member of the band. The press stopped referring to him as 'ex-Faces' guitarist'. He was now known as 'Rolling Stone Ronnie Wood'. Bill Wyman was even moved to comment how much he'd enjoyed making the album, mainly because of Ronnie's presence. The album's first single release, the mildly disco-orientated 'Miss You', shot straight to number one in the States and went on to become one of the band's best-selling singles of all time. For Ronnie, everything seemed to be turning gold. Except, of course, in his private life, which had become just a little tarnished by the death of his friend John Belushi.

To promote *Some Girls*, the Stones had played live on television for the first time in ten years. Naturally, the show had to be *Saturday Night Live*, America's hottest-rated TV programme of the seventies. The band was booked to open the first show of the fourth season. Within the industry it was billed as a meeting of the gods, since *Saturday Night Live*'s two principal players, John Belushi and Dan Ackroyd, had only just completed nine triumphant nights in their guise as the Blues Brothers, supporting Steve Martin at the Universal Amphitheatre in LA. Their first album, *Briefcase Full Of Blues*, was currently sitting at number one. The Stones were there to promote their return-to-form album. It seemed that all concerned were on a roll.

Dressing rooms were repainted and furniture specially hired by the network in anticipation of the Stones' arrival. Ronnie and Mick repaid their generosity by 'shocking and revolting' ABC's president, Fred Silverman, when the pair openly French-kissed live on air. At least, that was how it looked to millions of viewers, including Silverman. Ronnie remembers it differently. 'We were playing "Beast of Burden". I was in the middle of a solo, eyes closed, when suddenly I felt this horrible, slimy tongue in my mouth. It was Mick, French-kissing me on live TV. And that's my single worst memory of the band.'

Not that anyone would have believed the truth, namely that Jagger had an off-the-wall sense of humour. For when the Stones were first starting out there'd been all sorts of rumours about their sexuality, rumours which were actually on a par with the Oldham-inspired buzz that they were all dying of leukaemia. In fact, the only Stone who'd taken bisexuality even semi-seriously had been Brian Jones.

Ronnie had already ingratiated himself with Belushi while living in LA, and the pair had often played the blues together in the comedian's soundproof bunker, which he called 'The Vault'. It had been Ronnie who'd invited Belushi along to compère the New Barbarians' shows. The tour, despite being sold out, was a financial disaster, because of Ronnie's insistence on touring in true Stones style: a lavishly equipped jumbo jet, fleets of stretch limos, the best suites in the most expensive hotels and hot and cold running alcohol. He paid for the lot.

So naturally Ronnie was bound to be questioned by the authorities, along with Robert De Niro and Robin Williams, when Belushi's body was discovered in the notorious Chateau Marmont Hotel. All four had been regularly seen in the days leading up to Belushi's death, and had been named as clients by celebrity drug dealer Kathy Smith – later convicted of supplying and assisting Belushi to inject the dose that killed him. Along with De Niro and Williams, Ronnie was cleared of any involvement in Belushi's death, but the impression was given that he was heavily involved with cocaine. As indeed he had been.

'It was just too fucking available,' Ronnie now says. 'Packets and bleeding packets of it, everywhere you went. That's not an excuse.

I mean, I never saw Bill Wyman take much more than an aspirin, but if you lived in LA in those days and you were in the business, you did coke. It was as simple as that. As easy as having a beer, even a cup of tea.'

Which is a little disingenuous, because he'd been snorting cocaine long before going to live in LA and carried on long after he'd moved to New York. The difference, perhaps, was that everyone – except for a few police relegated to traffic duty – saw drugs as being part of LA life, as they'd been ever since the city had become entertainment capital of the world. No hanging around street corners necessary, for the best Colombian flake would be delivered to you by stretch limousine. It was easier than ordering a pizza – and infinitely more stylish.

In fact, Ronnie had become addicted to crack cocaine after being introduced to it by Bobby Keys, who'd become friendly with some Colombians. Crack was new on the scene, and the dealers had generously provided a free sample, knowing their new friends would inevitably come back for more. Apparently, Ronnie took a long time to realize how addicted he'd become, which partly explains his woeful fourth album, *1 2 3 4*. The crack pipe should have got a credit. 'I was trying to move with the times, using synthesizers and drum machines. Only time I ever strayed from my roots. Everyone's allowed one indiscretion.'

And then his life really changed.

Ronnie first met Josephine Karslake, in late 1977, at a party in London. Krissie was at home in Los Angeles with baby Jesse James.

Jo was a successful model with a two-year-old son and an unhelpful ex-husband, and by his own account Ronnie fell in love the moment he first saw her. Jo was less impressed. She wasn't a Stones fan – actually she liked the Bay City Rollers – and Ronnie was behaving like an adolescent schoolboy in trying to impress her. To begin with, she flatly refused to believe he was a member of the band, saying she'd been to one of their concerts and couldn't recognize him.

'Look,' Ronnie said, grabbing a recent Stones album, 'that's me!'

Still unimpressed, Jo told Ronnie she worked at Woolworths in Oxford Street.

Ronnie explained to her that he and his wife were having problems, which was true, but the biggest and most insurmountable problem for Krissie turned out to be Jo herself. The day after they'd met, Ronnie spent two hours waiting for Jo outside Woolworths, asking every employee when she'd be finishing work. When the penny finally dropped, he went round to her flat.

'I saw another side of him then,' Jo remembers. 'He wasn't bumptious any more, but more shy and abashed. And much more genuine.'

That misunderstanding cleared up, they spent a few weeks together before Ronnie decamped back to America, leaving Jo worrying that he'd seen her as just another groupie.

Had people known about Ronnie's fling? Of course they had. The London music scene is small and very incestuous. Certainly, all of Ronnie's closest friends knew – and suspected it was actually far more than a casual affair. As Richard Barnes said: 'He called me up and talked all about his "girlfriend". I knew then it was serious – he'd never used an expression like that before!'

Those suspicions were confirmed a month later when Ronnie invited Jo to Paris for the weekend. They arranged to meet at the hotel in the afternoon. Jo arrived deliberately late, for although she, too, had fallen in love, she had no intention of falling into the groupie trap.

Which was a bit of a wasted gesture, since Ronnie didn't show up until 6 a.m. the following morning, with Keith beside him. During the flight, they explained, their Concorde had developed engineering problems, shaking and vibrating so hard that Ronnie's dinner had fallen into Keith's lap. So it was that Jo's first real introduction to her future life was when she opened the door to see Ronnie standing there with a strung-out Keith in tow. A few minutes later Keith was injecting heroin with a heartfelt sigh of 'God! I needed that.' But only injecting into a muscle, for Keith always believed that you could avoid total addiction as long as you stayed away from the veins. On the other hand, he is one of the very few people with enough mental toughness to eventually kick a heroin habit without too much trauma.

Jo's introduction to life with the Stones can't have been too disturbing. For the weekend stretched into the following week, and then the next month when Ronnie insisted she accompany him to the Pathé Marconi studios, where the Stones were recording *Some Girls*. Jo called the model agency in London and cancelled all her bookings.

At the beginning of March 1978 a Mercedes sports car with Krissie Wood inside smashed through a shop window in Richmond High Street. That's Richmond, Surrey, as opposed to Richmond, Virginia, for Krissie was back in England. She was staying at the Wick Cottage, without Ronnie, for they were effectively living apart. But she was not totally on her own because the car was being driven by Charlie Heckstall-Smith.

'He was a musician,' remembers a family friend. 'Not greatly talented, but very good-looking. I'd stopped trying to understand what Ronnie and Krissie were doing. Anyway, Charlie was driving Krissie – her car – back to the Wick Cottage. He was her boyfriend, lover, whatever. And you know what? She still didn't think her marriage to Ronnie was over!'

Krissie believed that nothing would ever really split them up. I mean, how wrong can you be?'

On 8 March Krissie was lying in bed in the London Clinic when the door to her private room opened and Ronnie appeared. An eyewitness remembers that he moved very slowly and seemed to have trouble concentrating. He talked of this and that, Krissie trying with difficulty to follow him with her eyes as he moved around the room – she was in plaster and traction – and then he asked for a divorce. A moment later the door opened and one of the nurses walked in, and told Ronnie: 'The lady in the car outside wants to know if you're going to be much longer.'

From the very beginning Jo seemed to see her role in life as staying as close to Ronnie as she possibly could. Except for one more brief meeting at the Wick Cottage, that hospital visit was the last Krissie and Jesse saw of Ronnie for several years. Krissie still keeps a blurred colour Polaroid of Ronnie holding a tiny Jesse. 'That was it, he came to say goodbye to both of us. Ronnie was in tears, so was I. We'd been together so long, I always thought it would be for ever. I think we were young, too young and too inexperienced, and fame is not an easy thing – it takes away a certain freedom of privacy. Nobody's ready for that and the men themselves could deal with it, they could justify it, but as a woman with a man before, during and after – it's quite a trip.'

If there was to be any consolation, it would be that Krissie and Ronnie's relationship had lasted far longer than anyone close to them had believed possible. It had survived numerous affairs, some extremely public. It had survived a definite rivalry between them, not least over clothes. But it hadn't survived the transition from adolescence to adulthood – or what passes for adulthood in the rock world, where so many performers and their wives take a little longer to grow up. For Krissie, they were still as they'd always been, two kids hanging out in West London. She'd never really felt comfortable in Los Angeles: it was too great a reminder of how far Ronnie had progressed in the year she wasn't with him. He'd become a Rolling Stone without her and that had begun to hurt, to make her feel insecure, which had led to increasingly frequent and public arguments. She'd found that being the wife of a Rolling Stone was as much curse as blessing: the band was bigger than everyone except, perhaps, Mick and Keith. Her husband wasn't the central star he'd been with the Faces.

For his part, Ronnie simply needed to move on, and to have the love of a woman with none of the emotional baggage Krissie carried with her. He also needed looking after, especially now that he was living so far away from home, and Jo seemed more than willing and able to fulfil that role. He flew back to LA the day he said goodbye to Krissie, accompanied by Jo and her son Jamie, who was almost the same age as Jesse.

As part of the settlement, Krissie was given the Wick Cottage. She unwisely sold it several years later for less than its market value, saying that she wanted to rid herself of her past and start a new life away from rock 'n' roll, which she felt had robbed her of everything. But in fact ever since she was sixteen, Krissie's entire life had been rock 'n' roll. She'd grown up a music chick and matured into an R&B old lady. Nothing was to change.

Soon after her divorce Krissie began dating Thin Lizzy's lead guitarist, Brian Robertson. She was to witness the band's leader, Phil Lynott, die of drug addiction when his body simply gave up and his memorable last words to a nurse were: 'There's no chance of a wank, then?'

In retrospect, perhaps Krissie herself was hooked – not so much on drugs, but on musicians, who can likewise be horribly addictive. But in the event she was to devote herself to bringing up Jesse, who has turned out to be totally unaffected by Son-Of-Rock-Star Syndrome. Instead, he is a polite, well-mannered, level-headed and gifted young musician now to be heard on Art Wood's revamped Quiet Melon album, *Money Due Melon*, on the track 'Knee Deep in Nephews', which brings together Jesse and all three Wood brothers. His memories of childhood include a sad amount of waiting in hotel lobbies for a father who never showed up. Ronnie was sinking fast into full-blown drug addiction.

On February 22 1980 Ronnie and Jo were arrested on the Franco–Dutch island of St Maarten, in the eastern Caribbean, for possession of 260 grams of cocaine found hidden in a tree in the garden of their rented house in Philipsburg. It was during a period that Jo describes as their 'try anything' stage, although she's quick to stress that never included needles, for aside from anything else, Ronnie is terrified of them.

'We'd met these two guys who said they had loads of coke,' she recounts, 'and we invited them back to the house we were renting and did the usual thing of staying up all night. In the morning they asked to borrow our car, and we agreed because we were going to get some sleep. What we didn't know was they had hung their stash of coke in a sock in a tree in the garden. There was about 250 grams' worth. A neighbour saw them take the car and noted the number plates, then called the police.'

The police arrived and Ronnie naturally thought the complaint had been about the noise. But within minutes they had miraculously found the sock hanging in the tree and happily charged Ronnie and Jo with

trafficking in opium. Ironically, Ronnie had first noticed the two characters immediately after the plane had first touched down. 'I could tell they
were eyeing us up. I was carrying this giant ghetto-blaster through
Customs and one of the Customs officers followed us all the way to the
house – they definitely had it in for us. Then we saw one of the guys at a
casino a couple of nights later – turns out he was also a croupier. They
kept on trying to sell us some coke for thousands of dollars and
eventually came to the house. It was a set-up – they'd driven off leaving
both their jackets behind with convenient traces of coke in them.'

Jo and Ronnie were taken to the local police station. 'Leaving our
nanny, Jayne, in charge of a crying Jamie and Leah with orders to call
the Stones office and arrange for my lawyers to fly out immediately,'
Ronnie remembers. 'I was still stupid enough to think the authorities
would realize we'd been set up, but they were all in it together. I was still
saying I'd be happy to help them out, but they just took my shoelaces
and left me in my cut-down jeans and a shirt, marched me down a pitch-
black corridor and shoved me into a cell, slammed the door and that was
that. And then the same Customs guy turns up grinning at the window
of my cell.'

The only small comfort was that having stayed up for several nights,
both Ronnie and Jo needed their rest – although the cells were a far cry
from the sheltered luxury that life with the Stones offered. A single stone
block with no blanket and no pillow. A stinking metal bucket. And for
Jo at least, the constant fear of being the only woman in a black, male
prison – and a white one at that. 'I was convinced I was going to be
raped until one of the inmates realized who Ronnie was. This one guy
asked if in fact I knew Ronnie Wood, so I said yes. "And Keith
Richards?" he asked. So I said yes again, and the guy's eyes lit up. "Well,
I was with 'em on the '75 tour!"'

Instant bonding – and since the inmate was big enough to be able to
reach through the bars and, by using a stick, pass messages between
Ronnie and Jo's cells, neither felt totally isolated. As Ronnie recalls: 'I
worked out that if I stood on tiptoe and looked through the bars at a
certain time of day, and our new mate could get Jo to do the same, then
we could wave to each other. It was the only way I knew she was
still alive.'

Ronnie's lawyers had flown in on the first available flight, only to
discover that Ronnie and Jo had been arrested on the Dutch side of the
island, which meant that they were subject to 'parish law' and needed to
be represented by a Dutch official. A deal was finally struck with a local
Dutch firm of lawyers, who arranged a hearing before a judge. Ronnie
and Jo were interviewed separately, and luckily their stories matched up.

The judge concluded that they were innocent and ordered their release. It had taken six long, boring and, for Jo, terrifying days.

'I saw the croupier before I got out,' Ronnie says sourly. 'He'd obviously fucked up because he was in a cell. One of the officials turned to me and said: "Did this man try to sell you drugs?" And I looked him right in the eye and said, "Fucking right he did!"'

Grabbing the kids and the nanny, and never asking questions, Ronnie and Jo fled paradise and within twelve hours were back in New York, where a relieved Jo told her husband: 'That's it, I'll never touch anything again!' Whether the croupier was charged with any offence is unknown.

Although equally shocked by the ordeal, Ronnie was not about to offer the same promise.

To make matters worse, the Stones were due to go back on the road to promote their new album, *Emotional Rescue*. Ronnie's being busted hadn't helped. The band felt that he had let them down – even Keith, who more than anyone could recognize the signs of self-destruction and was now trying to reorganize his own life. Mick Jagger, when asked about the band's plans for promoting the album, would say: 'There might not be a Rolling Stones.'

18
'Rod even tried to buy a round'

In 1983 *Undercover* was another hit album for the Stones, making number three in the US charts and number four in the UK. But a major blow to Ronnie's bank balance occurred the following year when Mick Jagger announced that he wasn't prepared to promote *Undercover* by touring, as he wished to 'devote time to his solo pursuits'. As if in confirmation of Ronnie's junior-partner status, in June 1984 he was excluded from a band meeting held at Munro Terrace, Chelsea, where the group's future was discussed. It was reluctantly agreed to allow Mick freedom to spend time with his and Jerry Hall's new baby, Elizabeth, while promoting all his extracurricular work – commencing with his first solo album and a single, 'State of Shock', a duet with Michael Jackson. This meant postponing all Stones work for the foreseeable future. Naturally, the press announcement of Jagger's plans sparked off more 'Stones to Quit' rumours, all of which he vehemently denied. However, the rumours were fuelled by a disgruntled Keith Richards and Bill Wyman, the latter quoted as saying: 'I've lost touch with who Mick is now. He's just a business associate who has his share of five votes.'

Note the use of the word 'five'. Wyman was far too scrupulous to make a mistake: as far as the outside world was concerned, Ronnie was a full member of the band. He did, however, let his true feelings show, including his frustration at Ronnie's seeming indifference to the proposed lay-off: 'Woody is difficult because he's so shallow . . . great for a laugh, but you can't talk to him.'

Considering Ronnie's true status within the band, the comment was more than unfair. The only way he could keep his position was by remaining distinctly neutral, the hired foil between Mick and Keith. This was Stones business – the real Stones, that is, the guys who'd been together for nearly twenty years – and in their eyes Ronnie was still paying his dues.

Keith, although privately furious at what he saw as Mick's selfishness, restricted himself to the occasional muted comment until finally losing his temper openly in May. 'If Mick tours without the band I'll slit his throat!' he raged. Unlike Ronnie, though, Keith was at least financially independent.

At this time Jagger was also busy with a solo pursuit outside music: his autobiography. For this he was reputedly paid £3 million – not all up-front – but eventually he had to return the advance, because Bill Wyman, who kept the Stones' diary, refused to help him with the dates – or anything else very much. Wyman was planning his own book, the excellent *Stone Alone*. He was not about to collaborate with the man who had stopped the Stones touring. There are rumours that a first draft of Jagger's autobiography is hidden away in a safety-deposit box some-where, but his solo creative career demonstrates that being lead vocalist for the world's greatest rock 'n' roll band is a tough act to follow.

Ronnie can be forgiven for feeling impotent. He hadn't been consulted about the band's future, nor was he involved with a recent settlement with Allen Klein, their former manager, which added considerably to the others' personal fortune – even to the estate of Brian Jones. No reason why Ronnie should have been involved, of course, but it all emphasized how much of a new boy he was. He was beginning to feel distinctly superfluous to the band's needs, whatever they were. And Wyman's jibe did little to cheer him up, especially in the light of a looming cash crisis. 'They're all financially secure,' Ronnie was heard to complain, talking of his colleagues, 'they're content with the accomplishments they've made at their ages. But I'm younger, I've still got lots to do. I don't want to sit around the house when we could be on the road.'

He soon discovered that the game was played strictly to the Stones' rules, and that his future included an unpaid lay-off. To an extent, he was on his own.

Between 1980 and 1984 Ronnie's personal decline continued, with cocaine being the usual drug of choice, although not exclusively so. He'd become adept at turning any household utensil into drug paraphernalia, including the cardboard centre of a toilet roll. Even though his musical contribution was as strong as ever, his behaviour now had Keith seriously worried. The band had managed to get together for a winter tour in 1981 which stood to net £50 million. Keith tried to counsel Ronnie in his own inimitable way – otherwise known as a good smack – which led to several punch-ups. A few years older than Ronnie, Keith has always tended to see himself as his big brother, with all the attendant rights and privileges. But Ronnie now seemed to be spiralling down and down, totally out of control. And as always, the band had to come first.

'That's one boy who hasn't got much longer, the way he's going,' Keith was heard to say about Ronnie, as he began helping Mick draw up a list of possible replacements.

Ronnie thought he'd managed to hide the worst of his excesses. For example, he'd empty a cigarette, mix cocaine with the tobacco and suck the mixture back into the paper tube, then smoke an apparently innocuous cigarette – especially when his nose wasn't working too well. It's a measure of how far he'd gone that he thought he could fool Keith Richards about his drug-taking.

He couldn't. Keith – whose drug of choice at that time was opium – had distrusted crack cocaine from the very start. With his experience of drugs, who could possibly argue? Ronnie became increasingly paranoid as he tried to hide his habit. A trusted friend was someone who'd smoke crack with him. Anyone who wouldn't was likely to tell Keith and therefore viewed with suspicion.

By 1983 Ronnie had been marginalized: he would find himself billeted separately from the rest of the Stones, not just on another floor but in a different hotel. He realized that he could no longer take his position in the band for granted. Keith had given him a final warning: either quit smoking crack or leave the band. During the tour of 1982 Jagger added an ominous clause to the Stones tour contract which read: 'Anyone found in possession of drugs in any part of the backstage area will immediately be banished from the vicinity whatever his capacity.'

Moreover, Jagger was widely rumoured to be looking for Ronnie's replacement in the shape of the American guitarist George Thorogood. But even Jagger couldn't take the Stones continuing as a band for granted. The rift between him and Keith was growing ever wider, as the tension over his solo pursuits demonstrated.

'I saw the way things were going,' Ronnie was to say years later, 'and wondered how long I'd be in a job. It was fucking awful. You had Mick and Keith, who'd been childhood mates, who'd started the world's best fucking band, written some of the world's best fucking songs . . . and they were just drifting further and further apart and leaving me in the middle looking for a new job, when I'd already landed the best job of my life. But it was obvious that neither wanted to be the one to say: "That's it, let's split", because they both still cared about the band and each other. It was just Mick got to believing that Keith hated him and vice versa, which was bollocks – they were just pissed off, both of them.'

And Ronnie needed money. The failure of the New Barbarians' tour to promote his third solo album, *Gimme Some Neck*, following poor sales of its predecessor, *Now Look*, had left him relatively broke. Apart from the wage he got from the Stones, his only other source of income was the royalties from the Faces' albums, and the songs he'd co-written with Rod Stewart. Not bad – but not enough to support his lavish lifestyle. For although he wasn't making anywhere near the money the rest of the Stones were, he was determined to live in exactly the same way as his closest mates, Keith and Mick. And while the Stones' follow-up albums to *Some Girls* had done well – a US and UK number one in 1980 for *Emotional Rescue*; a US number one and UK number two for *Tattoo You* in 1981; a top-five position for the live album *Still Life* in 1982; and the 1983 success of *Undercover* – Ronnie rarely managed more than one co-writing song credit per album. Aside from touring, his income derived from air-play royalties, for in those pre-CD days back catalogues weren't anywhere near as vigorously marketed as they are to day.

By late 1983 Ronnie was addicted, strung out and facing the prospect of a Stone-less existence. No tours were scheduled and a question mark was hovering morbidly over his and the band's musical future. He'd already moved with his family to Manhattan's Upper West Side. New York was less sybaritic than Los Angeles; it felt more real and more like London.

'The biggest difference to me between London and Los Angeles,' Ronnie explains, 'was that LA lacked momentum and inspiration. It was also spaced out. In London you don't need a car to go and visit friends. I felt like one of those early convicts sent to Australia! On the other hand, LA could be creative and if I hadn't moved there I'd never have got to hang out with people like my great buddy Jim Keltner – who introduced me to Bob Dylan – and Ringo. People like Bobby Keys, of course, Jimmy Caan, Jack Nicholson and Dennis Hopper – it's that old creative thing between actors and musicians. And later on Sly Stone was my neighbour, so there was never any complaints about the noise! But the other problem was that in Los Angeles there are all these really slimy people, like the [drug] dealers . . . you can have all the security, all the gates and fences, and they'll still find a way to crawl into your home, slide back the doors to your bedroom and wake you up, saying: "I've got some more for you!" But one time, after we'd been up for about five days, me and Jo had finally managed to get rid of all these crazy people and hit the sack, when the chauffeur woke me up, saying: "Mr Wood, the canyon's on fire" – we were living in Mandelville Canyon then. And I was going: "Wha? Wha? Go away!" while he was saying: "No, no, you have to get out now." You could take enough possessions to fill a jeep – for me a few paintings and guitars. And we got out. I looked back and the sky was black except for a little patch of light above my house. Then the fire came, turned left at my garden, went along a little and then turned right. It was the only house saved. Someone had actually been killed once where the bedroom was, in a mudslide. And then I found out we were right in the earthquake epicentre . . . I mean, I always used to think epicentre was a supermarket . . . no, there we were, bang in the middle. So me and Josephine decided to move to New York. We took a brownstone between Rivermead and West End. You went out the front door and people were there – back in LA you'd have to go ten or fifteen miles to find human life on their feet!'

Ronnie left behind an intact house – and a mural of Father Christmas above the fireplace. 'I painted him sort of wedged into the wall,' he recalls with a chuckle. 'It was Father Christmas meeting his doom!'

Safely ensconced in New York, Ronnie did two more things towards recovery. First, he checked himself into a rehab clinic. 'It's funny: even now I look back and think I was never out of control,' he said recently. 'I've always known what I was doing – but no one else did! Plus I had Jo, who I wouldn't exactly say saved my life, but she certainly brightened it up.'

It's that quiet self-confidence again, the innermost belief that wherever he is in life is exactly where he's meant to be – and that everything will be all right in the end. However, this time he did take things seriously. What seems to have been the trigger wasn't so much his own appreciation of how far things had gone wrong as the threat of being fired from the band that had become his life – even if that band might not exist for very much longer. Either way, it worked. Like so many other rock stars before and since, Ronnie returned home officially clear of drugs. More importantly, he came home with a better understanding of himself – which led to step two: 'I knew I had to get busy. I needed to know the boundaries I was expected to work with.'

Admirably, Ronnie returned to school – actually an art workshop in San Francisco where he studied every day for three weeks from 10 a.m. to 5 p.m.

'I went to San Francisco to learn about woodcuts and monotypes, which gave my art a new lease of life. I completely committed myself to working hard, it became my other definite priority. With no Stones work coming in for the foreseeable future, I had to seriously think about making my art work for me.'

Ronnie held his first exhibition in Dallas on 28 November 1984 at the Foster Goldstrum Gallery. It was entitled 'Portraits' and in addition to silk-screen prints of the Stones, it also featured John Belushi, John Lennon, Chuck Berry and, oddly enough, Sid Vicious. The show, a runaway success which continued until January 1985, established the trend of rock musicians who also make art. However, it has to be said that Ronnie Wood's work is far more painterly and accomplished than that of, say,

Brian Eno or David Bowie. But his line drawings are still the best, as befits a man whose favourite artists include Dürer, Rembrandt, Daumier, the architect Le Corbusier and the children's book illustrator Arthur Rackham.

In January 1985 Ronnie and Jo were married at St Mary's Church in Denham, Buckinghamshire. Keith Richards and Charlie Watts were the two best men. The guests included Ronnie Wood look-alike Gary Holton, star of Channel 4's *Auf Wiedersehen Pet*, Rod Stewart, Jeff Beck, Ringo Starr, Peter Frampton, Peter Cook, who'd become one of Ronnie's closest friends, and the family: Lizzie, Archie, Art and Ted. Archie was in a wheelchair, having had a leg amputated because of thrombosis in 1980. When he had been told that his leg would have to go because of old age, he'd responded: 'The other one's just as old, isn't it?'

Naturally enough, no Ronnie Wood wedding could pass off without some sort of incident. In this case the vicar, the Reverend Peter Crick, was so overcome by the array of rock stars facing him that he launched into a diatribe about their overall godlessness. At which point the Irreverent Peter Cook began haranguing him back, as an outraged E. L. Wisty. All this to the background noise of Eric Clapton and Patti Boyd screaming at each other outside the church.

And afterwards, Archie entertained the wedding party for a full hour, telling joke after joke until: 'Everyone was in hysterics,' Ronnie says fondly. 'He was magic that day, was Dad. It reminded me that whatever he'd done for a job, Dad was always an entertainer. I remember looking over at Peter [Cook], one of the funniest men this country ever produced, and he could hardly stand, he was laughing so much. Special day, that. I mean, just getting Rod, Jeff and me in the same room as the best of mates was pretty good. Rod even tried to buy a round. Of course, the bar was free, but a nice gesture nonetheless.'

In 1986 the Stones began work on a new album, *Dirty Work* – all except for Mick Jagger, who was still busy with his personal business interests. This meant the preparation was largely left to Keith and Ronnie: working up the songs without a singer; choosing session musicians; and arranging the studio. It all reminded Ronnie of his early days with the singer-less Faces. But it did enable him to claim a co-writing credit ('Had It With You') on the B side of the Stones' obvious filler single, a cover of 'Harlem Shuffle'. Eventually Ronnie would clock up four co-writing credits on the album. When Mick did arrive, the atmosphere was decidedly tense. Keith was furious with him for releasing a solo album during the opening sessions for *Dirty Work*, publicly commenting: 'It is a totally inappropriate time to release a solo effort.'

The ill feeling between Mick and Keith looked set to run and run, leading inevitably to rumours of a Stones break-up and a Faces reunion. This latter rumour stemmed from the Faces' brief get-together at the end of Rod Stewart's sold-out Wembley show in July, in aid of the multiple sclerosis-stricken Ronnie Lane, for whom Bill Wyman covered on bass. The Faces' reunion never happened, but the rumours persist to this day and there have been the odd Faces' appearances here and there – the Brit Awards in 1986 and two shows in Ireland in 1987, Wyman again on bass, prompting Ronnie's comment: 'Bill, mate, you've left the Stones to join the Faces! At least I did it the right way round.'

It's a moot point whether Mick and Keith would have settled their differences without Ronnie. It is true, however, that he really worked to get them talking to each other again.

'I'd be over visiting Mick, or he'd be at mine, and I'd call up Keith, say a few words then pass the phone to Mick, who's not the kind of bloke to back off. But he did find it hard to believe Keith wanted to talk to him. Then I'd go out the room and leave them to it. I'd do the same if I was with Keith. And eventually everyone was mates again. After one of these times Mick came bouncing into the room all smiles, saying: "I can't believe it, Keith doesn't hate me!"'

But it was not in time for Live Aid, for which Mick and Keith played separately – Mick with David Bowie in London, and Keith joining Ronnie and his old LA neighbour, Bob Dylan, in Philadelphia. 'Dylan changed the set list just as we were walking up the ramp on stage,' Ronnie remembers, 'and played all these fucking songs that Keith and me hadn't rehearsed. But what could we do – walk off the fucking stage? I mean, this was Bob Dylan and I'd have played the spoons if he'd wanted.'

A year after they married, Ronnie and Jo moved back to England. Ronnie might believe that his entire life is preordained, but after several years of surviving forest fires (which destroyed half his neighbourhood and stopped just feet from Ian McLagan's front door), earthquakes and landslides in Los Angeles, garbage strikes, brown-outs, freeze-ups and muggers in New York, America began to seem just a little dangerous for the kids. The Wood family returned to England in the summer of 1986, settling in a beautiful Georgian mansion on Richmond Green, Surrey, until persistent – but justified – complaints about the noise from the neighbours to the Council forced Ronnie to move to his present homes in County Kildare, Ireland, and on Kingston Hill, not far from Richmond.

'I told him to buy a place far enough away from people so that he wouldn't annoy them,' says Lizzie. 'He bought a lovely place over there [Ireland]. He wanted me to move there but I didn't want to. I've got my flat in the grounds whenever I want it.'

The story of Ronnie and Jo's 'eviction' from Richmond made a light-hearted feature in the *News of the World*, with a picture of them sitting on the steps of the house like two little waifs.

Less humorous were the headlines in January 1992 reporting that Jesse, then fifteen, had been savagely slashed by a twenty-strong gang wielding Stanley knives in a completely unprovoked assault near the Kingston Hill house. When his son stumbled indoors covered in blood, Ronnie was shocked so badly that he almost fainted. Jesse had to be rushed to hospital, where he underwent urgent plastic surgery to his hand. It was his Uncle Art who had driven him there, for if Ronnie had taken him someone at the hospital would have made a phone call and photographers from every tabloid newspaper would have been on the scene within the hour.

Later the police issued a statement saying that they suspected Jesse had been targeted because of his famous father. The assailants, who might even still be proud of their cowardice, were never found.

Mick and Keith's feud was finally resolved in 1989 by the release of Mick's second solo album, *Primitive Cool*, and Keith's first, *Talk Is Cheap*. Both accepted that in terms of talent, the whole was greater than any individual part. As if to prove them right, the entire band, including Mick Taylor, was inducted into the Rock & Roll Hall of Fame at a ceremony in New York. Middle-aged and mellow, they even spoke fondly about Brian Jones. It seemed time for Ronnie to become a shareholder in one of the world's most exclusive and lucrative businesses, Rolling Stones Inc, which he did when Bill Wyman finally left.

The next few years established the Stones as the biggest-grossing rock band of all time with further successful albums – *Steel Wheels, Stripped* and *Voodoo Lounge* – and sell-out world tours of incredible proportions, leading to the ongoing *Bridges To Babylon* tour.

And now Ronnie has a piece of the action. He's still having parties, big fucking parties, mostly in Kildare, but occasionally at his Kingston Hill mansion. The latter's called Homewood, but you'd never know it because fans keep on stealing the sign. His real home has definitely become the estate in Ireland. and no longer just for tax purposes.

'I love it, my favourite place in the whole world. Got my new stables – had quite a few winners recently – and Josephine loves it here too. And the pub in my garden reminding me of my old Dad – we lost him a few years back – called Yer Father's Yacht. Magic.' In Kildare he can enjoy privacy and still lead a relatively normal life: no rubbernecking tourists and none of the crazies that so many rock stars inevitably attract.

So what kind of man is Ronnie Wood? First off, he's generous to a fault and loves company. That said, his path is littered with people wondering why their new best friend has suddenly vanished from their lives. He doesn't do it deliberately, but his natural charm, which makes a person feel they're the most important person in the world, Ronnie's world, inevitably leads to hurt. His speaking voice, a cross between the cracked tones of a whisky priest and the insistence of Richard Burton, could talk anyone into anything – and possibly often does. If Ronnie's a man who finds it hard to say no, he finds it equally hard to take no for an answer.

'Ronnie finds it hard to pin himself down – he likes too many people,' says family friend Richard Barnes. 'That's hard on the people close to him. He's not the kind of man to sit and watch TV with just one other person. He likes to share things – he likes to watch the Marx Brothers, but he has to have loads of people over to share it with him. He's certainly not someone who'd go to the cinema on his own – he's got to have someone to share humour with him. He never wants to neglect anyone, he's loyal, he's a butterfly who flits around a lot and is comfortable with anybody – certainly more than anyone else in the business.'

Ronnie's still also a wild man who will always find a way to live on the edge. No matter that Jo always tours with him, making it plain that family business is at least as important as the Stones, Ronnie needs the buzz of the extreme. How many other people would check into a health farm before a birthday, in order to tune up their body for forty-eight hours of excess? Everyone's getting older. 'I saw Dennis Hopper the other day,' Ronnie says, grinning. 'Asked him if he still did dope. "No, man," he said, "I gave it up years ago. All I have to do now is shake my bones and I get high!"'

In many ways Ronnie's approach to life recalls one of those legendary American or Japanese tourists who have only twenty-four hours to see Europe. He has always known that time began running out on him from the moment he was born. His great loves, besides music and family, are his art and horses. But, looking at his paintings and prints, you get the impression that he's holding something back, keeping some part of himself deliberately hidden. By contrast, his sketches are far more revealing of the man. So, behind the bonhomie, Ronnie Wood can be a very private person, as indeed are most millionaire rock stars. That sense of a guarded self runs throughout his life. Very, very few people have ever known where they truly stood with him.

On occasion he can be disconcertingly direct, and a sudden insight verging on the cruel is even more shocking when delivered with the same smile that also praises. The man is something of a watcher and, like all watchers, has learned to bide his time. But he still does his best to avoid confrontations – they get in the way of music. And he's still, perhaps, getting used to how much power comes with being a Rolling Stone.

For the Rolling Stones Organisation is worth hundreds of millions, in terms of back catalogue, royalties and merchandising alone. That's gross, of course, and business expenses are heavy. And the money isn't actually in a bank somewhere, for the figure also refers to future earnings. Nonetheless, it represents a different type of power from that which comes with being a rock and cultural icon. That kind of money buys an awful lot of favours. Rock iconhood fosters a near-fanatical following. Put the two together and the result can almost be menacing. Of course, menace was an early Stones trademark. But it's still surprising to discover, when you research and write a book like this, how much awe the Rolling Stones still inspire in people of all ages and from all walks of life.

As for Ronnie, he says: 'I never had any misgivings about joining the Stones. It had to be. When I went over to Munich to audition, I just walked in, told them the song and how we were going to play it. And Charlie Watts said: "Get him, he's already bossing us about!" I was never resentful about being on a wage in the beginning. Told myself I was the youngest member. Everything comes to he who waits.'

Ronnie had been waiting since before he used to drive around in the old Bentley he bought for £500, listening to *Beggar's Banquet*, his favourite Stones album. He'd been waiting since he was seventeen and first saw the Stones play live in Richmond. The dream came true. Ronnie Wood went from wheelbarrows to Lear jets in around thirty-five years.

Nowadays his only unfulfilled musical ambition is to play a perfect version of 'Guitar Shuffle', which he first heard performed by his hero Big Bill Broonzy.

Meanwhile Woody is still on tour.

Where are they now?

Still alive, but no longer making headlines, are:

Kim Gardner. He runs the Cat and Fiddle pub on Sunset Boulevard, Los Angeles, and enjoys outraging Californian palates with stewed ox-tail, sausage and mash and steak and kidney pudding. He still plays bass in his spare time away from the kitchen. When Bill Wyman left the Stones, Ronnie was asked for his suggestions for a replacement and instantly suggested Willie Weeks.
Ronnie: 'It was only after that I thought: Oh fuck! I should have thought of Kim. But then I thought: No, he's got too much loyalty to his pub.'

Tony Monroe runs a successful sheet-metal business in the north of England. He hasn't seen Ronnie since he was fired from the Birds. He occasionally plays and sings in a local pub. His wife still makes the best meat pies in the world.
Ronnie: 'Did we replace him? No? Probably just as well then.'

Ali McKenzie is a glazier in West London. He no longer sings.
Ronnie: 'Ali's great, still pops round to see my mum.'

Jack Jones is a newsagent, also in West London. He's been in various come-backs of the Creation, none of which lasted.

Ian McLagan, based in Austin, Texas, continues to be a successful session player – most recently on tour backing Billy Bragg.

Kenney Jones runs a polo club in Surrey, where he lives. Ronnie: 'Fucking riveting game, polo, innit? I've never been so excited, I don't think.'

Art Wood is a graphic designer, looks after Ronnie's artworks and has reformed Quiet Melon.

Ted Wood tours the world as the drummer with Bob Kerr's Whoopee Band.

Krissie Wood is studying alternative medicine and yoga, and still lives in Richmond.

Picture credits

Clockwise from top left: page 1: Lizzie Wood, Lizzie Wood, Art Wood; page 2: Art Wood, Lizzie Wood, Tony Monroe; page 3: Ali McKenzie, Ali McKenzie, Tony Monroe; page 4: Tony Monroe, Ali McKenzie, Tony Monroe, Tony Monroe; page 5: Tony Monroe; page 6: David Wedgbury, Tony Monroe, Tony Monroe; page 7: Ali McKenzie, David Wedgbury; page 8: Phil Smee, Kenny Pickett, Ron Wood; page 9: Art Wood, Phil Smee; page 10: Shirley Arnold, Shirley Arnold; page 11: Krissie Wood, Ron Wood, Krissie Wood; page 12: Reg Pippett, Angie Wood; page 13: Angie Wood, Angie Wood, Angie Wood; page 14: Reg Pippett, Reg Pippett; page 15: Reg Pippett, Reg Pippett, page 16: Reg Pippett, Reg Pippett, Reg Pippett.

Index